Captain Labaume

A

CIRCUMSTANTIAL NARRATIVE

OF

The Campaign in Russia,

EMBELLISHED WITH PLANS

OF THE

BATTLES OF THE MOSKWA

AND

MALO-JAROSLAVITZ.

CONTAINING A

FAITHFUL DESCRIPTION OF THE AFFECTING AND
INTERESTING SCENES, OF WHICH THE AUTHOR
WAS AN EYE-WITNESS.

BY EUGÈNE LABAUME,

*Captain of the Royal Geographical Engineers, Ex-Officer of the Ordnance
of Prince Eugene, Chevalier of the Legion of Honour, and
of the Iron Crown. Author of an Abridged
History of the Republic of Venice.*

TRANSLATED FROM THE LATEST FRENCH EDITION.

THIRD EDITION, CONSIDERABLY IMPROVED.

LONDON:

PRINTED FOR SAMUEL LEIGH, IN THE STRAND,
BY W. CLOWES, NORTHUMBERLAND-COURT.

Captain Labaume

A French Officer's First Hand Account of the
Invasion of Russia & Retreat from Moscow

Eugene Labaume
and
T. Dundas Pillans

LEONAUR

Captain Labaume
A French Officer's First Hand Account of the Invasion of Russia
& Retreat from Moscow
by Eugene Labaume
and
T. Dundas Pillans

First published under the title
The Crime of 1812 and Its Retribution

Leonaur is an imprint of Oakpast Ltd

Copyright in this form © 2014 Oakpast Ltd

ISBN: 978-1-78282-267-7 (hardcover)
ISBN: 978-1-78282-268-4 (softcover)

http://www.leonaur.com

Publisher's Notes

Contents

Introduction (1912)

By W. T. Stead

I have been asked to write a few words of introduction to Mr. Pillans' translation of Lieut.-Colonel Labaume's narrative of *Napoleon's Russian Campaign of 1812*, and I comply with the greatest pleasure.

Labaume was a lieut.-colonel in the French Army. He went through the campaign from first to last. He records what he saw and heard and suffered with the downright simplicity of one who was a soldier without ceasing to be a man. He is a first-hand witness of events which have been artistically treated by Verestchagin on canvas, and by Count Tolstoi in his great prose epic of *War and Peace*.

The most striking chapters in the book are those which describe the ghastly catastrophe of the headlong rush of the wreck of the Grand Army across the territory which Napoleon had desolated. Like a wounded mastodon, crippled and bleeding at every pore, the once invincible army staggers blindly, madly, through the snow, intent only on escape, until at last, a mere shadow of its former self, starving, frost-bitten, despairing, it reaches safety in Prussia. More vivid word-painting may be found elsewhere, but here are the words of a man who saw it all and who tells us what he saw.

It was not, however, from my desire to commend Labaume's narrative, which Mr. Pillans has put into excellent English, that led me to respond so willingly to the translator's request that I should write a brief introduction to this notable book. What tempted me was the opportunity which such an introduction affords of saying a much-needed word on the subject of Labaume's narrative.

There is a strange and pestilent habit among some Englishmen of ignoring all the great services which Russia has rendered to the cause of human progress and the liberty of nations, because, forsooth, Russia is an autocracy which is now only beginning to be tempered by constitutionalism and a semblance of parliamentary institutions. The Centenary of the 1812, which is to be celebrated as a great national and indeed international festival this year at Moscow, ought to afford all such atrabilious critics material for serious reflection. For, as Madame Novikoff once remarked, it was in the glorious year 1812 that Moscow was offered up as a burnt sacrifice on the altar of European, freedom. It was the Russian campaign which broke the power of Napoleon. After the retreat from Moscow, Leipzig and Waterloo were but the corollaries of a solved problem. That which all Europe with Britain to back her, failed to do, the Russian people accomplished by a heroism of patriotic devotion, attested by incredible sacrifices, of which it is well that the world should be reminded this year.

Let me quote two authorities, one English the other French, as to the services which Russia—unregenerate, despotic Muscovite Russia—rendered to the cause of European freedom.

The Englishman, George Canning, speaking in Liverpool in 1814, on this subject, made the following pertinent observations:—

> By what power, in what part of the world, has that final blow been struck which has smitten the giant to the ground? I suppose by some enlightened republic; I suppose by some nation which in the excess of popular freedom considers even a representative system as defective unless each individual interferes directly in the national concerns; some nation of enlightened patriots, every man of whom is a politician in the coffee-house as well as in the Senate. I suppose it is from such a government as this that the Conqueror of Autocrats, the sworn destroyer of monarchical England has met his doom. I look through the European world in vain; I find there is no such august community. But where was the blow struck? Where? Alas for theory! In the wilds of despotic Russia. It was followed up on the plains of Leipzig by Russian, Prussian and Austrian arms.

Let it not be said that Russia being invaded merely defended her own fatherland. The defence of Russia was the work of 1812. The liberation of Europe was achieved in 1813, and achieved through the initiative, the high resolve and self-sacrificing ardour of Russia.

M. Alfred Rambaud, the French historian of Russia, pays homage to the nation which banished the nightmare of Napoleonic domination. He says:—

> The power which had struck hardest for the freedom of Eu-

rope was most poorly compensated. It is an incontestable fact that, of all the Allies, Russia showed herself the least grasping. It was she who had given the signal for the struggle against Napoleon, and had shown the most perseverance in pursuit of the common end. Without her example the States of Europe would never have dreamed of arming against him. Her skilful leniency towards France finished the work begun by the war.

It is well to be reminded by these facts, when differences of opinion as to the necessity of isolated and temporary acts of policy, in countries where England and Russia find themselves face to face with Oriental anarchy, seem to have blinded many good-hearted but wrong-headed people, as to the many incalculable services which Russia has rendered to mankind.

One more observation and I have done. In this book we see war at its worst, war uncontrolled by rules and regulations; war in which armed men pillaged undefended cities, outraged helpless women, burned down the villages of harmless peasants. War nowadays, despite occasional outbursts of panic-roused savagery in the ranks of the Italian invaders of Tripoli, is a comparatively humane operation. The proceedings of armies in the field are confined in their ever narrower and narrower limits. Almost everything that Napoleon's Grand Army did, excepting when actually engaged in active combat, now lies under the ban of all the civilised Governments of the world. And to whom is it that we owe this great advance? We owe it not to humanitarian England nor to chivalrous France. We owe it, first and foremost of all, to that much-abused and much-maligned Russia which in 1874 summoned the Brussels Conference to define the laws of war, and which in 1889 and 1907 carried on the same noble mission at the Conferences of the Hague.

Napoléon Buonaparte

Translator's Preface

The writer of the following narrative says of Napoleon that he will be for historians "the riddle of the human heart." But there is a greater enigma connected with his career, and that is the growth and persistency of what is known as the "Napoleonic Legend." How is it that this evil genius, who kept Europe in a turmoil for twenty years; who bled France almost to death; whose armies passed like a blighting pestilence from Lisbon to Moscow; whom no treaties could bind; to whom the strongest ties of human affection and gratitude were as gossamer when they stood in the way of his insatiable ambition,—how is it that this modern Attila has become for many the embodiment of human greatness, and that in the Christian era people are to be found to worship the memory of the murderer of the Duc d'Enghien and the wholesale violator of the moral law?

The answer is to be found in the cunning of the man himself, and the credulity of his dupes. After having shown himself to be the greatest liberticide in history, he devoted his well-merited exile in St. Helena to spinning a web of ingenious sophistries to prove that instead of being the Demon of Discord he was in reality the Apostle of Peace. He, the suppressor of liberty, posed as the champion of Liberalism in Europe; and the emancipator of the nations from the tyrants who oppressed them. The astonishing effrontery of the claim assured its success, for the bulk of mankind are prone to believe that which is asserted with emphasis, even when unsupported by proof.

Napoleon Bonaparte began as a Jacobin, and ended as one, for the spirit of Jacobinism is the spirit of tyranny. It matters not whether that spirit is manifested in the rags of a *sans-culotte* or under the imperial purple, and "a Robespierre on horseback" is probably the most dangerous of the breed.

His early successes were due far more to the smiles of Fortune than to his own deserts. At Brumaire he would have been irretrievably lost but for the ready wit of his brother Lucien, and at Marengo his rout was certain but for the timely intervention of Desaix and the splendid charge of Kellerman. He himself believed that he was born under a lucky star.

With all his undoubted genius, it was the limitations of his knowledge which caused his downfall. France and her people he knew by heart, but his ignorance of Spain, Russia and England precipitated his ruin. With regard to the first, his short-sighted treachery roused the latent fire of Spanish patriotism, the flames of which scorched his laurels and set Europe in a blaze. The snows of Russia were the winding-sheet of his reputation, and in his insane hatred of England he launched those famous decrees which carried ruin to the trade and commerce of Europe, and ranged the whole of the middle classes against him.

When his star began to be veiled behind the clouds of his own arrogance and conceit, his fall was like the descent of a meteor. An edifice which it had taken twenty years of bloodshed and treachery to erect fell with a crash in little more than two. The Russian catastrophe of 1812 was the precursor of the abdication of 1814, and Waterloo only gave him the *coup de grâce*.

He was pre-eminently lucky in the circumstances of his early career. He then commanded an army imbued with revolutionary fervour—an army of political dervishes who went forth conquering and to conquer in the sacred names of Liberty, Equality and Fraternity. He was the incarnation of the Revolution, the apostle of the regeneration of enslaved peoples. He had against him incompetent generals, commanding armies of serfs. At the close of the war the positions were reversed. He had become the enslaver of nations, and the nations themselves were in arms against him. He began by warring on kings, he ended by warring on peoples.

Of all the crimes and blunders which he committed none exceeds in turpitude the Russian campaign of 1812. It was unprovoked and entirely gratuitous. It was commenced *à cœur leger,* like another war in later times, which brought on France almost equal disasters, and which was, by the way, the *damnosa hæreditas* of the "Napoleonic Legend." Designed to be carried on at the expense of the invaded country, no forethought was displayed for the supply of his army or the security of its retreat. Instead of the fertile plains and sunny skies of Italy, he found the forest-clad, barren swamps of Lithuania, lying under gloomy skies, which brooded over a fire-blackened waste. The results of his colossal recklessness were seen in the destruction of half a million of men, a veritable holocaust of Nations, offered at the shrine of the man who basely fled to Paris, leaving his victims to the tender mercies of barbarous Cossacks and an infuriated peasantry.

This year, (1912), on the 23rd of June, a century will have elapsed since Napoleon crossed the Niemen to commence this wicked and wanton war.

To those who worship at the shrine of the Moloch of Militarism (that bloody idol to which have been sacrificed so many millions of the human race) I commend this narrative. Those also who still believe in the "Napoleonic Legend" may find in the following pages matter for reflection.

The centenary of the Moscow campaign seems a fitting occasion to republish, in an English dress, this graphic description of one of the most ghastly episodes in history; which stands on the same evil eminence as the destruction of Carthage and Jerusalem, and will remain for all time a sinister example of the miseries which can be inflicted on mankind by the diabolism of unbridled ambition.

Preface

I describe what I myself have seen; eyewitness of one of the greatest disasters that have ever befallen a powerful nation; spectator and participator throughout the whole course of this terrible and ever-memorable campaign, I do not pretend to present the facts with artistic effect and coloured with exaggeration. I recorded day by day the events which unfolded themselves before my eyes, and I only seek to communicate the impressions I received. It was by the glare of burning Moscow that I described the sack of that city; it was on the banks of the Berezina that I recorded the fatal passage of that river. The plans of the battlefields that accompany this work were executed upon the spot by order of Prince Eugene.

It is almost impossible to realise the difficulties which I had to surmount in order to preserve my memoirs. Engaged, like my comrades-in-arms, in continual fighting; perishing from cold, tormented by the pangs of hunger; victim of every kind of suffering; uncertain at the dawn of each day whether I should see its close, my mind seemed to concentrate itself upon the desire to live to describe my experiences. Possessed by this indescribable craving, each night when seated before a smouldering fire in a temperature of 20 to 25 degrees below zero, I recorded the events of the day. The same knife that had served to cut up a piece of horseflesh to allay the pangs of hunger, I employed to fashion a pen out of a raven's feathers; a little gunpowder, diluted in the hollow of my hand with melted snow, furnished me with a substitute for writing materials.

I have written my narrative without spite and without prejudice; but I cannot deny that in describing this enterprise—one of the most deplorable which ambition ever conceived—I have had a hundred times to repress my indignation against the author of so much evil. At the same time, the admiration due to his past greatness, and the recollection of the memorable victories of which I was a witness, and in the glories of which I participated, have imposed upon me the duty of restricting myself to facts in my impeachment of the conqueror, and scrupulously to refrain from abusive declamation.

Having continually before my eyes the spectacle of this host of warriors, miserably perishing in distant deserts, I have only been sustained by the idea of paying homage to their constancy; to a courage which has never been denied, and to deeds all the more heroic in that they neither redounded to the advantage of their country nor reaped glory for themselves. I shall be content if I have been able to show by this enthralling narrative, that in the midst of such overwhelming disasters our brave soldiers were always worthy of themselves; that they failed in nothing of their ancient renown, and that, always formidable to the enemy, they were only vanquished by the elements.

CHAPTER 1

France After Tilsit

Those who search our annals for the most brilliant period of our glory will, without question, find that France was never more powerful than immediately after the Treaty of Tilsit. At that time Spain, under the name of our ally, was in reality one of our provinces, supplying us with men, with money and with ships. Italy, wisely governed by a prince who was not only a good soldier but an able administrator, was subject to the same laws as the rest of the Empire, enjoyed a prosperity as great as our own, and recalled with pride that her legions had displayed in the first Polish campaign a splendid courage which procured for France a glorious peace. Alarmed by our colossal aggrandisement, Germany, unable longer to oppose herself to our success, only sought to assure her existence by accepting all the great changes which had overthrown the Germanic constitution.

England alone, the persistent foe to an ambition so fatal to her own, saw in Napoleon's achievements only danger for herself and oppression for the Continent. Determined to place bounds to this inordinate ambition, she represented to each of the Northern Powers how vital it was to their interests to stay the rapidly increasing progress of our overweening preponderance. Vain attempt! These sovereigns, deceived by their courtiers, did not possess the experience necessary to convince them that they must all combine to crush the giant who would devour them.

After his return from Tilsit, the mania for invasion suggested to the victor the idea of kindling in Spain an unjust war, which was doomed later on to blast his laurels, and afford his enemies the longed-for opportunity of annihilating so dangerous a power.

A weak prince was the nominal ruler of that unhappy Peninsula;

• St Petersburg

SCALE OF MILES

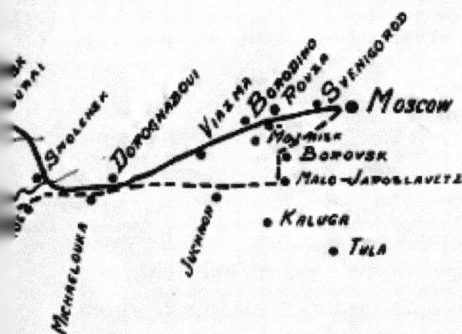

0   25   50   75   100   200

SVENIGOROD

• Moscow

VIAZMA
BORODINO
ROUZA

DOROGHABOUI

SMOLENSK
MOJAISK
• BOROVSK
• MALO-JAROSLAVETZ

MICHELOVKA
JUCHNOW
• KALUGA
• TULA

ROUTE OF FOURTH CORPS TO MOSCOW ————

· · · · · FROM MOSCOW ————

IN THE RETREAT THE FOURTH CORPS FORMED PART OF
THE GENERAL ARMY AND FOLLOWED THE SAME ROUTE

DISTANCES

FROM KOVNO TO MOSCOW ···· 783 MILES

" MOSCOW - KOVNO ···· 774 "

TOTAL   1,557 "

but a perfidious favourite, a traitor to his country, and basely ungrateful to his royal benefactor, was the actual governor of the State; and by the most craven subservience to the foreigner disgraced the nation whose rights he seemed to have usurped, only to subject it to a long and shameful servitude. The credulity of the father and the timidity of the son facilitated these criminal designs, and he played off one against the other. Under the pretence of stopping those quarrels, Napoleon, feigning peaceful intentions, promised his mediation, repaired to Bayonne, and seized both monarchs so that he might dispose of their crown. The proud Castilians, indignant at such an outrage, from being faithful allies became irreconcilable enemies; they immortalised themselves by their constancy in misfortune; while we, on the other hand, lost our reputation for invincibility by attempting to accomplish a design utterly opposed to sound policy, and which presents in the history of a civilised nation an instance of ingratitude so monstrous that no parallel can be found for it in the records of barbarous peoples.

Spain, although bordering upon France, was little known; the character of its inhabitants was known even less; this ignorance misled the conqueror, and led him to attempt a sinister invasion of which all the evils are subordinate to the fact that it was, together with the campaign of Moscow, the prime cause of the events which resulted in the deliverance of Europe. It is no part of my plan to give a resume of an aggression which led to a struggle between two nations equally generous; who had always been united by mutual esteem, and who still would be so if a perfidious despot had not founded his power upon the hatred of Peoples. This struggle, memorable for its ferocity and its vicissitudes, should afford the historian a splendid subject for his pen, and the soldier a vast field for study.

At present I confine myself to observing that Providence seems to have prompted Napoleon to these two iniquitous wars in order to teach the Spaniards and the Russians how fatal must be an alliance with evil men, reserving as her last lesson in morality the luring on of her instrument from blunder to blunder, in order to show humanity that while tyranny is a crime against all mankind, it can easily be defeated by a general uprising under the banners of Justice.

While Napoleon vainly endeavoured to drive the English from the Peninsula, a new storm burst over Germany. Austria, who had been so often humiliated, could not accustom herself to the shameful yoke which her defeats had imposed upon her. The revolt of the Spaniards, and the numerous army with which England supported them, afforded her a favourable opportunity to recover her lost possessions, and to resume that political preponderance which she valued so much.

The new war with Austria was for France only a fresh field for the achievement of military glory. Landshut, Eckmühl and Ratisbonne,—a series of brilliant successes, paved the way for the most memorable of her victories; the field of Wagram repeated the prodigies of Austerlitz, and in one campaign secured for France the most decisive results.

The Treaty of Vienna not only gave us peace, but placed under our domination opulent provinces; it extended the boundaries of Würtemberg and Bavaria, and seemed to foreshadow the complete restoration of Poland. But this treaty, enforced by a power which threatened the general security, would have contained the germs of another war, had not the most august and most unexpected of alliances crowned the fortunes of the victor.

The sovereign of Austria, wearied with a resistance which had proved so fatal to his arms, bowed to the inevitable by yielding to a man before whom everything yielded. He sacrificed his glory and even his blood to obtain peace, realising thus those fabulous times when magnanimous princes offered up their daughters to avert the plague which devastated their countries.

Of all the good fortune which destiny bestowed upon Napoleon, this marriage was, without question, the most extraordinary, since it secured the position of a man, who, emerging from the ranks, had allied himself with a powerful monarch; but nothing satisfied with such an elevation, he was dazzled by it, and deliberately threw away all its results, in the mad endeavour to surpass the limits of his brilliant destiny. Thus, utterly wanting in wisdom, that which appeared to add to his greatness only became the cause of his ruin.

This epoch was without doubt the most astonishing of all those which occurred during the life of Napoleon. What man could then have enjoyed more glorious and more peaceful days! From a simple citizen he had seen himself raised to the first throne in the world; his reign had been one long series of victories; and as the summit of his happiness, a son, the most ardent of his desires, was born into the world to succeed him. Even the peoples who were bound beneath his yoke were beginning to be reconciled to it, and seemed desirous of preserving the crown to his house. All the foreign princes who were subjected to his power had become his vassals, maintained his troops, and paid tribute to satisfy his luxury and extravagance. In fine, all obeyed him. He lacked nothing that could contribute to his happiness.

Nothing, that is, if one can be happy without love and without justice; but, never having known these feelings, he found neither felicity nor repose. Abandoned to a restless spirit and to chimeras of an insatiable ambition, he listened to nothing but the promptings of his tumultuous passions; to satisfy which he sighed for the unattainable, and disregarding others he forgot everything until he forgot himself.

The Continent appeared to have accepted in good faith all the great changes which Napoleon had effected; and the vulgar, whose restricted vision rarely penetrates to the dark recesses of kingly ambition, believed that the extraordinary alliance of this man with an archduchess would crown his immoderate desires; and above all that the softening influence of fatherhood would lead him to see that a throne was consolidated not by blood and tears, but by wise institutions, which securing attachment to his government would ensure its permanence. Never had mortal combined easier and more certain means to realise the happiness of the world. It sufficed him to be just and prudent; founding its hopes on that, the Nation accorded him that unbounded confidence which he afterwards so cruelly abused. Posterity will decide whether the worst crime of Napoleon consisted in the direct evil he committed, or in his omission to confer upon mankind those blessings which he could command, but which never so much as crossed his mind.

This man, who will be for historians the riddle of the human heart, would have been admired by the whole world if he had devoted to a proper object the exceptional abilities which he cultivated for the enslavement of mankind. But far from meditating with calmness and moderation upon the beneficent application of his genius, he conceived enterprises beyond the compass of human power, and to realise them he forgot the host of victims whose sacrifice they would involve. Tortured by sombre visions, the slightest contradiction irritated him, and the bare idea that a nation existed sufficiently determined to turn a deaf ear to all his overtures, and to resist his sinister influence, was a reflection that tore his heart asunder and poisoned the brightest moments of his glory. To crush an enemy whom he could not reach, he extended in vain his arms to the two confines of Europe; hardly had he thought to grasp this enemy at one point, when it escaped him at another; furious at seeing his project foiled, he aspired to universal domination, for the sole reason that a people isolated from the Continent knew how to profit by its fortunate position to exempt itself from his intolerable yoke.

In the hope of realising his fatal system, he extended France in all directions beyond her natural boundaries; he formed chimerical designs, and professed to entertain a dread of Russia under the pretence that, desiring to seat herself upon the ancient throne of Constantine, she would thus command the two seas that encircle Europe He then arrogated to himself the *rôle* of prophet, warning France of remote misfortunes, and sacrificing the present generation to the problematical welfare of generations yet unborn.

Deluded by the brilliance of his fortune, he despised the advice of the wisest counsellors; ability was only recognised in those who would agree with his insane pretensions; and with him the most subservient courtier became the most useful subject. Despot over his people and his army; himself the slave of his own desires, he aspired to universal dominion, and carried his ambitious projects to the extremities of the pole. A defective judgment conducted him to an unsound policy, and led him to make in the north, as he had already done in the south, a dangerous enemy, out of the most loyal and powerful of his allies.

Intoxicated with success, he persuaded himself that he was the object of envy to all the Powers; judging her by his own standard, he thought that Russia viewed with secret jealousy the union contracted between the most ancient and the most recent of empires. Full of this idea, he pursued his devastating plan; and wishing, as he said, that his dynasty should soon become the oldest in Europe, he sought to consecrate his usurpation by dethroning all the legitimate princes, to bestow their crowns upon his brothers, who, too feeble to second his tyranny, only shone around him as pallid satellites shine around a baleful sun.

CHAPTER 2

Napoleon Rudely Rejects Russian Offer

The Treaty of Tilsit was merely a truce for those who knew the character of Napoleon. In comparing the continually increasing power of the two great empires, it was universally recognised from their common splendour that one or the other would overthrow the colossal edifice which both appeared desirous of uprearing. Formerly the distance which separated them inevitably tended to keep their interests apart; but the conquests of France having made her Russia's neighbour, everything portended their approaching rupture.

For more than two years each had maintained towards the other a hostile attitude; until at last Napoleon, having reinforced the garrison of Dantzig, formed several *corps d'armée,* completed the cavalry, the train of artillery and the whole military organisation, considered himself in a position to complain of Russia; and conveniently forgetting that he had, in defiance of treaties, invaded Holland, the Hanseatic cities, and above all the Duchy of Oldenburg, over which Alexander's brother-in-law had legitimate rights, he charged him, as a grave offence, with having renewed commercial relations with England.

Nothing, however, in the shape of hostile action was taken, with the exception of the famous *senatus consultum,* which organised the Empire on a military basis. The country thus found itself on the verge of the most perilous struggle in which it had ever been engaged; one half of Europe was about to march against the other, without Napoleon having deigned to inform the Senate, and without that body having been allowed to express an opinion on a war in which France was about to pour out her blood and her treasure.

Public opinion was as yet uncertain as to the motive and the object of all these armaments. Our differences with the Russians, in view of the climate of that country, offered so few advantages and involved such great risks, that it was difficult to imagine that we would ourselves provoke aggressions where we had so much to lose and so little to gain. It was believed, on the contrary, that the three great Empires were about to combine to effect the partition of Turkey, and thus strike a disastrous blow at the English possessions in Asia. But those who were aware of the dissatisfaction of Napoleon at the refusal of the Senate of St. Petersburg to give him Alexander's sister in marriage, had no doubt whatever that our preparations were directed against the North. The mission of Colonel Czernichew, and particularly his hasty departure, following upon his insidious attempts to discover the secrets of the State, were proofs positive that there would shortly arrive a terrible struggle between the rival powers, of which the shock would overturn the world.

Thenceforth France continued her gigantic armaments; innumerable *cohorts* passed from the banks of the Tagus to those of the Oder, and the same soldiers who had recently camped on the fertile plains of Lombardy, at the end of three months found themselves transported to the arid sands of Poland.

In these circumstances all eyes were turned towards Prussia; and the whole world waited with impatience to see which side she would espouse; her cities, her territories, were all occupied by our armies; nevertheless the weight of our alliance seemed so opposed to her policy, and above all so injurious to her interests, that in spite of the subjection to which she had been reduced, she hesitated to pronounce herself; when, to the universal astonishment, she finally decided in our favour. Those who knew how Napoleon contracted his alliances, remarked that Prussia had only adhered to us when she saw Berlin pressed from all sides, and when the Duke of Reggio, (Marshal Oudinot), was on the point of entering it as a conqueror. Shortly afterwards the king found himself obliged to abandon his capital and to leave it to the tender mercies of the French general.

At the same period another treaty was disclosed, between France and Austria, the principal clauses of which provided that each of the contracting Powers was to furnish to whichever might be attacked an auxiliary corps of thirty thousand men. And as Napoleon alleged that he was menaced by Russia, he asked and obtained the promised contingent, which was placed under the command of Prince Schwartzenberg. Thus Napoleon coerced the kings as Robespierre had tyrannised over the Peoples; under each of them nobody dared to remain neutral; love of peace appeared to them treason, and moderation was held to be a crime.

If surprise was felt at seeing the Austrians and the Prussians accepting our alliance, much more was experienced in learning that Sweden had rejected it. This Nation, which was perhaps the only one interested in seconding our expedition against Russia, was so disgusted with our invasion of Pomerania, and with the aggression made against the trade of Stralsund, that she declined to avail herself of a unique opportunity for avenging the fate of Charles XII., preferring to renounce the provinces of which she had been deprived rather than to engage with us in treaties which, owing to the bad faith of our leader, she had no guarantee would be kept.

The roads of Germany swarmed with troops, who in their march maintained the most rigid discipline, all converging towards the Oder. The King of Westphalia, (Jerome Bonaparte), at the head of his guard and two divisions, had already passed that river, as had also the Bavarians and the Saxons. The first corps was at Stettin, the third marched in the same direction, and the fourth, on arriving at Glogau, replaced the Westphalians, who left for Warsaw.

The organisation of our army since its formation was imposing; and if I were to enumerate all the nations which composed it, I should recall the descriptions of Homer when he speaks of the different peoples who marched to the conquest of Troy. In the month of April the Grand Army included nine corps of infantry, each composed of at least three divisions (the first had five) and one of cavalry; to these must be added the Imperial Guard, consisting of about fifty thousand men, and four grand corps of cavalry bearing the name of "reserve." The total of our forces, exclusive of the Austrians, might amount to four hundred thousand infantry and sixty thousand cavalry. Nearly twelve hundred guns, distributed among the different *corps d'armée*, constituted the force of the artillery.

The Prince of Eckmühl, (Marshal Davoust), had for some time held the command of the five divisions which formed the first corps; the second was entrusted to the Duke of Reggio; the third to the Duke of Elchingen; (Marshal Ney), the fourth, known as the Army of Italy (including the Royal Guard), was commanded by the viceroy; (Eugene Beauharnais), Prince Poniatowski, at the head of his Poles, formed the fifth corps. The Bavarians, incorporated in the sixth, were under the orders of Count Gouvion Saint-Cyr. The Saxons counted

as the seventh corps, and had for leader General Reynier. The Westphalians, marching under the orders of their king, took rank in the
army under the name of the eighth corps. With regard to the ninth,
only its framework was formed, but it was known that it was intended for the Duke of Belluno; (Marshal Victor), lastly, the tenth corps,
placed under the orders of the Duke of Taranto, (Marshal Macdonald),
was composed of the Prussians, commanded by General Grawert, and
of the division Grandjean, among whom the only Frenchmen were
Generals Ricard and Bacheler, and the artillery.

The Russian forces opposed to us were divided into two parts,
described under the names of First and Second Army of the West; one
was commanded by General Baron Barclay de Tolly, and the other by
Prince Bagration. They consisted of forty-seven divisions, inclusive
of eight of cavalry. The Emperor Alexander, who with his whole staff
had arrived at Wilna on the 26th of April, had been for some time
prepared to repel all our attacks. But those who had long made a study
of our system of warfare unceasingly urged him not to risk a battle,
being convinced that Napoleon's ambition would lure him into savage regions, which would be, during the rigours of winter, the tomb
of his army.

Although Prussia had declared for us, prudence made it necessary
to distrust an alliance contracted under compulsion; and the French
garrisons stationed in the various fortresses remained therefore always
vigilantly on their guard; particularly at Glogau, which was the place
assigned to several corps for the passage of the Oder. Its vicinity to
Breslau, where the King of Prussia had retired with the rest of his
troops, naturally gave rise to uneasiness, and compelled the governor
to secure himself from a *coup de main* which would have been fatal to
the designs of France.

The fourth corps, which had come from Italy, under the style of
"Army of Observation," seemed by its title to be charged sometimes
with marching in advance of the Grand Army, sometimes on its flanks,
and again uniting with it when important emergencies demanded its
support. Having had the honour of belonging to it, I have deemed it
necessary in the first place to describe its operations, as its isolated manoeuvres were of high importance and came specially within my own
knowledge; besides which this corps participated in the big engage-
ments which distinguished our march on Moscow. As to the calamities of the retreat, it is only too well known that they were common
to the whole army.

The viceroy, before proceeding to take command of the fourth corps, which in the meanwhile was under the orders of the Duke of Abrantès, (Marshal Juno), was called to Paris, where his conferences with the emperor led to the belief that he was destined for duties even higher than those of the leader of an army. For some time a report had been current that Napoleon, wishing to end the war in Spain himself, had announced to his council that he intended, in the event of his having to leave the capital, to entrust this young prince with the government of the Empire. But these lofty hopes, which indeed after the repudiation of his mother, (the Empress Josephine), appeared to have little foundation, were speedily shattered, for the viceroy, seven or eight days after his arrival in Paris, having received his instructions, left for Poland, and arrived at Glogau on the 12th of May.

During the day on which this prince remained in that town he reviewed the troops placed under his orders, and was very satisfied with the fine appearance of the fifteenth division, composed entirely of Italians; it might then number more than thirteen thousand men; the soldiers of which it was formed seemed such seasoned veterans, that General Pino, although first captain of the Royal Guard, considered himself honoured by such a command.

The rendezvous of our corps was at Plock, where the Bavarians had already arrived, and it was towards that town that the Viceroy, passing through Posen, directed his steps. His arrival having preceded by some days that of his army, he employed the interval to reconnoitre the Bug and the Narew, and to unite by a system of defence the line which the latter river described with the lakes which extend from Augerburg to Johannisburg The prince in particular visited the fortress of Modlin, whither the King of Westphalia had also repaired; the dispositions which they made seemed to indicate that Volhynia was to be the theatre of war. But, a few days later, the emperor having arrived at Thorn, became the cynosure of all eyes wherever he appeared. The viceroy hastened to tender him his homage, and on returning made all the preparations necessary for a movement on the 4th of June.

On that day our corps began its march on Soldau, where it arrived on the 6th. A two days' halt was ordered, which was utilised to construct the ovens for the bakeries. We then advanced upon Villemberg, where a forty-eight hours' halt was also made. In three days' marching we reached Rastenbourg, a pretty little town surrounded by lakes, where the army found some supplies; since leaving Glogau we had not encountered one larger or more populous. From Rastenbourg we went to Lotzen; then to Oletzko, the last town in Eastern Prussia. Two leagues farther on we entered the Duchy of Warsaw, and at once noticed the striking difference between the two States; in one the houses are clean and well built, in the other they reek with a fetid stench and are wretchedly constructed. The inhabitants of the first are civil and hospitable; those of the second only consist of filthy and disgusting Jews; as to the small Polish nobility, their misery is prejudicial to their dignity. The great nobles, whose existence is very different, are splendid, brave and generous; their high sense of honour and their love of country will always make them veritable heroes. The peasant class are few in number; this want of population, combined with the barrenness of the soil, results in Poland being badly cultivated; its sandy territory, covered with rye, appears to be stricken with sterility.

On arriving at Kalwary we found merely a large hamlet full of Jews; at Marienpol, the same population. Wearied with their revolting aspect, and above all by their number, we said that Poland was nothing but Judaea where one sometimes chanced to meet a few Poles.

During this march Napoleon left Thorn, and visited the fortress of Dantzig, which his spirit of domination led him to regard as the most important in his Empire; from there he went to Osterode, rapidly passed through the towns of Liebstadt and Kreustenbourg, in the neighbourhood of Eylau, Heilsberg, and Friedland, the scene of his greatest military glory; he reviewed numerous divisions, visited the fortress of Pillau, and a few days afterwards, marching with the centre of his army he passed along the Pregel as far as Gumbinnen.

The emperor hoped by these armaments to impose on Russia, and compel her to bend to his will, while he wished to rid himself of all who could establish order and cement peace. Alexander, on the other hand, by an excess of moderation, rare indeed amongst powerful monarchs, agreed that France should maintain a garrison in Dantzig; but he required with reason that Prussia should be evacuated, so that there should remain between the two Empires an independent State. Such were the wise and moderate stipulations which Napoleon called "an arrogant and altogether extraordinary demand," and upon the formal refusal of Russia to receive the embassy of General Lauriston without the acceptance of these preliminary conditions, he rushed into the room in a fury, and bellowed in the frantic manner which the slightest contradiction always evoked, "the vanquished give themselves the airs of victors; fatality impels them; let destiny be fulfilled." And there and then, leaving Gumbinnen, he repaired to Wilkowiski (22nd

June 1812), where he issued the following proclamation as an order of the day:—

> Soldiers!—The second Polish war has commenced; the first ended at Friedland and Tilsit. At Tilsit, Russia swore eternal alliance with France and war against England. Today she violates her oaths! She refuses to give any explanation of her strange conduct in demanding that the French eagles shall repass the Rhine, thus leaving our allies to her mercy.
> Russia is drawn on by Fate. Her destinies must be fulfilled. Does she, then, think us degenerates; are we then no longer the soldiers of Austerlitz? She places us between dishonour and war. The choice cannot be doubtful. Forward then! Let us pass the Niemen; let us carry war into her territory. The second Polish war will be as glorious to the French arms as the first; but the peace which we shall conclude will carry with it guarantees and put an end to the sinister influence which Russia for fifty years has exercised upon the affairs of Europe.

This proclamation, remarkable for an excess of bluster and above all for the mania which Napoleon had for assuming in his utterances the pose of an oracle, reached us at Kalwary. Though it was merely a monotonous repetition of the ideas expressed on so many previous occasions, it excited the ardour of the troops, who are always ready to swallow anything which flatters their courage. Proud of being about to enter Russian territory they were delighted that in commencing the second Polish campaign they were about to leave behind them the river which had previously marked the limits of the first. The word Niemen inflamed the imagination, everyone burned to cross it: and the desire was all the more natural, inasmuch as, apart from our spirit of conquest, the miserable condition of the Duchy of Warsaw added each day to our privations and sufferings; and to put a stop to our grumbling the enemy's country was held up to us as a promised land.

The Russian Army opposed to ours was formed into six grand corps: the first of 20,000 men was commanded by Count Wittgenstein, and occupied Rossina and Keidanoui. The second, under the orders of General Bagawout, also of 20,000 men, held Kowno. The third, of 24,000 strong, was at New-Troki, and was commanded by General Schomoaloff. The country between New-Troki and Lida was occupied by the fourth corps, commanded by General Tutschkoff. These four corps, with the guard at Wilna, formed what the Russians called

"The First Army of the West." The second army was composed of the fifth corps, the strength of which amounted to 40,000 men; of the sixth corps, that of Doctorow, numbering 18,000 men, and Platow's Cossacks. This second army, of which Prince Bagration was the commander-in-chief, was encamped at Grodno and Lida and distributed throughout the whole of Volhynia. General Marckoff organised in this province the ninth and fifteenth divisions, which were to form the seventh corps; but this general, recalled to the army of the centre, resigned the command in Volhynia to General Tormasow, who created a new corps destined to act against the Duchy of Warsaw.

CHAPTER 3

Privations and Difficulties Begin

Such was the position of the Russians beyond the Niemen when the King of Naples, (Marshal Murat), who commanded the whole of our cavalry, removed his quarters two leagues on the other side of that river (23rd June), having with him the two corps of cavalry commanded by Generals Nansouty and Montbrun, each composed of three divisions. The first corps took position at the opening of the forest of Pilwisky. The second corps and the guard followed. The third, fourth and sixth corps advanced by Marienpol to the extent of one day's march. The King of Westphalia directed himself upon Grodno, with the fifth, seventh and eighth corps, by returning along the Narew, and faced the army commanded by Prince Bagration.

The pontoons, under the orders of General of Artillery Eblé, arrived the same day close to the Niemen. Napoleon thereupon, in the disguise of a Polish soldier, examined from the heights which dominated Kowno the most suitable point at which to effect the passage of the river; and towards eight o'clock in the evening the army placed itself in motion; three companies of *voltigeurs* of Morant's division crossed the Niemen, and protected the construction of three bridges, which were thrown across this river, where five years previously the two emperors had sworn eternal friendship!

At dawn of day, that is about one in the morning, we were in Kowno. The general of division, Pajol, having pushed the advanced guard farther forward, sent a battalion to occupy the town, and drove before him the enemy's cavalry, which retreated as we advanced. During the 24th and 25th the army never ceased crossing the three bridges constructed in a single night. At the same time Napoleon, who had arrived at Kowno, ordered the construction of another bridge across the Wilia in the immediate vicinity, while the King of Naples marched towards Zismori, and Marshals the Prince of Eckmühl and the Duke of Elchingen betook themselves, the first to Roumchichki and the other to Kormelow. Finally, on the next day (27th June) our light horse were only ten leagues from Wilna.

The day following, towards two in the morning, the King of Naples continued his march, supported by General Bruyères' cavalry division and by the first corps. But the Russians retreated in all directions behind the Wilia, after having burnt the bridge, together with the magazines containing the food supplies. A deputation of the leading inhabitants of Wilna having presented themselves before Napoleon, handed him the keys of the town, which he entered towards midday. Instead of remaining there, he rode to the outposts of General Bruyères to ascertain in what direction the enemy had retired. They were being pursued upon the left bank of the Wilia, when in a cavalry charge the hussar captain, Octave de Ségur was wounded, this distinguished officer being thus the first prisoner to fall into the hands of the Russians in this campaign.

The place which Napoleon had selected for crossing the Niemen was extremely advantageous, Kowno being commanded by a high mountain situated upon the bank held by us, and descending abruptly to the town. Even had this position been less favourable for us, it was no part of the Russian plan of campaign to oppose themselves to our initial efforts. It is stated with regard to this subject, that the Emperor Alexander had taken all the necessary measures to dispute the passage of the Niemen; but at the moment when the attack was about to commence General Barclay de Tolly, throwing himself at the feet of his master, implored him not to join issue with so formidable an army to whom no effective resistance could be made; and urged him to allow Napoleon to pass like a torrent, reserving all their forces for the time when the enemy would begin to be weakened.

I cannot vouch for the truth of this story, but thus much is certain: that Alexander, having remained for six weeks at Wilna, reviewed his armies, made elaborate arrangements, reconnoitred the principal positions on the Niemen that were capable of defence, and then suddenly abandoned this line without fighting, and ordered a retreat upon the Dwina and the Dnieper.

On arriving at Wilna, we were enabled to read the proclamation which had been issued by the Emperor of Russia, when he learnt that the French troops had crossed the Niemen; it displays so vividly the nobility and equity of this sovereign, that in comparing it with that of Napoleon, published at Wilkowiski, a complete insight can be obtained into the characters of those two potentates upon whom the eyes of the whole world were fixed. Here is the proclamation:

Wilna, 25th June 1812.
For a long time past we have observed, on the part of the Emperor of the French, manifestations of hostility against Russia; but we have always hoped to assuage them by conciliatory and pacific means. At last, seeing the continual renewal of these manifest provocations, notwithstanding our desire to preserve tranquillity, we have been compelled to complete and to concentrate our armies. Nevertheless we still flattered ourselves that a reconciliation might be effected by remaining within the frontiers of our Empire, without violating the peace, and merely with the object of defending ourselves. All these conciliatory and pacific methods, however, have failed to preserve the repose which we desired. The Emperor of the French, in suddenly attacking our army at Kowno, has been the first to declare war. Seeing thus that nothing can make him accessible to the desire of maintaining peace, we have no alternative but to oppose our forces to those of the enemy, invoking the aid of the Almighty as the Witness and Defender of the Truth. It is unnecessary for me to remind the leaders, the officers and the soldiers, of their duty and their courage; the blood of the valorous Slavs runs in their veins. Warriors! you defend religion, fatherland and liberty. I am in the midst of you. God is against the aggressor.

While our whole army was concentrating around Wilna, the second Russian corps under General Bagawout retreated upon the Dwina; Count Wittgenstein also retired upon Wilkomir, as the Duke of Reggio, by marching upon Janow and Chatoui, had forced him to abandon the Samogitie, On the 28th, an action took place close to Develtovo, the cannonade being very heavy. The enemy did not maintain his position; driven by our troops as far as the Dwina, he recrossed the bridge over this river with such great precipitation that he had no time to burn it.

The Russians were repulsed beyond the river, while the fifth, seventh and eighth corps, under Prince Poniatowski and the King of Westphalia, captured Grodno. The dilatoriness displayed by the latter in conducting his operations allowed the Second Army of the West, under Prince Bagration, to entrench itself in a strong position, and to withstand all our attacks. By the skilful use of numerous bodies of Cossacks under Platow, there is no doubt that he might long have held the provinces committed to his charge, if, after the evacuation of Wilna, Bagration had not been ordered to return so as to effect a union with General Barclay de Tolly. With a view to preventing this junction, the Prince of Eckmühl was immediately detached from our centre to march towards Minsk, and thence to direct the operations of the King of Westphalia, with which the emperor was extremely dissatisfied; but Jerome, refusing to submit to an order which so grievously wounded his *amour propre*, threw up his command, and obtained permission to return to his dominions.

On the 29th of June, the fourth corps, which had up to then remained in observation behind the Niemen, at last saw this longed-for river. On arriving at Pilony, the place selected for its passage, we found the viceroy, the Duke of Abrantés, and all the staff, who, in very rainy weather, were engaged in constructing a bridge. The artillery of the Royal Guard were in position on the plateau which commanded the opposite bank; a wise precaution, but unnecessary, as several reconnaissances beyond the Niemen proved that on that side all was perfectly quiet.

We were relieved thenceforth from all anxiety as to the success of the crossing, as Lt.-Col. Bataille, *aide-de-camp* to the viceroy, who had been sent on a mission to Napoleon, informed us that our troops, after having passed without hindrance through the defile of Kowno as far as Roumchicki, had arrived at Zismori without fighting; that the Russians had only made a very feeble defence of their positions between Roui Kontoui and Wilna, and that above all, not having constructed any redoubt upon the heights, which are about two leagues beyond that town, the emperor had made his entry on the 28th preceded by the Polish lancers of the 8th regiment, commanded by Prince Dominic Radziwill. The commandant reported that the suburbs had suffered a little from the operations of war, but that order having been promptly restored everything had resumed its normal course, and that this large and populous town not only afforded supplies for the army, but conditions favourable for Napoleon's designs.

Our stay at Pilony, during very wet weather, was characterised by such extraordinary misfortunes, that, without being superstitious, every one looked upon them as a sinister omen of future misery. In this frightful village the viceroy himself was without a lodging. We were huddled under wretched sheds, exposed to all the inclemency of the weather. The scarcity of provisions seemed to foreshadow what we should one day have to endure from the horrors of famine; the rain descending in torrents, overwhelmed men and horses, who were absolutely without shelter; the former survived, but the latter were destroyed, All round our bivouacs they could be seen lying dead in hundreds, while on the roads nothing was to be seen but dead horses, waggons overturned, baggage scattered all about; and it was in the month of June that we experienced these horrors of cold, rain and want! This storm prevailed everywhere and continued the whole night; it is said that at Zismori a thunderbolt falling in the camp of the infantry of the guard destroyed several men. Such disasters were of gloomy augury for the future; there was universal apprehension, but the sun appearing once more upon the horizon dispersed the clouds, and from that moment the fine weather appeared as if it would be unending.

The day following (30th June), the thirteenth and fourteenth divisions, commanded by Generals Delzons and Broussiers, peaceably effected their passage. The Royal Guard, under General Theodore Lecchi, followed by Pino's division, crossed on the 1st of July, and thus all the combined Italian troops passed over the Niemen in presence of the viceroy. They responded to this honour with spontaneous acclamations, and the prince must, on his part, have experienced great satisfaction in seeing the soldiers whom he had trained pass into the enemy's territory; but above all, in observing that at six hundred leagues from their native land they maintained the same order and discipline as when exercising in front of his palace.

Hardly had we set foot on the opposite bank, when we seemed to be breathing a new air; the roads, however, were pretty bad, the forests gloomy and the villages deserted; but our imagination, excited by the spirit of conquest, led us to view everything with enchantment!

After a two hours' march over marshy ground, we arrived at the hamlet of Kroui, the *château* and houses of which are built of wood. I note this fact for the last time, for in Russia all the villages are so constructed; when they are otherwise built I will record the circumstance. We found here some brandy, which the soldiers pillaged with avidity. As there were no Jews among the inhabitants the houses were deserted, which showed us that the enemy, desirous of desolating the country on our whole line of march, had taken the inhabitants and the cattle away with them.

The next morning (2nd July) we received orders to march on

Zismori to rejoin the high road by which the emperor had passed. On arriving at that large hamlet, we only found there some Jews terrified at the horrible tumult occasioned by our passage. Our original instructions were to halt there, but on the arrival of the viceroy, the staff continued its march to establish itself at Melangani, leaving Pino's division at Zismori, and those of Generals Delzons and Broussier in the environs of Strasounoui. The day following (3rd July) we marched towards Rouicontoui, a wretched village where on the left we beheld a little wooden *château*. The Prince did not stop there, but went to sleep at a farm close to where the road branches off to New-Troki.

We were disagreeably surprised at seeing our advance guard leaving the road to Wilna and taking that to New-Troki; everyone exclaimed against this *contretemps*, saying that a fatality seemed to attach to our corps, which, having need of repose, found itself forbidden to enter a town where we expected to refresh ourselves after a long and painful march. This hope having been dissipated, we sought to console ourselves by the idea that we should be directed to Witepsk and Smolensk, and that these two cities would enable us to forget Wilna.

After weary hours of continuous marching through forests and over muddy tracks, we at last arrived at New-Troki (4th July), situated on a hill and surrounded by lakes. This pleasing situation offered a striking contrast to the country we had traversed, and everybody remarked the fine effect produced by a large convent built upon the summit of the mountain which commanded the town. Others were struck with the density of the forests, and the clearness of the water which never froze. All those who had artistic tastes were lost in admiration of this lovely country. In the midst of the lake stood an ancient *château* in ruins, the embrowned mass of which projected on one side over the surface of the water, and on the other stood out against the rosy sky.

Troki appeared to be an enchanted resting-place; but the illusion ceased the moment we entered it. Scarcely had we reached the first houses, when a troop of Jews, followed by women, children and old men with long beards, threw themselves at our feet to implore us to deliver them from the rapacity of the soldiery, who, swarming through the houses, stole or destroyed everything they could lay their hands upon. We could only give these poor wretches very cold comfort. The town contained no magazines, and our soldiers who had for so long been without rations only subsisted on what they could pillage. This gave rise to an extreme disorder, fatal to discipline, which is almost invariably the certain precursor of the ruin of an army.

The houses in Troki had been dismantled by the inhabitants, who, in fleeing, had carried off everything. Those of the Jews, disgusting by their filth, were sacked by our troops, so that this place, so delightful in its aspect, was, so far as we were concerned, associated with everything repulsive; we could not even find straw on which to lie down, and it was necessary to go a distance of four leagues to obtain fodder for the horses.

As it seemed probable that we should have to stay at Troki, the headquarters of the army having been established at Wilna, the Viceroy repaired to that town, where he had long conferences with the Emperor. Several officers also obtained leave to go there; and there it was that one could see the tricks which Napoleon resorted to in order to assure success. By the most gaudy promises he roused the enthusiasm of the populace, and thus obtained from them the greatest sacrifices. The nobility also seconded with all their power those who asserted that they were fighting to secure the independence of Poland and restore to her the splendour of the times of Ladislas and Sigismund.

The sight of the Polish standards planted on the walls of the ancient capital of the Dukes of Lithuania evoked the enthusiasm of all the inhabitants, and thrilling memories of the ancient glory of their country. Nothing could be more stimulating to ideas of greatness than to see on the banks of the Wilia the same warriors who had consecrated their time of exile and added lustre to the Polish name on the banks of the Nile, the Tiber, the Tagus and the Danube. On all hands the air resounded with cries of joy; wherever they went the people followed them in crowds; every one wished to gaze on them; to engrave on their hearts the image of those brave compatriots, and to march under the same flag.

Napoleon having received the members of the university in a body, inquired of the rector as to the different sciences which were taught in this celebrated seat of learning. He next resolved to reorganise the civil administration, entirely upset by the departure of the functionaries, and by the removal of the archives of the town. After the French fashion he divided the invaded provinces into prefectures, appointed inspectors, receivers, commissaries of police, and above all *intendants* to accelerate the receipt of the numerous requisitions. But that which he had most at heart was to induce the Lithuanians to make a levy *en masse*, in order to form new corps. To all peasants who would revolt against their masters he offered arms, and sought, as at the commencement of our Revolution, to stir up civil war between the populace and the nobility.

These measures had a certain effect in the town where the emperor commanded in person, but in the hamlets and the country districts they resulted in nothing favourable to his plans. Nevertheless, Napoleon did not allow a day to pass without urging the Lithuanians to aid him. In order to impose upon them, he endeavoured to astonish the vulgar. In the same audience he would speak of shows and of religion; of war and the arts; then mounting his horse, he would rush about at all hours of the day; then he would return to his cabinet, after having ordered the construction of a bridge or some fortifications; and finally, in the middle of the most serious occupations, he would affect to concern himself with matters of utter frivolity.

The commission formed for the general administration of the whole of Lithuania was at first composed of only five members, but Napoleon increased the number as his partisans multiplied. The day on which this commission was established he issued three proclamations. The first, which was addressed to the people, announced the installation of the Provisional Government, and emphasised the gratitude which was due to its creator. The second urged the clergy to stimulate the zeal of the nation, and by fervent prayers to obtain from God blessings and mercy. The third, having for its object the recall of the Lithuanians in the Russian service, was couched as follows:—

Poles!—You are under the Russian flag: this service was permissible so long as you had no longer a country, but today all is changed. Poland has been resuscitated; it is for her complete restoration that we now fight; it is to compel the Russians to recognise the rights of which you have been deprived by injustice and usurpation. The general confederation of Poland and of Lithuania recalls all Poles from the service of Russia. Generals, officers and soldiers of Poland! hearken to the voice of your country; abandon the banners of your oppressors; hasten to our side so that you may range yourselves under the eagle of Jagellon, Casimir and Sobieski! The country demands it; honour and religion give the same command.

The committee of the government established at Wilna, which without doubt only lent itself to Napoleon's designs with the object of alleviating the misery of the people so afflicted with the horrors of war, occupied itself with indefatigable zeal in promoting the success of the administration. The department of Wilna had already been formed, and the invaded territory divided into eleven *sub-prefectures*. This organisation, so advantageous in appearance, was productive of no good results: the country districts were ravaged; the villages were deserted, all the peasantry had fled into the woods, and no one was seen but a few miserable Jews, clothed in rags, who, prompted by the spirit of avarice, preferred to expose themselves to the violence of our soldiers rather than abandon their squalid homes. As an illustration of the disorder which reigned in the midst of this pretended administration, I may mention that the *sub-prefect* of New-Troki, coming from Wilna to take up his duties, was stopped by stragglers, who stripped him of his belongings. His own escort consumed his provisions and stole his horses, and he arrived on foot and in such a miserable condition, that everybody took for a spy the man who had come to be the magistrate of the town.

The brilliant hopes which had at first been conceived commenced to be damped when it was seen that the leader of our expedition aspired to a new crown; and that powerless to establish anything on a firm basis, he talked of nothing but the conquest of vast provinces, and the subjection to a common law and the same sceptre of countries differing *in toto* in their customs and their physical condition. Shutting his eyes to the absence of discipline in his armies, he caused the ruin of the rich and the despair of the poor, and finally reduced the Lithuanians to regard as their oppressor the man who had announced himself as their liberator. As to ourselves, he accumulated on our heads the hate of every nation thus causing the crushing weight of his tyranny to fall on those who were its chief victims.

While all these events were happening at Wilna, Warsaw witnessed a spectacle which would have been magnificent had it not been prompted by a man who played fast and loose with the enthusiasm of nations, and whose undigested schemes failed for want of a little reflection and wisdom. The unhappy Poles, misled by bombastic promises, assembled in their capital (28th June) and formed a Diet. The assembly having met, a committee drew up an eloquent report, and an orator enlarged upon the importance of the duties which had been confided to them. In his exordium he reminded his audience that in days gone by, Poland, situated in the centre of Europe, had been a famous Nation, mistress of a vast and fertile territory, made illustrious by the twofold glories of war and art; maintaining for centuries with unconquerable determination the barriers which the barbarians sought to break through in order to enslave the civilised world. He said that the crown of Poland had been the object of general ambition as the highest of honours, and that if discord sometimes broke out, these passing clouds only overshadowed Poland herself and never carried tempest into foreign lands.

He next gave a long recital of all the miseries which had been endured by their beloved country through Russian ambition, by successive partitions, which were an outrage against a once powerful nation; above all, he recalled the final calamity, when Poland saw herself annihilated by a triple partition, and when Warsaw heard, amidst the horrid yells of a ferocious conqueror, the groans of the population of Praga, who were exterminated by sword and fire. He showed that this triumph of brute force had destroyed the moral rights of nations, and that expediency having thus been established as the basis of the government of the world, would in future be the sole standard of international morality. Lastly, that Russia, trampling without intermission on Poland, was gradually advancing towards Germany, which she aspired to dominate.

After this rapid review, the orator recited, in language perhaps less glowing but not less energetic, all the reasons which should unite Poland to France.

Europe requires repose after twenty-five years of disturbance. Her system will be incomplete, the reward of her sweat and blood cannot be assured, so long as the caverns of the north can vomit forth upon her the hordes whose nature can no longer be disguised. They are no longer the men whom necessity drove from their savage dens, impelling them towards those happier lands which offered them enjoyments unknown to their inhospitable clime. In them a blind instinct took the place of the arts which refine and defend civilised peoples; but here, alongside of this barbarism, are found the arts of a polished nation. Russia has availed herself of the service of Europeans; she has learnt from them all that is necessary for attack and defence, to create and destroy. From every point of view Russia has made herself the equal of Europe in order to become her master. At home, superstitious and docile slaves are the instruments of a government accustomed to every crime. For a century past at its command their sinews have strained to undermine all the dams whose destruction is threatened by this raging torrent. How often have not the Russians burst through those barriers, either for their own selfish aims or at the insane invitation of princes, against whom they bore weapons concealed beneath their treacherous assistance! For fifty years past Russia has repeatedly deluged southern Europe with her armies. The Empire of Constantinople remains shattered upon her half-extinguished crescent.

He ended with this impassioned peroration:

Henceforth the sons of the Peasts and the Jagellons can repossess themselves of the name of which their ancestors were so proud; the name before which those will tremble who for a time, by fraud and violence, have made themselves our masters. Ah, doubt not that this land, once so prolific of heroes, is about to recover all her glory. She will again bring forth another Sigismund, another Sobieski; her star will burn with a brighter and a purer lustre, and the nations brought to do us justice will recognise that to flourish in the soil of Poland, the seeds of all the virtues have only to be cultivated by an emancipated people.

The commission then submitted the Act of Confederation, the principal clauses of which were directed to the constitution of a new kingdom constructed out of those portions of ancient Poland which had been torn from her, and to the recall of all Poles from the service of Russia. Finally, it was arranged that a deputation should wait upon the Emperor of the French to secure his powerful protection for the cradle of renascent Poland.

This deputation, on being admitted to his presence (11th July) on the eve of his departure from Wilna, submitted to him the Act of Confederation of which we have spoken; but the conqueror only made evasive promises, and was perhaps shocked that the noble Polish nation did not grovel at his feet to obtain the honour of forming part of the great Empire. The freedom which was demanded appeared to cause him uneasiness and surprise; he seemed to dread the moment when this assembly which he had convoked, and which appeared to second his designs, might become not altogether subservient to his will, for the distinctive character of tyrants is never to do good except with misgiving; often to take umbrage at their own creations, and to resent all independence even when it is the work of their own hands. Napoleon, therefore, promised nothing, and exacted as a preliminary enormous sacrifices, and a devotion which the Poles were not inclined to offer until they had assured the certainty of their future welfare. Even before his arrival Napoleon had demanded that the provinces subjected to Russia should declare for him, and finally he gave it to be understood that Gallicia must be renounced, as he had guaranteed to Austria the integrity of her dominions.

If all these vast projects had been conceived by a sober brain, more mindful of the welfare of the peoples than of selfish ambition, there can be no doubt that gigantic as they were, they might have been accomplished. Napoleon had reached such a height of power that it was no longer necessary for him to achieve his objects by means of war. With an adroit, prudent and above all brilliant policy, he could have made durable conquests even more extensive than those which he had accomplished by force of arms; it is here that posterity will recognise that he was blinded by an excess of prosperity, since he employed the most tremendous weapons only to precipitate his fall, while he might have achieved success without risking anything or compromising himself But, foe to all that required patience and reflection, he recognised nothing but force, and Heaven decreed that he should in his turn be crushed by the very force which had up to then been the foundation of his power.

Thus the brave Poles, despairing of their country, looked on all these plans as chimerical, when they saw that Napoleon, with an ambition more excessive but less honest than that of Charles XII., aspired to the Crown of Poland, and that he only offered them his support in order to profit by their hatred of Russia. And this fortunate conqueror, insecurely seated on the most glorious throne in Europe, seemed to show by his disquiet that he was conscious of being unworthy of the supreme rank to which fortune had raised him. Instead of maintaining himself there by the exercise of justice, and by the glamour inspired by the encouragement of art and science, he thought to overturn the world, and from north to south renew those savage wars of the Middle Ages when despots only reigned by fomenting trouble and discord, and by promising their subjects the plunder of their neighbours.

CHAPTER 4

Dreadful Privations of French Army

While Napoleon remained at Wilna, the Prince of Eckmühl was sent towards Minsk, with instructions actively to pursue Bagration, who was endeavouring to effect a junction with the army of Barclay de Tolly. By this movement we prevented that general from gaining the Dwina, and drove him towards Mohilow upon the Dnieper, continually harassed by the first corps and by Grouchy's cavalry. All our other corps, composing the centre, had followed the direction of Dinabourg. As to the fourth, the two French divisions and the Royal Guard took the road through Paradomin to Ochmiana; but the viceroy, Pino's division and all the cavalry, marched upon Rudniki. This last movement appeared necessary owing to advices that the Hetman Platow, at the head of four thousand Cossacks, finding himself separated from the corps of Bagration, would be forced to debouch by the Lida road in order to effect his junction with the Russian Army which had evacuated Wilna.

On receiving this information the viceroy put himself *en route* (7th July); but the road to Rudniki was found to be so bad that the cavalry of the Royal Guard was obliged to seek another. It is impossible indeed to give an idea of the difficulties which were presented by this road, formed entirely of trunks of fir trees laid upon marshy ground. In marching over these trunks the horses separated them, and falling between the openings, broke their legs. If, in order to avoid this difficulty, we attempted to pass either on the right or the left, we were engulfed in the bog, from which it was impossible to emerge.

The staff, after having lost several horses of its escort, managed to get through this dangerous passage, and arrived at Rudniki in the middle of the night. On the morrow (8th July) we continued our march towards Jachounoui, to regain the high road; thence we went to Mal-Solechniki; but the prince would not halt there, and rode on at a brisk trot to sleep at Bol-Solechniki, where he hoped to receive some news about the Cossacks whom he had been instructed to pursue. On the day following, we continued our route and got as far as a fort near Soubotniki.

Circumstances here compelled the viceroy to halt. The nature of the roads had prevented the thirteenth and fourteenth divisions, as well as the Italian troops, from following us, so that only the light horse remained with us. The order of march, which had been sent to them, was, owing to a misunderstanding of the messenger, returned to General Dessoles, our chief of the staff, in consequence of which those troops, being without instructions, remained in their positions while it was believed they were on the march. Finding that they did not arrive, officers of intelligence were dispatched in all directions, who, after a diligent search, succeeded in withdrawing Pino's division from the morass of Rudniki and conducted it towards Ochmiana. The viceroy, on his part, having searched vigilantly for the Cossacks, retraced his steps, and in his march to Jachounoui picked up the thirteenth and fourteenth divisions, which next day (12th July) debouched at Smorghoni, and united themselves at last with the rest of the troops composing the fourth corps.

The town of Smorghoni is of considerable size, although almost all its houses are of wood. A small stream, crossed by a bridge, separates the fort from the town. The Jews, who form nearly the whole of the population, are much addicted to trade; and this town, although very depressing, was welcome to the whole army for the sole reason that we were there able to purchase bread and beer.

The day's rest which we enjoyed at Smorghoni was employed in the construction of a bridge across the Narotsch, to enable us to proceed direct to Vileika. This work had hardly been completed when our instructions were altered, and the major part of the troops marched upon Zechkevitschi, where we passed the night.

(15th July.) The road to the large village of Vileika is very sandy, and runs through woods. Just before reaching this hamlet we crossed the Wilia on a bridge of rafts. This river is here of no great size or depth, but its banks are very steep, especially the one on which stands Vileika. On entering the village, General Colbert, commanding the advance-guard, took possession of some abandoned magazines. As the enemy had only recently quitted this position, the viceroy redoubled his vigilance for fear of a surprise, and took particular care in the selection of a camping-ground.

While we marched on Vileika, the King of Naples, supported by the second and third corps, drove the First Army of the West from position to position behind the Dwina, and compelled it to retreat to the entrenched camp of Drissa. On our right, the Prince of Eckmühl continued to follow Prince Bagration. and had arrived at Borisow on the Beresina without fighting. Towards our extreme left Marshal the Duke of Taranto also obtained some signal advantages, and took entire possession of the Samogitie.

This behaviour of the enemy, in always fleeing before us, was variously interpreted. To some it appeared the effect of weakness, to others the result of a premeditated plan. The former said:—

Where, are these Russians who for fifty years have been the terror of Europe and the vanquishers of Asia? The power of Russia is nothing but a fraud, concocted by subsidised scribblers or lying travellers. It exists only in the imagination, and her prestige has vanished the moment we have attacked her.

But those whom experience had accustomed to penetrate the future replied, that it was not wise to despise an unbeaten enemy; that of a surety his flight was deliberate, with the object of reducing our forces, and depriving us of the means of recruiting them by luring us far from our own country. These sagacious reasoners said:—

It is on the elements that the Muscovites rely as their most potent allies. Why should they seek to fight us, when they know that winter will force us to abandon all our conquests?

The enemy himself explained the motive for his retreat by disseminating broadcast, on the banks of the Dwina, the following proclamation:—

Soldiers of the French Army!—You are being forced to plunge into a new war; it is sought to persuade you that it is because the Russians refuse to do justice to your valour. No, comrades; they recognise it, as you will one day see on the field of battle. Remember that, if necessary, one army will succeed another, and that you are four hundred leagues from your base. Do not be deceived as to our first movements; you know the Russians too well to suppose that they flee before you; they will accept

46

battle and it will be difficult for you to retreat. We tell you, as comrades—return to your native land *en masse*; do not believe the mendacious statement that you are fighting to secure peace. No, you fight for the insatiable ambition of a sovereign who does not desire peace (otherwise he could long since have obtained it), and who plays with the blood of the brave. Return to your homes; or if, meanwhile, you desire an asylum in Russia, you can there forget such words as conscription and levies, and all that military tyranny which never permits you for an instant to escape from its yoke.

This document contained such undoubted truths that every one was astounded that its circulation was permitted. Others regarded it as spurious, and believed that it had been drawn up to evoke "the reply of a French grenadier," and it would have been a subject of pleasantry in the army, and of contempt for the enemy, had it not been long known that a blind obedience towards his leaders is the first virtue of the soldier, and that every Frenchman, true to his flag, makes it a point of honour to fight to the death all who are held up to him as the enemies of his country.

In continuing our movement we arrived at Kostenevitschi, a wretched little village where, with the exception of the post office and the house of the parish priest, there was nothing but a few tumble-down hovels thatched with straw. The Royal Guard encamped around this village, although the Viceroy had established his quarters two leagues farther on. On the following day (17th July), after a five hours' march by a fairly good road, we arrived at the town of Dolghinow, the population of which consisted almost entirely of Jews; and this enabled us to procure a few bottles of brandy. Our continual march and a long absence of this stimulant impel me to mention an apparently insignificant fact; but from the importance which we attached to it one can judge of the extent of our needs and the difficulties of satisfying them.

We next marched upon Dokzice, about seven leagues distant. This town, the population of which also consisted of Jews, is well built and contains a church and a small wooden *château*. The extremities of the town are situated upon two hills, between which runs a small marshy rivulet. On the day of our arrival we noticed thick smoke arising behind the *château* in which the prince was quartered. The flames quickly burst out in all directions, and devoured in an instant several of the neighbouring houses; but the army took prompt measures to extinguish the fire, which was rapidly got under, thus relieving all apprehensions.

Since quitting, near Smorghoni, the road to Minsk and the Dnieper, we had turned off to the left in order to gain the Dwina, and follow the movement of the centre of the Grand Army, which was marching in that direction. General Sebastiani, commanding the advance-guard, drove the Cossacks as far as the Dwina, supported by the corps of the Duke of Reggio; but the enemy, who were within their entrenched camp at Drissa, having learnt that our *chasseurs* were off their guard, threw a bridge across the river, over which there passed five thousand infantry and as many cavalry, commanded by General Koulniew, and in the combat which followed General Saint Guriez was surprised and taken prisoner, and the rest of his brigade saved themselves after sustaining considerable losses.

In approaching Beresina where we were to sleep (20th July) the road continually ascended, conducting us gradually to the river of that name, which flows through the most marshy plain in Europe. In leaving this town, all the houses of which are built in a single line, the road continued through a species of peat, over which branches of fir trees had been placed to solidify it, leaving openings to allow the water to flow through.

From the Beresina up to the Oula the ground was always very boggy. The road which runs alongside one or the other of these rivers, forms a line of twenty to twenty-five leagues, passing continually through marshes and immense forests. Pouichna was one of our halting places, as was also Kamen; the first of these hamlets is remarkable for a large wooden *château* ; the second for a considerable eminence, situated in its midst, which commands the whole plain. At Botscheikovo we struck the banks of the Oula (23rd July). This river is connected with the Beresina by the Lepel Canal, which is much used for trade, and all the more useful in that it affords communication with the waters of the Dnieper and the Dwina, uniting thus the Baltic and the Mediterranean. It gives life to the interior of Lithuania by bearing on its surface the products of the most divergent climates, and by facilitating the exportation of native commodities. The Oula runs between very high banks. Beyond the bridge there is a magnificent *château*, the finest we had seen since our entry into Poland.

It was with surprise that we continued so rapid a march without fighting. The Russians adopted with regard to us the tactics of the

Parthians towards the Romans. Being unable to contend against the conquerors of the world, they lured them into the interior of their country, burning and destroying all that could be serviceable to the enemy, so as to inflict on him the horrors of famine and all the bitterness of a rigorous climate. We advanced every day without hindrance, and with as much security as if we were traversing Bavaria or Saxony.

Chapter 5

Action Near Witepsk

The impunity accorded us by our adversaries appeared altogether incomprehensible, and the most contrary and often entirely erroneous conjectures were expressed as to its meaning. However, since our crossing at Kamen several officers who had been sent to Ouchatsch, where the Emperor was established, reported that Generals Lefebvre and Nansouty, having taken Disna and Polotsk, had forced the enemy to abandon his entrenched camp of Drissa, and hastily to ascend the Dwina towards Witepsk, so as to avoid being cut off by our corps, which, passing along the two banks, advanced against that town. The orders which they brought led us to conclude that we should soon encounter resistance. These conjectures were soon turned into certainty, when reconnaissances made towards the mouth of the Oula and upon the road to Bezinkovitschi proved that the Cossacks were hovering on our flanks. The viceroy at once sent forward the advance-guard and the light horse to the banks of the Dwina (23rd July), where the Russians had assembled in considerable strength, under the orders of General Ostermann.

Shortly afterwards, the prince mounted his horse, accompanied by his *aides-de-camp*, and followed the movement of the advance guard. On arriving at Bezinkovitschi the enemy retreated and passed the Dwina at this point with the cavalry and a few guns. While we were in this town, the Russian sharpshooters, ambushed in the houses of the village on the other side of the river, harassed us with a continual fusillade; and it was here that Colonel Lacroix, passing through the principal street leading to the river, received a shot that broke his leg. After this reconnaissance the viceroy returned to sleep at the Château of Botscheiko. During the evening he had long conferences with General Dessolles, which led to the supposition that a night march was in contemplation, but the order was not issued until the following day.

(*24th July.*) After a march of five hours and crossing a little stream called the Svetscha, our force arrived at Bezinkovitschi. This small town was already full of troops, mainly the two divisions of cavalry under Generals Bruyères and Saint-Germain, who had come by the Oula road. This large body of troops, marching upon Witepsk, had little effect in dismaying the enemy, who, separated from us by the Dwina, boldly manoeuvred his cavalry and fired on our *voltigeurs*, who advanced to seize the ferryboat which had been removed to the other bank.

The viceroy having been ordered to make a feigned crossing at this point, placed two guns in position to protect the sappers charged with the construction of the bridge, and the marines of the Royal Guard under Captain Tempié. These brave men, animated by their leader, threw themselves into the water, and in spite of the enemy's fire, endeavoured to capture the ferry-boat. At last our batteries and some sharpshooters placed upon the bank succeeded in overawing the Russians to such an extent that they evacuated the houses in which they were concealed, and allowed us to bring back the boat unmolested, and complete the bridge which was being constructed by our engineers.

In this interval a division of Bavarian cavalry under General Preyssing, having discovered a ford two hundred paces below the bridge, effected a passage. The river had hardly been passed when the squadrons ranged in order of battle were supported by several companies of infantry which had crossed by the ferry; they placed themselves in motion, driving the enemy before them, who at our approach took to flight, burning everything behind them.

We were watching these manoeuvres, when a report was spread that the emperor was about to arrive. The courier who had brought the news was followed immediately by another, who confirmed it; next came some saddle horses, artillery officers, and generals of the Guard; then the town, which was already full of troops, was in a few minutes crowded; and in the middle of the tumult Napoleon appeared. On his arrival he descended to the river where the bridge was being erected. He drily condemned its construction, and then crossed the bridge, joining the Bavarians who had halted in the middle of the plain. Marching with them, he instructed them to advance and then returned to Bezinkovitschi. There is no question that he took this course in order to draw the enemy's attention to this point, so as to diminish opposition when he attacked Witepsk by the opposite bank; or perhaps in the hope of disturbing the march of the Russian Army in its return up the Dwina after it had left its entrenched camp at Drissa.

It is impossible to realise the tumult which reigned at Bezinkovitschi as the general staff arrived. This confusion increased in the middle of the night. The number of troops which flocked in from all sides, and the rapidity with which they were sent forward, left no doubt that we were on the eve of a battle. The cavalry commanded by the King of Naples formed the advance-guard; Delzons' division (the thirteenth) followed immediately in support.

(*25th July*). Orders having been received to march to Ostrowno, our staff was proceeding thither when we heard a heavy cannonade, and soon after one of General Delzons' *aides-de-camp* arrived at full gallop, and announced to Prince Eugene that the enemy had been encountered near Ostrowno, and that an obstinate combat was in progress at the moment of his departure. The *aide-de-camp* had hardly finished his report when the din of cannon was redoubled, and the viceroy promptly ordered a halt of the baggage train, and, followed only by his principal officers, hastened towards Ostrowno to join the King of Naples, who had with him the cavalry divisions of Bruyères and Saint-Germain, supported by the infantry of the thirteenth division. On arriving, however at Soritza, the action was found to be over; fourteen guns had fallen into our hands, and the large number of dead left upon the field testified to the resistance of the vanquished, and to the valour of the 7th and 8th Hussars, who on this occasion covered themselves with glory.

At three o'clock in the morning (26th July) the prince repaired to the King of Naples at Ostrowno. The fourth corps encamped around him, and the cavalry, placed in advance, watched the manoeuvres of the enemy. Towards six o'clock the chiefs of the army, followed by their respective staffs, marched towards the outposts, and went over the ground where the combat had occurred on the previous evening. They had hardly traversed it when reports were received that Ostermann's corps, comprising two divisions, was in position, and the viceroy directed the thirteenth and fourteenth divisions to support the cavalry commanded by the King of Naples. The hussars sent out as scouts, having discovered obstructions at the entrance to a wood, returned to inform us that the enemy appeared resolved to defend it obstinately.

As a matter of fact, the firing of skirmishers was heard on all sides, and the Russian cannon, stationed on the route, enfiladed our foremost columns. General Danthouard immediately advanced our guns, and it was in this exchange of shots that the captain of the 8th Hussars, Ferrari, former *aide-de-camp* to the Prince of Neuchatel, (Marshal Berthier), had a leg carried away. The King of Naples, galloping to all points where his presence would be useful, ordered an attack to be delivered by our left, with the object of dispersing the cavalry stationed at the extremity of a wood. Although this movement was well conceived, it had by no means the successful result which was expected. The hussars, to whom its execution was entrusted, not being in sufficient strength, found themselves obliged to retire, but in perfect order and without loss, before numerous squadrons who were preparing to charge.

While these operations were proceeding on the left, the Russians attempted to break our right, which the viceroy perceiving, sent against them the thirteenth division, which successfully checked their progress. Our artillery, advantageously posted upon some rising ground, secured our line from being forced.

Our right seemed well guarded, when a sudden attack accompanied by appalling yells was made upon our left and centre. The enemy, advancing *en masse*, had driven in our skirmishers posted in the wood, and forced the artillery to retreat with precipitation, while the Russian cavalry took advantage of level ground upon our left to deliver a vigorous charge upon the Croats and the 84th Regiment. Fortunately, the King of Naples arrived in time to check the movement. Two battalions of the 106th, held in reserve, supported the Croats, while General Danthouard, combining in the highest degree ability and courage, and Captain Bonardelle, revived the spirits of the artillerymen, and by skilful dispositions enabled them to resume the offensive, which they had temporarily lost.

Matters having been restored upon the left and the centre, the King of Naples and Prince Eugene visited the right wing and put it into action. The Russians, concealed in a wood, opposed the strongest resistance to the 92nd Regiment, which, although posted on an advantageous eminence, remained inactive. In order to stimulate it the Viceroy sent the adjutant, Commandant Forestier, who succeeded in inducing it to advance; but its march seemed to be too slow for the fiery valour of the Duke of Abrantés; and that intrepid general, accustomed to the chief command, left the prince in order to infuse energy into the regiment upon whom all our eyes were fixed. His presence, or rather his example, electrified all hearts, and in a moment we saw the brave 92nd, headed by General Roussel, charge and overthrow all in their way, and penetrate into the wood which the enemy appeared to have barred against us.

Upon our extreme right it was seen that a Russian column sent to turn us, had retreated as soon as we had captured the wood. The King of Naples then ordered the cavalry to charge this column in order to cut it off, and compel it to lay down its arms; the difficulties of the ground caused the cavalry to hesitate for a moment; but the King, whose impetuous character would have desired the execution of the order to be as prompt as the thought, put spurs to his horse, and drawing his sword cried, in stirring tones, "Let the bravest follow me." This heroic action filled us with admiration; everyone hastened to second him, and we should have succeeded in capturing the column had not deep ravines and thick brushwood enabled it to escape and rejoin the corps from which it had been detached.

Although the success of the combat was assured, it was still too risky to attempt to traverse the large wood in front of us, at the end of which were the hills of Witepsk, where it was said the whole of the Russian army was encamped. The matter was under consideration when a tremendous noise was heard in our rear. No one knew its cause, and anxiety was mixed with curiosity, when, beholding Napoleon in the midst of a brilliant suite, our fears were dissipated. From the enthusiasm which his presence always evoked, it was supposed that he was about to complete the glory of a successful day.

The King of Naples and the prince hastened to meet him, and informed him of the events which had occurred and the measures they had taken. Napoleon, the better to form an opinion, rode rapidly towards the most advanced posts of our line, and from an eminence observed for some time the enemy's positions and the nature of the ground. His piercing glance took in the Russian camp and penetrated their plans. Hence new dispositions, directed with complete *sang froid* and executed with order and rapidity, moved the army into the middle of the forest. Proceeding at full trot, we debouched at last towards the small hills of Witepsk at the moment when day began to close.

The thirteenth division, which co-operated with this manoeuvre on the right, in marching through the wood encountered a pretty strong resistance from the enemy, who only retreated gradually; and his numerous sharpshooters made us pay dearly for the ground we gained.

Broussier's division (the fourteenth) followed the high road, but arrived very late in the position selected between the road and the Dwina. As to the fifteenth division and the Italian guard, which formed the rest of the infantry of the fourth corps, they had been placed in reserve a little behind the fourteenth.

The army having come to a halt, Napoleon established his quarters in the village of Koukoviatschi. The King of Naples and Prince Eugene encamped in a wretched little *château* near the village of Dobrijka, surrounded by the corps under their command.

At dawn on the following day (27th July) our troops marched on Witepsk. The Russians, in retreating towards this town, fired several cannon shots at us, which did little harm. They next deployed on the summit of a large plateau situated near the town, which commands all the roads leading to it. From the hill upon which we were placed the enemy's lines could easily be seen, and above all his numerous cavalry ranged in order of battle at the extremity of the plain.

Broussier's division led the advance, and it was broad daylight when it crossed a little rivulet which separated us from this plain, and took up a position upon rising ground facing the plateau occupied by the Russians. At the same time the 16th Chasseurs-à-cheval, having gone on in advance, were charged by several squadrons of Cossacks of the Guard; and this regiment would have been totally defeated had they not been extricated towards the left by two hundred *voltigeurs* commanded by Captains Guyard and Savary. The gallantry of these warriors attracted the attention of the whole army, which, encamped upon a range of hills formed like an amphitheatre, watched their exploit, and rewarded their valour with approving shouts. Napoleon, who witnessed this fine feat of arms, sent to ask what corps these soldiers belonged to. He was told that they were of the 9th Regiment, and that three-fourths of them were *enfants de Paris*. "Tell them," said the emperor, "they are brave men; they all deserve the Cross of the Legion of Honour."

The 16th Chasseurs, retiring upon the fourteenth division, were covered by the 53rd Regiment, commanded by Colonel Grosbon. This division, formed in square, presented an impregnable front to the enemy, to break which he concentrated all his efforts. This circumstance threw our ranks into some confusion; but Napoleon being present, this could not long continue. Posted on an eminence he watched all the manoeuvres, and with perfect coolness ordered all that he deemed necessary to achieve the victory. He directed a regiment of cavalry to retire in order to enable the thirteenth division to cross a bridge. This retrograde movement caused some agitation in our rear, composed of a rabble of camp followers, people who are easily alarmed, and who, always apprehensive of their safety are more a source of annoyance than of benefit to an army.

The thirteenth division having advanced, wheeled to the right. The viceroy marching at their head led them to the rear of the fourteenth, upon the heights which commanded the plateau where the enemy was posted. These heights not being occupied, we advanced without difficulty, and arrived to take up a position on the summit, and found ourselves face to face with the Russian camp, only separated from it by the River Loutchesa, the steep banks of which formed so deep a ravine that it was impossible to bring on a general action. We feigned nevertheless to be desirous of engaging by detaching some light troops, who succeeded in passing the ravine and establishing themselves in a small wood. But these troops, not being supported, went no farther, and returned to their corps as soon as the guns ceased firing and the divisions were no longer under arms.

This suspension, at the moment when the armies were *en prise*, excited general astonishment, and every one inquired for the Emperor and what were his instructions. While these questions were being asked, a portion of the first corps of the Imperial Guard came to join us. From this some concluded that Napoleon only awaited the union of all his forces to make a serious attack, while others were convinced that the Duke of Elchingen and Montbrun's cavalry, advancing by the other bank of the Dwina, would turn the position of Witepsk and cut off the retreat of the Russians. As it was not executed, this movement was doubtless found to be impracticable.

At last, night having fallen, the troops bivouacked on the spot where they had taken position, and each related the honourable deeds by which his corps had distinguished itself. In all these stories it was noted with satisfaction that the combat, although glorious, had not been deadly. At the same time, among the few killed was Colonel Liedot of the Engineers, a man truly worthy of the corps to which he belonged. During the Egyptian expedition he was conspicuous for his courage; and in the construction of the fortresses in Italy, he showed that camp life had not been incompatible with the development of scientific knowledge.

The determination with which the Russians had maintained their positions, and the concentration of a large part of our troops upon the same point, led us to suppose that the morrow would be devoted to a general action; but imagine our surprise when at early morning (28th July) we found that the enemy had effected his retreat. The army immediately followed in pursuit, with the exception of the Imperial Guard, which was established in Witepsk, where it seemed that the Emperor meant to remain. This town was almost deserted; the Jews alone were left, and a few people of the lowest order. Cossacks were discovered on the opposite side of the route, and they were promptly pursued by General Lefebvre, commanding the light horse of the Guard.

CHAPTER 6

Lying Report of Alexander's Assassination

Witepsk, the chief town of the government of that name, is situated between hills and the banks of the Dwina, and formerly contained twenty thousand inhabitants. The principal buildings, from their pleasant position, afforded us the most agreeable prospect. For two months, Poland and Lithuania, over a distance of three hundred leagues, had presented to us nothing but deserted villages and a devastated country. Destruction seemed to precede our steps, and on every hand the entire population fled at our approach and resigned their abodes to clouds of Cossacks, who, before abandoning them, destroyed everything they could not remove. Thus, long subjected to the most fearful privations, we viewed with envy these clean and elegant houses, where repose and abundance appeared to reign. But we were deprived of the repose upon which we had counted, and had to resume the pursuit of the Russians, leaving our left in the town which had been the object of our desires and most cherished hopes.

In following the movement of the advance-guard, we were astonished to observe the perfect order in which Count Barclay de Tolly had evacuated his position. We spread ourselves on all sides over an immense plain, without being able to discover any signs of his retreat—not a single waggon abandoned, not a single dead horse, not even so much as a solitary straggler to indicate the route taken by the enemy. We were still in this uncertainty, probably unique, when Colonel Kliski found a Russian soldier asleep under a bush. This discovery appeared to us a godsend, and the viceroy availed himself of it to interrogate the prisoner, who gave us some information about the direction taken by the column to which he belonged.

With a view to make certain, the prince rode on in advance; but having found nothing in that direction worthy of notice, we resumed our march, and returned at full gallop to the high road which, from Witepsk, continued up the Dwina. We found it covered with numerous cavalry; the King of Naples lost no time in rejoining the viceroy; and, having concerted their measures, they directed the movements of their respective corps. That day the heat was excessive; clouds of dust, raised by the horses, made the march appalling; it was necessary to halt, and a wooden church was selected for the purpose, where the King of Naples, the prince and General Nansouty had a long consultation.

The vanguard having received instructions to continue the pursuit, it was not long before we learnt that at last the Russian Army had been encountered. The whole army immediately continued its march and came up with the enemy; but the Cossacks, who formed his rearguard, seeing our artillery advance, beat a retreat, contenting themselves with firing a few cannon shots when they found a favourable opportunity. They manoeuvred thus as far as the other side of Aghaponovchtchina, where our corps and the cavalry halted. In the neighbourhood of this village, on a hill towards the left, there was a mean *château*, where Napoleon was lodged, who had come from Witepsk to rejoin us as soon as he had heard that we were engaged with the Russians.

Never did bivouac present a more martial appearance than that of Aghaponovchtchina. The emperor, the King of Naples, and the prince were under one tent; the generals, lodged in miserable cabins constructed by the soldiers, camped with their officers along a rivulet, the muddy water of which was eagerly sought after; for during the three days that had elapsed since we were on the battlefield, the heat had been intense, and we had had nothing to eat but execrable bread and some roots; but the victory redoubled our strength and rendered us insensible to every privation. As to our troops, they bivouacked around the *château* upon rising ground From afar the enemy could see our numerous fires, the glare of which lit up the obscurity of the night.

Early next day (29th July) the search for the Russians was resumed. The emperor returned to Witepsk, where he intended to remain long enough to carry out his plans regarding Lithuania. On arriving at the junction of the road from Janowitschi with that from Sourai, the King of Naples left us, with all the cavalry and the fourteenth division. The viceroy, continuing his march, proceeded towards the Dwina, followed by the thirteenth and fifteenth divisions, the Royal Guard and the brigade of Italian light horse commanded by General Villata.

We were on the point of entering Sourai, when some *chasseurs* informed us that a convoy of the enemy, weakly escorted, was attempting to pass the river to gain the Waliki-Luki road. The viceroy at once ordered his *aide-de-camp*, Desève, to follow the *chasseurs* and capture it. This order was promptly carried out, for two hours afterwards, the aide-de-camp returned, bringing the news that the convoy was in our hands.

The town of Sourai, although built of wood, was nevertheless one of the best we had met with. The population, almost wholly composed of Jews, was numerous and industrious, so that they were able to supply us with articles of which we were in sore need; the shops were well stocked, which was very lucky for us, as everything pointed to our remaining in this little town.

Sourai, without being a military station, was nevertheless a very important place, situated at the point where the Casplia joins the Dwina. Here the high roads from St. Petersburg and Moscow divide, and the town thus forms two *têtes-de-pont* which guard the road to Witepsk. During our stay here several engineer-geographers arrived, who made a plan of the river and neighbourhood.

The thirteenth division, which had followed us, was encamped on the other side of Sourai; a portion of the fifteenth with the Foot Guards remained in the town; the Cavalry Guard, under General Triaire, crossed the Dwina and made a reconnaissance in force upon the Waliki-Luki road. The enormous quantity of provisions which the dragoons brought in from the expedition proved that the country afforded abundant supplies for the cantonments.

On arriving at Sourai, the viceroy was told that another Russian convoy, strongly escorted, had taken the road to Veliz. He at once directed Baron Banco, colonel of the 2nd Regiment of Italian *chasseurs*, to take with him two hundred picked men, and start immediately in pursuit. This detachment, after marching nine leagues, arrived at Veliz just as the convoy emerged from the town, and attempted to cross the bridge over the Dwina. The chasseurs promptly charged the escort. They were repulsed five times by the infantry, and by detachments of cavalry much stronger than themselves; but at last the valour of the Italians prevailed, and the whole convoy was taken, while five hundred Russians were obliged to lay down their arms. This victory cost us some wounded, amongst them six officers, one of whom died of his injuries.

While Napoleon was at Witepsk, endeavouring to organise Lithuania, and the troops of the centre of the army were cantoned between the Dnieper and the Dwina, we learnt that the Prince of Eckmühl had been attacked at Mohilow. Bagration, taking advantage of the repose which the action of Borisow had afforded him, crossed the Beresina at Bobruisk, and marched upon Novoi-Bickow. On the 23rd July at daybreak a swarm of Cossacks surprised us, and captured about a hundred of the 3rd Chasseurs, including the colonel. The alarm at once spread throughout the camp, the *générale* was sounded, and our soldiers at once flew to arms. General Sieverse, with two divisions of veterans, directed all the attacks. From eight in the morning until five in the afternoon firing was kept up on the fringe of the wood, and at the bridge which the enemy was attempting to capture.

At five o'clock the Prince of Eckmühl advanced three battalions of *élite*, placed himself at their head, overthrew the Russians, recaptured the positions which they had taken, and energetically pursued them. The losses were about equal on each side; but Prince Bagration, who had only accepted this engagement to protect his retreat and facilitate the passage of his troops across the Dnieper, withdrew to Bickow, crossed the river, and thence directed himself towards Smolensk, where the Russian armies were to effect their junction.

General Kamenski, with two divisions, attempted to unite himself with Prince Bagration. Not succeeding in this, he re-entered Volhynia and joined the corps commanded by General Tormasow. These troops forming one army, marched upon the seventh corps, towards Kobrin, and surrounded on all sides the Saxon general, Klengel, who had with him two regiments of infantry and two squadrons of horse. Compelled to yield to forces so much superior to his own, he nevertheless only surrendered after a stubborn combat, hoping always that he might be rescued by General Reynier; but the latter, in spite of his utmost efforts, only arrived after the capitulation.

While we sustained checks upon our right, we were more fortunate on our extreme left. The Duke of Taranto, commanding the second corps, pushed reconnaissances upon the Riga road, and by the skilful dispositions of Generals Grawert and Kleist obtained some signal advantages over the Russians. A few days after, General Ricard, having been detached towards the right, took possession of Dunabourg, which the enemy abandoned, after having made complete preparations for defending it.

The most glorious action for our arms was that of the second corps. The Duke of Reggio advancing on Sebei, encountered Witt-genstein's army, reinforced by the corps of Prince Repnin. The combat took place at the Château of Jakoubovo. Legrand's division sustained a strong attack until ten at night, and by the valour of the 26th Light Infantry and of the 56th of the line, inflicted considerable losses on the Russians, who nevertheless next day attempted the passage of the Dwina. The Duke of Reggio thereupon ordered General Castex not to oppose them, and the enemy fell into the trap. On the 1st of August they proceeded towards Drissa, and formed in order of battle before the second corps. Fifteen thousand men, forming the half of Wittgen-stein's army, had passed the river, when they were assailed by a masked battery of forty guns, which pounded them with grape for half an hour. At the same time, Legrand's division joined in the action, while just as it had turned in our favour Verdier's division arrived at the *pas de charge* with fixed bayonets. The Russians were hurled into the river, losing three thousand men and fourteen guns. In pursuing their *débris* on the Sebei road, we counted two thousand dead, among whom was General Koulniew, a very distinguished officer of light troops.

During his sojourn at Witepsk, the emperor had several houses opposite his palace demolished in order to form a large esplanade for reviewing his troops. Having assembled the grenadiers of the Foot Guards, he ordered them to recognise General Friant as their colo-nel, (killed afterwards at Waterloo). Never has appointment been more unanimously approved. The complimentary and gracious words with which Napoleon accompanied this distinction, were only exceeded by the enthusiastic delight which the grenadiers manifested at the an-nouncement. They saw in this dignity a fresh proof of the esteem for their corps, composed in great part of the veterans, who in Italy, Egypt and Germany had fought under the eyes of their leader himself. But General Friant, although highly sensible of this honour, begged, and obtained permission, to remain in command of the second division which he had himself formed, and which since the opening of the campaign had always found itself in the van.

At this time a rumour was spread that the Emperor of Russia had been assassinated at Waliki-Luki by his courtiers. It is asserted that Napoleon, with an air of satisfaction, announced this news at one of the receptions which he held at Witepsk. We afterwards learnt that this lie had been circulated by him with the object of neutralising the effect produced by the vigorous proclamation published by Alex-ander, in which he appealed to all the People of his mighty Empire to rise against the perfidious enemy, who, after violating the soil of the fatherland, was advancing against the ancient capital to destroy and annihilate the glory of its illustrious founders. All these shameful dodges were, however, absolutely futile, and did not even come to the knowledge of a population, which, fleeing *en masse* at the approach of the French Army, could not possibly feel the effects of this pitiable trick, nor be corrupted by specious promises, the object of which was to stir up a frightful discord, by raising the masses against the nobility, and stifling in the hearts of the upper classes the attachment and fidelity which they owed to their sovereign.

CHAPTER 7

Entry into Smolensk

Since the affairs at Veliz, the viceroy, having felt the necessity of reinforcing the detachment of chasseurs which he had left there, sent General Villata to that point with a battalion of Dalmatians. Veliz, situated at the junction of two main roads, one of which leads to St. Petersburg and the other to Smolensk, was subject to frequent apparitions of Cossacks. It was also the most advanced position to which the French army had yet penetrated. Moreover, the population of the town, entirely Jewish, supplied us with the prime necessaries of life, while throughout the neighbourhood nothing was to be found but poverty-stricken villages. We were enjoying the carelessness engendered by good living, when Colonel Banco, who was familiar with the Russian language, was informed by spies that the enemy intended to attack the brigade. Acting on this news, General Villata secretly made his preparations for receiving him, while publicly assuming an air of perfect security. The Cossacks, having appeared at break of day before Veliz, expected to find every one asleep; but the Dalmatians, who were under arms, issued from their ambuscade, and opened a fire which overthrew several horsemen. The Cossacks, dismayed by such a reception, took to flight, and abandoned the attempt to surprise the position.

At this period the heat was so intense, that Napoleon, in spite of his impatience to reach the enemy, found himself obliged to give the army a rest. Those who had been through the Egyptian campaign asserted that the sun of that country was not more burning than that of Russia. The troops stationed at a distance from streams suffered cruelly. The soldiers, in order to obtain water, dug in the earth with their bayonets, but even when they were lucky enough to find any, it was so muddy that it could only be drunk after being filtered through their pocket-handkerchiefs.

The fourth corps, having halted at Sourai for ten days, resumed its march on the 9th August, and took the road to Janovitschi, where it was expected that the fourteenth division would be found. On the eve of this movement Prince Eugene sent his *aide-de-camp*, Lt.-Col. Labedoyère, (condemned by court-martial, and shot after Waterloo), to the King of Naples. On his return, Labedoyère confirmed the news of the sanguinary engagement which General Sebastiani had had with the enemy near Inkovo, and its vexatious results for us; for it appeared that our cavalry had suffered greatly, and that besides several guns, we had lost a superb company of *voltigeurs* of the 24th Light Infantry. It was added, indeed, that without the courage and daring of the Prussian lancers, our losses would have been much heavier. General Sebastiani was much censured for this affair, for, although informed of the superior force of the enemy, he considered nothing but his own courage, and, disregarding every warning, persisted in risking the action.

The viceroy having passed two days at Janovitschi (10th August), our sappers, commanded by General Poitevin, repaired the bridge over the little river that traversed the town. This bridge was so bad that it was too risky to use it, and the horses and vehicles were obliged to cross the river by a ford, although the bottom was extremely muddy and the banks were very steep.

In proceeding towards Liozna a slightly undulating plain is crossed; next several copses are traversed and a rivulet is passed, which runs through a hamlet situated halfway to the Château of Velechkovitschi, where the army halted (11th August). The soldiers encamped under some heights which surround the château. On the following day, the road as far as Liozna, running through marshy meadows, presented great obstacles to our convoys, particularly to the artillery, owing to rain having fallen heavily for two days. I may remark that these violent storms were the only ones that we encountered, and during the rest of the campaign, until we reached Moscow, we scarcely ever suffered inconvenience from this cause.

Around Liozna, a large village full of mud, we crossed on the 12th August, by a rickety bridge, a small stream the course of which forms a thousand bends, and separates the village at a quarter of a league towards the northwest, from the *château* where Prince Eugene was lodging. Our troops availed themselves of the camp which had been formed by the Duke of Elchingen's corps, and which was found between the village and the *château*.

To reach Liouvavitschi, there was a more direct road than the one we took; but several obstacles presented by the ground forced us to seek another, which, however, was itself not exempt from difficulties; for we were obliged to pass through several defiles, and across muddy fields, and tracks made through the middle of the forests. Before arriving at this town, we crossed over a most detestable bridge, and passed along a road so muddy that the horses could hardly get through it.

On entering Liouvavitschi, we saw the cavalry of the King of Naples return from the environs of Roudnia and Jorkovo, but instead of following the road to Razasna it turned to the left, as if to pass the Dnieper at a point much higher than that towards which we were proceeding. The reunion of the whole army upon the banks of that river manifestly indicated the intention to cross it, and attack Smolensk by the left bank, so as to capture the town, the fortified portion of which was upon that side. The order was soon given to rendezvous around Razasna, where several bridges had already been thrown across the river.

Before arriving there we traversed an almost desert country; we saw no village upon the road, and rarely met with houses where we could stop. The road was laid over a quagmire, in which we were forced to abandon part of our baggage. After infinite trouble, we arrived at last at this Dnieper, the Greek name of which—the Borysthenes—conjured up in our minds grand and poetic ideas. But these illusions were soon dissipated when we saw a commonplace river flowing in a very narrow bed.

These waters are so closed in, that the river is only visible when one strikes it. The banks, also, are extremely steep and inaccessible.

Around Razasna, all the different corps of the Grand Army, one part of which came by way of Orcha and the other by Babinovitschi, effected their junction. The emperor had reached Razasna on the morning of the 13th August. On that day he lined up the divisions of the corps of the Prince of Eckmühl, which had come from Mohilow, and, after having inspected them, he dispatched them on the road to Smolensk. This immense concentration of men upon the same point, while increasing our misery, redoubled the confusion and disorder which reigned on all the main roads. Wandering soldiers searched in vain for their regiments, and at last officers, carrying urgent orders, could not deliver them owing to the congestion of the roads, which occasioned an appalling tumult upon the bridges and in the defiles.

Leaving the town of Liadoui (a place remarkable for being the last in which we found Jews), and crossing a small stream, above which is a vast plateau, entirely commanding the town, we continued our march as far as Smiaki. The viceroy wishing to encamp in this hamlet, gave the order to halt, while the other corps of the Grand Army marched upon Smolensk, and from the cannonade which was in progress we concluded that the town was being vigorously attacked.

On the morrow (16th August) we remained in the same position. During the whole day, numbers of troops continued to pass through, advancing towards the front. Towards six o'clock in the evening, we had to leave Smiaki and march for three hours to Krasnoë, a small village where there are some stone houses, and where the Viceroy established posts of communication; but he did not remain there, and continuing the route, we traversed the neighbouring small river of Katovo. The prince established his bivouac under a large avenue of trees, surrounded by his divisions. At daybreak (17th August) we continued our route, and bivouacked a league beyond the post of Korouitnia, in a birch-wood, situated on the shores of a lake.

Our camp presented an extremely picturesque *coup d'œil*, the viceroy having raised his tent in the midst of this copse. The officers slept in their carriages; those who had none, cut down trees and built huts, while their comrades lit fires to cook the food. As to the soldiers, some went marauding, others washed their linen on the banks of a limpid brook, and the rest, after their long march, amused themselves by making war on a small flock of geese and ducks, which had escaped the voracity of the Cossacks.

It was here that we learnt that after a bloody engagement the town of Smolensk had been committed to the flames by the Russians, and abandoned to the victors. This event was a sinister omen, and made us realise to what extremities a people could resort when it is determined not to submit to foreign domination. The following day we approached this unhappy town, but a league before we reached it, the viceroy caused us to encamp in a wood near the Château of Novoidwor, where he was joined by the emperor. Here one of my comrades, coming from Smolensk, gave me the following description of the events of which he had been an eyewitness:—

The position which we maintained up to the 13th of this month (August) had led the enemy to suppose that we intended to attack Smolensk by the right bank of the Dnieper. But suddenly the emperor, by a prompt and unexpected manoeuvre, passed his whole army to the left bank. During the 14th, the King of Naples, commanding the vanguard, was joined by the corps of the Duke of Elchingen, who in the morning had passed the Dnieper near Krasnoë, and engaged the 25th Russian division, consisting of five thousand infantry and two thousand horse. Krasnoë having been taken, Grouchy's cavalry delivered several magnificent charges upon the flying enemy, and took some guns and many prisoners. After this success Napoleon appeared with his army before Smolensk on the morning of the 16th. This town is surrounded by an ancient embattled wall, eight thousand yards in circumference, ten feet thick and twenty-five feet high; flanked at intervals by enormous towers, which form bastions, on most of which heavy guns were mounted.

The Russians, still believing that we would advance by the right bank of the Dnieper, had retained a large portion of their troops on that side; but seeing us arrive by the left bank, they believed themselves to be outflanked, and returned in all haste to defend Smolensk at the principal point of attack. This they were all the more eager to do, as Alexander, in quitting the army, had instructed Baron Barclay de Tolly to join battle in order to save the town.

After having passed the 16th in reconnoitring the place and its neighbourhood, the emperor assigned the left to the Duke of Elchingen, resting on the Dnieper; the Prince of Eckmühl commanded the centre, Prince Poniatowski the right; while the Guard and the fourth corps were held in reserve. The Westphalians were also expected, but the Duke of Abrantés, who commanded them, had by a mistaken movement lost his way.

Half of the following day was occupied in observations. The enemy occupied Smolensk with thirty thousand men; the remainder were in reserve on the right bank, communicating by means of the bridges, constructed below the town. Napoleon, aware that the garrison, placed under the orders of General Doctorow, would take advantage of any respite to strengthen its position, ordered Prince Poniatowski to advance, having Smolensk on his left and the Dnieper on his right. He directed the establishment of batteries to destroy the bridges, and by that means to intercept communication between the two banks. The Prince of Eckmühl attacked the entrenched suburbs, defended by seven or eight thousand infantry.

In the afternoon General Bruyères' light horse drove the Russians, and took possession of the plateau nearest the bridge. There, a battery of sixty guns was established, and fired so accurately upon the masses on the opposite bank that they were compelled to retire. To reply to this battery, two of twenty guns each were brought into action. The Prince of Eckmühl, having been ordered to carry the town, confided the attack on the suburb on the right to General Morand, and that on the suburb on the left to General Gudin. After a brisk fusillade the two divisions stormed the positions, and pursued the enemy with rare intrepidity as far as the covered way, which they found strewn with corpses.

On our left the Duke of Elchingen captured the trenches occupied by the Russians, and compelled them to re-enter the town and seek refuge in the towers, or on the ramparts, which they obstinately defended; but they were finally dislodged by shells which set the defences on fire. Count Sorbier, commanding the artillery of the Guard, by mounting enfilading batteries, made it impossible for the besieged to occupy their covered ways.

General Barclay de Tolly, seeing then that the assault of the town was about to be delivered, although the breach was not yet practicable, reinforced the garrison with two fresh divisions, and two regiments of infantry of the Guard. The fight lasted until the end of the day. Soon afterwards columns of smoke and a great burst of flames were observed, extending in an instant to the principal quarters of Smolensk, which, in the midst of a lovely summer night, presented a spectacle such as can only be likened to that which the inhabitants of Naples behold during an eruption of Vesuvius.

An hour after midnight, the *débris* of the town were abandoned. At two o'clock in the morning our first grenadiers formed for the assault, when, to their great surprise, they advanced without encountering resistance, and discovered that the place was entirely evacuated. We took possession of it, and found on the walls several guns which the enemy had been unable to remove.

It would be impossible adequately to describe the horrible scene of devastation presented by the interior of Smolensk. My entry into this town will be the epoch of my life. Picture to yourself all the streets, all the squares, encumbered with dead or dying Russians, and the flames lighting up far and wide this frightful spectacle.

On the morrow (19th August) we entered Smolensk by the suburb which extends along the river. On all sides we marched over nothing but ruins and corpses. Of the palace, still burning, nothing was left but walls cracked by the heat, and under their fragments the blackened remains of the inhabitants whom the fire had devoured. The few houses that remained were overrun by our soldiers, and on the threshold was seen the homeless tenant, who, with the remnants of his family, lamented the slaughter of his children, and the loss of his all. The churches alone offered some consolation to the unhappy people who were without other shelter. The cathedral, famous throughout Europe, and highly venerated by the Russians, became the asylum for those who had escaped from the fire. In this church, close up to the altars, were entire families lying on rags. On one hand could be seen an old man expiring with his face turned towards the statue of his tutelary saint; on another, poor little infants to whom their mothers, crushed by misfortune, gave suck while bedewing them with their tears.

In the midst of this desolation, the passing of the army into the interior of the town offered a striking contrast. On one side was the degradation of the vanquished, on the other the arrogance bred of victory; the first had lost everything, the others, rich with spoil, and having never known defeat, marched proudly to the sound of martial music, striking with mingled fear and admiration the miserable remnants of a subdued populace.

The struggle at Smolensk deprived the enemy's army of twelve thousand men, of which a third were left in the town. Although we were the assailants, this loss was triple that of ours. Lying beside one French soldier could be seen the bodies of five or six Russians. A fact so remarkable will be understood when one remembers that the Muscovites always get drunk before a battle; also that their sharpshooters, more daring than dexterous expose themselves to danger without doing much harm to their adversaries. According to all accounts, the enemy had several generals killed. On our side, Generals Zaionsheck, Grandeau, and Dalton proved by their wounds how greatly they had contributed to the victory.

Measures were promptly taken to repair the large bridge over the Dnieper, which had been burnt, and which communicated with the other part of the town, not one single house in which remained standing. It was at the end of the suburb by which we had arrived that the fourteenth corps and Grouchy's cavalry forded the river with all their artillery. During this interval other bridges were constructed, and they so greatly facilitated the passage, that on the same day the light horse, with the artillery under the orders of the King of Naples, were upon the road to Moscow in pursuit of the enemy.

The troops of Prince Eugene and those of Count Grouchy, having crossed the river, encamped on the height commanding the town, past which runs the mail road which leads to St. Petersburg from Porietsch. This was a position of the highest importance, and it was a matter of universal astonishment that the enemy had not better defended it. By maintaining it our march would have been arrested, inasmuch as it covered the high road to Moscow, and would have prevented us from remaining in the town, which it entirely commanded.

While the centre of the army pursued its triumphant march, Count Gouvion Saint-Cyr was gaining important victories on the Dwina. After the affair at Drissa, General Wittgenstein having been reinforced by twelve battalions, resolved to take the offensive against the Duke of Reggio, who, foreseeing that he was about to be attacked, united the sixth Bavarian corps to the second. The attack was made on the 16th and 17th of August, but at the moment when the Duke of Reggio was taking his measures for repelling it he was struck by a bullet in the shoulder, the dangerous wound obliging him to quit the field, and transfer the command to General Gouvion Saint-Cyr.

The latter made all preparations for attacking next day at dawn, and, the better to deceive the Russians, he ostentatiously withdrew, to the left bank of the Dwina, all the baggage, with a large part of the artillery and cavalry which, reascending the river, repassed it during the night at Polotsk without being observed. The enemy, outwitted by this adroit manoeuvre, believed that we were retreating, and advanced to pursue us; but instead of finding us disposed to yield ground we appeared all drawn up in battle array, and our artillery opened fire. At the same time our infantry columns, under protection of the guns, attacked the left and centre of Wittgenstein's corps. The two divisions of Wrede and Roy, having combined their movement with courage and intelligence, issued together from Spas. Legrand's division, in position to the left of this village, was linked with that of Verdier, a brigade of which watched the enemy's right; lastly, Merle's division covered the front of the town of Polotsk.

The enemy, surprised at such excellent dispositions, nevertheless maintained a firm front, thanks to his numerous artillery; but on the approach of night, Count Wittgenstein seeing his centre and left broken, beat a retreat *en échelon* after desperately defending each position. It was by this obstinate resistance that he succeeded in saving his army, which, notwithstanding the most determined efforts, was utterly unable to resume the offensive. Had it not been for the woods which facilitated the escape of prisoners, we should have taken a considerable number; those which we did capture, were collected wounded on the battlefield, and from the number we found it was easy to estimate how heavy the Russian loss had been. Several guns augmented the trophies of a glorious day.

This victory was, however, dearly bought with the loss of several brave Bavarian officers, and above all by the mortal wounds of Generals de Roy and Sierbein. The generals, officers, and soldiers vied with one another in intelligence and bravery to secure the victory. Amongst the first, Count Gouvion Saint-Cyr in his report of the action especially commended Generals de Wrede, Legrand, Verdier (wounded), Merle, and Aubry; the last-named general of artillery particularly distinguished himself in the handling of this arm. Count Gouvion Saint-Cyr ended his report by requesting the emperor's recognition of the services of his officers. He thus did justice to all, except himself, about whom he preserved absolute silence; but his modesty only enhanced his reputation, and served to throw into stronger relief those great abilities which a few days afterwards were rewarded with a marshal's *bâton*, presented on the battlefield. While our left corps was gaining important victories on the Dwina, our centre was distinguishing itself by combats not less glorious.

The Duke of Elchingen having crossed the Dnieper (19th August) below Smolensk, united with the King of Naples to pursue the enemy. At one league from that town, he encountered a portion of his rearguard, formed by a division of Bagawout's corps, of about six thousand men. In an instant its position was stormed, and the bayonet covered the field with dead.

This corps, which protected the retreat of the Russians, having been forced to retire upon a second *échelon*, took up a position on the plateau of Valontina. But the first line was broken by the 18th Regiment, and towards four o'clock in the afternoon the firing extended to the whole rearguard, fifteen thousand strong. The Duke of Abrantés, who had lost his way on the right of Smolensk, made a false movement, and was unable to gain the road to Moscow with sufficient rapidity to cut off the retreat of this rearguard. Moreover, the first *échelons* of the enemy retraced their steps, and successively joined in the battle to the extent of four divisions. The Russians had all the more interest in defending this position, inasmuch as besides its actual strength it was regarded in the country as impregnable, because in the ancient wars the Poles had always been beaten there. Hence the Muscovites, owing to a religious tradition, associated this plateau with an assurance of victory, and had dignified it with the pompous title of "Sacred Field."

If the enemy attached a high importance to retaining it, our interest in capturing it was none the less, in order to harass his retreat and capture all his baggage train and vehicles full of wounded proceeding from Smolensk, the evacuation of which was protected by the rearguard.

At six in the evening, Gudin's division, sent to sustain the third corps against the numerous troops which the enemy hurried forward, debouched in column upon the centre of the position, and sustained by Ledru's division, carried it at the point of the bayonet. The 7th Light, the 12th, 21st and 127th, which formed Gudin's division, attacked with such impetuosity that the Russians were put to flight, convinced that they were engaged with the Imperial Guard. This valour cost the life of the brave general who led them. But his death was amply avenged; his division dealt great slaughter among the enemy, who, flying towards Moscow, left the "Sacred Field" covered with dead. A Russian general of division was taken in the *mêlée* by one of our infantry officers. Among the dead were found the bodies of Generals Skalon and Balla; and it was stated that the cavalry general Koff, who was mortally wounded, was as great a loss to our adversaries as any sustained by ourselves.

At three in the morning of the day following, the emperor distributed on the field of battle rewards to the regiments which had distinguished themselves; and as the 127th, which was a new regiment, had borne itself well, Napoleon bestowed upon it the right to carry an eagle; a privilege which up to then it did not possess, never having so far participated in a battle. These rewards, bestowed in the midst of the dead and dying, presented a spectacle of grandeur which made our exploits bear comparison with all the most heroic deeds of antiquity.

During the four days on which Napoleon remained at Smolensk, he reviewed the various corps which had distinguished themselves since the opening of the campaign. In this respect none deserved this honourable distinction more than the fourth. It was at length conferred upon us, and the chiefs of each division, with the exception of General Pino, who had left a few days before for Witepsk with the fifteenth, received instructions (22nd August) to draw up their soldiers under arms. All our army, in its best array, was ranged in order of battle in a vast plain a little above that on which we were encamped. Its splendid appearance, and above all, the memory of the brilliant affairs at Witepsk, secured for our corps rewards which were commensurate with its valour, and which testified to the munificence of the leader who deigned to bestow them.

CHAPTER 8

Burning of Viazma

Up to this time it was believed that the emperor, only desirous of restoring the Kingdom of Poland, would limit his conquests to the towns of Witepsk and Smolensk, which, from their position, closed the narrow tract comprised between the Dnieper and the Dwina. Every one considered that, in view of the approach of winter, these two rivers would serve as his line of defence; and if, instead of advancing farther, he had ended the campaign by the capture of Riga, had fortified Witepsk and Smolensk, and above all had organised Poland, which he had entirely conquered, there is no doubt whatever that in the following spring Napoleon would have forced the Russians to submit to his conditions, or at all events reduced them to run the almost certain risk of seeing both St. Petersburg and Moscow destroyed, since the French army was at an equal distance from both these capitals.

But instead of adopting this judicious plan, he was obsessed with the recollection of the fortunate issue of his last campaigns, when he dictated peace in the palaces of the sovereigns he had conquered. These glorious memories emboldened him to such an extent that he despised the counsels of wisdom, and determined, although six hundred leagues from France, with only worn-out horses, with neither means of subsistence, magazines, nor hospitals, to venture upon the desert route to Moscow; and as a last proof of recklessness, leaving on his left the corps of Wittgenstein, and in his rear a Russian army, cantoned in Moldavia, and ready to march against us immediately upon the ratification of the treaty of peace concluded with the Ottoman Porte.

That army having ceased hostilities with the Turks, was then commanded by Admiral Tschikagow, and without intermission detached fresh troops to reinforce the army of Volhynia, opposed to the corps of Prince Schwartzenberg. Napoleon, hoodwinked by a deceptive alliance, believed that the Austrians, obedient to his orders, would repel the corps of Tormasow, of Ertel and of Sacken, on the same heights where we had beaten that of Barclay de Tolly; and that consequently the allies laying waste the Ukraine, would penetrate into the governments of Kiow and Kaluga, and join us at the moment of our entry into Moscow. But their insecure position, and above all the operations of the Russian generals, exploded this grand scheme. Turn by turn conquerors and conquered, the combatants did nothing but manoeuvre, and according to the news received by the Grand Army, mutually yielded the territory they had abandoned. Thus the fortress of Bobrinsk was not surrendered, and the Austrians did not even see the banks of the Dnieper.

On leaving Smolensk (23rd August) we reached Volodimerowa. To the right of this village is a wooden *château* situated on an eminence, overlooking a marsh.

We all believed that it was the intention of the prince to march upon Doukhovchtchina in order subsequently to turn off toward Doroghoboui, where the centre of the Grand Army was established, but General Grouchy, who preceded us with his cavalry, announced that he had repulsed the enemy more than twenty leagues away. The viceroy thus being able to dispense with the necessity of going to Doukhovchtchina, decided to seek a route which would conduct us direct to Doroghoboui. This he found near Pomoghailovo, and followed with the more confidence as a Russian corps had passed along it in effecting its retreat.

This march was through an excellent country; strange to say cattle were seen feeding in the meadows; inhabitants were found in the villages, and houses that had not been sacked. The soldiers being in the midst of abundance forgot their fatigue, and thought nothing of the length of a march which had lasted for more than ten hours. At last we arrived towards evening at Pologhi, a village somewhat removed from the road we were seeking. The next day (25th August) we crossed the Vop, a small stream which would have attracted our notice if we could have foreseen how fatal it was to be for us in the future. One could understand, however, what it would be like in the winter from the difficulty we found in crossing it in the middle of summer. It was very deep, and the slopes which led down to it were so steep that the artillery could only pass with the greatest difficulty, and by doubling the teams of the guns.

Continuing our march, we again saw the Dnieper, the banks of which, marshy and covered with woods, reached almost to the hills upon which ran the road we were following. A league farther on the high towers of the fine Château of Zazélé could be seen; from a distance they give to this building the appearance of a town. Quite close to it was a lake, where Grouchy's cavalry refreshed themselves, which having arrived before us were encamped around the *château*.

From this place the viceroy sent officers to Doroghoboui, where Napoleon was stationed; but although General Grouchy had pushed his advance-guard well forward, it was not yet known whether communications were open as far as that town. The officers sent on the mission crossed the Dnieper below Zazélé, and rejoining the postal road to Smolensk, arrived safely at Doroghoboui, where the staff of the Grand Army had established its general quarters. This town, situated on a height, was a good military position, as it guarded the passage of two high roads against armies marching from Smolensk and Witepsk upon Moscow. So heavy, however, had the Russian losses been at Smolensk and Valontina, that in spite of these advantages the town was only feebly defended.

Our corps was on the point of entering Doroghoboui, when the viceroy received dispatches from the Emperor, and after reading them the Prince proceeded to select a suitable spot for our encampment. The want of water having obliged us to push on as far as Mikhailovskoe, we established ourselves close to this village (26th August). In our rear was the cavalry; in the centre the infantry of the Italian Guard, and upon our flanks the French divisions of our corps.

A league from Mikhailovskoe two villages were passed, situated in marshy valleys; we then entered the plain watered by the Dnieper, and followed the road to Blaghove, where we were to cross the river, having on our right the cultivated uplands upon which were situated several villages. The smoke which issued from the houses showed they had not been abandoned. In the distance we could see the inhabitants fleeing to the top of the hills, and watching with anxiety to see if we were coming to trouble the peace of their homes.

The source of the Dnieper not being far from Blaghove, the river is here quite narrow. We therefore passed it easily by a ford, and the only difficulty experienced by the artillery was in negotiating the banks, which, in common with all the rivers in Russia, are extremely high, so as to contain the floods caused by melting snow.

The viceroy did not cross until he had seen all his force pass the stream. The fourth corps, forming the extreme left of the Grand Army, was obliged to march by very indistinctly traced roads, and to prevent the force losing its way, the Prince instructed General Triaire, commanding the advance-guard, to indicate the route by means of vedettes of dragoons. This wise precaution was a godsend to the detachments, and especially to stragglers, who, being thus relieved of uncertainty as to the road they should follow, all arrived safely at Agopochina. Previously these unlucky beings, when left in the rear, found themselves in the midst of dense forests or immense plains, all intersected by similar pathways. Knowing nothing of the language of the country, they wandered helplessly through these vast solitudes, and sooner or later perished of hunger or fell by the knives of the exasperated peasants.

The village of Agopochina where we halted (27th August) is remarkable for a great *château* and fine church built of stone, the four *façades* of which are embellished with four peristyles. The sanctuary, constructed according to the Greek rite, was of immense value, and decorated with rare and curious pictures, which suggested to us the severe but correct style which the Greeks brought from Constantinople when they came to Italy in the fifteenth century to found schools of painting. At this village Commandant Sevelinge, who had recently arrived to join our staff, was sent to the King of Naples with important dispatches, but as the King did not receive these dispatches, and the *commandment* was never again seen, we sorrowfully concluded that he had fallen into the hands of the Cossacks.

The day following (28th August) we continued to march to the left of the main road. The route which we followed could never before have been traversed by an army. It was narrow, intersected by numerous ravines, and often dwindled to a mere footpath. On arriving at a village, the name of which we did not know, we found three different tracks; one straight in front of us, another to the right, and the third to the left. We took the last-named, and after a two hours' march it brought us to a deserted *château* situated a league beyond Bereski.

Early in the morning (29th August) we left the neighbourhood of this *château* in a very dense fog. From the frequent halts which the Viceroy ordered, and the reconnaissances which he constantly made upon the right, as if to ascertain whether there was gun-firing on the main road, we concluded that he was anxious to know whether Napoleon was experiencing obstacles to his march.

We now approached Viazma. This little town, which, by the way, is a large one for Russia, was in a favourable position for the enemy.

Built upon the bank of the river which bears its name, it is surrounded by ravines, and is situated upon a large plateau which commands at the same time the plain and the opening of the defile through which passes the road to Smolensk. The Russians profited but little by these advantages; they made only a feeble defence of the position, and after a slight encounter they set fire to the principal edifices and retired. We arrived just as Viazma burst into flames. Although by this time quite accustomed to fires, we could not help looking with pity on this unhappy town, which formerly contained ten thousand inhabitants. While it had only recently been founded, it contained more than sixteen churches; the houses, all newly constructed and very handsome, were enveloped in clouds of smoke, and our regret at its destruction was increased by the fact that since leaving Witepsk we had not met with a more charming and agreeable place.

The viceroy halted in the plain for two hours. From rising ground we could see clearly the progress of the conflagration, and hear the heavy cannonade which was being directed against the enemy beyond the town. A large body of cavalry, debouching from all quarters, was encamped in the environs. Prince Eugene by direction of the emperor crossed the Viazma, which is here only a small stream. We presently encountered one of its branches, the approaches to which were so boggy that it was impossible to ford it; and we had therefore to retrace our steps to a point where there was a wretched bridge; thence we reached the top of a hill, from which we saw at some distance a very handsome *château* and a large church. On arriving there we found that the former had been sacked by the light cavalry.

The day following (30th August) the army remained in its positions. The guns of each division were pointed towards the different roads by which the enemy might appear. The emperor was at Viazma, whence he directed the third corps to march in support of the King of Naples, who, so far, had pursued the Russians on the road to Moscow, without having been able to bring them to an engagement.

The Bavarian cavalry under General Preyssing led the way when the advance was resumed (31st August) and with them marched the viceroy and the staff. On our road we came to two handsome *châteaux*, which, however, had been entirely looted. We halted at the second, and found ourselves in a beautiful park, the walks through which were very delightful; the buildings had been recently redecorated, but they presented nothing but a scene of the most appalling destruction; nothing was to be seen but broken furniture; fragments of priceless porcelain were scattered about the garden; and engravings of great value, torn from their frames, were blowing about at the mercy of the winds.

The viceroy had pushed forward the light horse beyond the Château of Pokrow, but observing that the infantry were a long way behind he feared to endanger them; so, retracing his steps, he established himself at the *château*, where some provisions were found, and particularly a supply of oats and excellent forage.

Since the actions at Witepsk, the fourth corps had not encountered the enemy; we had not even seen those squadrons of Cossacks which, during the first Polish campaign, incessantly harassed our troops and intercepted our convoys; but after leaving Viazma it was necessary to proceed with more caution.

As a matter of fact, we were almost certain that we should soon meet with resistance. On the 1st of September, when only about one-half of our customary march had been accomplished, our advance-guard was checked by Cossacks; two or three cannon-shots heralding this encounter. Prince Eugene immediately threw the cavalry of the Italian Guard into order of battle, and, preceded by a cloud of skirmishers, they drove before them the enemy's squadrons, who retired as we advanced. They so continued to act as far as the environs of Ghiat, which the emperor had just taken. Above this town there was a small stream which they crossed, and a moment afterwards, as if to observe us, they ranged themselves in order of battle upon the plateau which commands the plain over which we had arrived.

The viceroy, after having ordered me to sound the fords through the river, directed the Bavarians to cross it at the point which had been found practicable, and which was situated between two small villages held by Cossacks. No sooner had the Cossacks observed this movement than they abandoned the villages and the plateau, which were promptly occupied by the Bavarian cavalry followed by their artillery. Arrived on this height, we saw that on all sides the enemy were taking to flight. They were at once energetically pursued, but as night was falling, our corps proceeded to take up its quarters in the little village of Paulovo, situated half a league from Ghiat.

The headquarters having remained for three days in this town, we stayed at Paulovo and Woremiowo (2nd and 3rd September). An order of the day was here published in which the Emperor, in granting repose to the army, invited it to take the opportunity to replenish its supplies, clean its arms, and prepare for the battle which the enemy seemed ready to accept; and looting parties were warned to rejoin the ranks on the following evening under pain of forfeiting the honour of participating in the fight.

Preparations for the Battle of Borodino

Napoleon, after the capture of Smolensk, was aware that Alexander, having concluded peace with the Turks, would very soon have the army of Moldavia at his disposal. In spite of this knowledge and the urgent advice of his best generals, he pursued his conquests without troubling himself about the future. The Russians, however, alarmed at the disastrous plan adopted by Barclay de Tolly, clamoured for a decisive battle. In these circumstances all eyes turned towards Prince Kutusoff, the glorious conqueror of the Turks, who, owing to a Court intrigue, was living in obscurity on his estates, while his victories had paved the way to a settlement with the Ottoman Porte.

This general, regarded by every Russian as the hope of the fatherland, assumed his new position on the 29th August at Czarevo-Saimiche. The officers and soldiers hailed with delight the return of this old veteran, so famous in the annals of Russia, as their leader. The inhabitants of Ghiat told us that his mere presence had filled the whole army with joy and hope. Hardly had he arrived, when he announced that the retreat was ended, and that with the object of saving Moscow, from which we were only four days' march, he had selected between Ghiat and Mojaisk a strong position, where one of those memorable battles would be fought which often decide the fate of Empires. Each side felt confident of victory. The Russians were inspired with the determination to defend their country, their hearths, and their children; we, on the other hand, accustomed to conquer, intoxicated with suc-

---

1. The great and sanguinary engagement called by the French the Battle of the Moskwa, is known to the rest of the world as the Battle of Borodino. Moskwa is the name of the river in the neighbourhood of which it was fought; Borodino is the village around which the most desperate fighting occurred.

cess, longed impatiently for the conflict, and in virtue of the superiority which courage gives over numbers, we only discussed on the eve of the battle what would be the fruits of victory on the morrow.

The staff had just entered the village of Woremiewo, where a fine *château* belonging to Prince Kutusoff was situated, when the viceroy, accompanied by several officers, set out to reconnoitre the environs. He had hardly proceeded for a quarter of an hour when it was found that the whole plain was swarming with Cossacks, who advanced as if with the intention of charging the group which surrounded him, but on seeing the dragoons who formed our escort they fled and did not reappear in the neighbourhood of Woremiewo.

While we remained in this village some soldiers of the 106th Regiment, in the course of a marauding expedition, seized a post-chaise in which were a Russian officer and surgeon. On being taken before the staff, the former asserted that he came from Riga, his native town, and that he was proceeding to the headquarters of General Kutusoff, who some days previously had replaced Barclay de Tolly. Although this officer was "decorated," and belonged to an influential family of Livonia, the prince declined to see him, suspecting with reason that he had risked capture in order to act the spy on our movements. Several peasants, surprised in the midst of the fields, in the neighbourhood of Mojaisk, where we knew the enemy was entrenched, seemed to change these conjectures into certainty.

After passing two days in Woremiewo, we left it (4th September) and passed through forests, where it was said that Cossacks had been encountered. Reports from the advance-guard confirming this statement, the viceroy was obliged to order a halt in a plain where we found ourselves on issuing from a wood, and where all our corps was assembled. The prince put himself at the head of the cavalry, the infantry following, and the Guard as a reserve bringing up the rear. On arriving close to the little village of Lowzos we were stopped by a small river. The Cossacks, drawn up on the other side, appeared to be forming into squadrons to oppose our passage, but our cavalry having reascended the ravine, the Russians feared lest we should fall upon their rear, and decided to beat a retreat.

During the whole of our march, we had heard on our right a heavy cannonade, which seemed to indicate that we were not far from the road along which Napoleon was marching, and the smoke of the guns and several villages on fire were to be seen in that direction. Close to the post station of Ghridneva was an immense ravine, which intersected the high road, and on the side opposite to us there rose a plateau, upon which the Russians had mounted batteries at the close of a sanguinary combat which had taken place during the day.

The enemy perceiving that the fourth corps was debouching on its right, employed a large force of cavalry to keep us in check under cover of a wood. The viceroy ordered Colonel Rambourg of the 3rd Italian Chasseurs to charge them, but the Cossacks, who were doubtless part of the regular army, observed this movement without dismay, and when the *chasseurs* were on the point of charging they issued from the wood, with loud yells of "*Hourra! hourra!*"—a war-cry which has since become famous, and which the Tartars utter when they rush on their foes. The Italian *chasseurs* received them without flinching; the *mêlée* was very sharp, but only lasted for an instant. The Cossacks having noticed the advance of the Bavarian light horse, abandoned the struggle and left several prisoners in our hands.

The Russians, maintaining their positions, delivered a hot fire from the summit of the plateau upon our corps as it advanced, and several shot fell in the midst of a group of officers belonging to our general staff. In spite of that, we reached the great ravine and effected our junction with the advance-guard of the Grand Army commanded by the King of Naples, We recognised him from afar by his white aigrette; and at the head of his troops he was conspicuous as the *beau idéal* of a dashing soldier.

Immediately Prince Eugene had satisfied himself of the presence of the King of Naples, he joined him to arrange their combined operations. They met in the midst of the batteries, and with complete *sang froid* continued their conversation while several persons in their vicinity were killed by the enemy's fire.

At the approach of night we returned to Lowzos, where the only shelter we had was afforded by some miserable barns covered with straw. Hunger redoubled our weariness, and there was nothing available to satisfy it. However, we were in touch with the entrenched camp of Mojaisk, where Kutusoff aspired to beat us; and he would certainly have succeeded if, without giving battle, he could have held us at bay for a few days before this formidable position.

The position of Ghridneva which the Russians had defended on the previous evening was evacuated during the night. The King of Naples, burning to pursue them (5th September), pushed rapidly forward. The fourth corps, which continued to flank the left of the army, followed the high road, keeping itself at a distance of about a league.

Leaving a forest infested with Cossacks, we passed through several villages which they had looted, and the desolation spread by their ravages wherever they went made it easy to follow their track. On arriving at the foot of some hills, we perceived on the summit some of their squadrons in battle array, around a very handsome *château* which commanded the surrounding country.

Towards this point the viceroy sent forward the Bavarians, who, in spite of the difficulties of the ground, arrived at the top in the most perfect order; but in proportion as our allies advanced the enemy retired; and while they were descending the other side of the hill our artillery fired on them with guns which had been placed in position on the terrace of the *château*. In following them through the wood we arrived at an open space, from which were distinctly seen long columns of Russians, who, driven by our troops, took possession of an immense plateau about half a league off, where it was confidently asserted Prince Kutusoff would at last try the fortune of battle. Upon our right was to be seen beneath us the Abbey of Kolotskoi, the huge towers of which gave to this building the appearance of a town.

The glazed tiles with which it was covered, struck by the rays of the sun, glittered through the thick dust raised by our numerous cavalry, and served to deepen the sombre and savage gloom which brooded over the surrounding country; for the Russians, intending to arrest our course before this position, had devastated in a horrible manner the whole plain on which we had to encamp. The green wheat had been cut; the forests hewn down; the villages burnt; in fine, we had nothing to eat, no food for the horses, and absolutely no shelter.

We halted upon a hill, while the centre of the army pursued the enemy with ardour, and compelled him to retire upon the plateau where he was entrenched. This inaction continued until towards two o'clock in the afternoon. At that hour the viceroy, followed by his staff, went to reconnoitre the approaches of the position which Kutusoff had chosen. We had hardly commenced to survey the line when our dragoons placed as skirmishers announced the arrival of the emperor. Immediately, his name flying from mouth to mouth brought every one to a standstill to await him. He soon appeared, followed by his principal officers, and took his stand upon an eminence whence he could easily survey the Russian camp. Napoleon having long and carefully observed this position, attentively examined the surrounding localities, and with a satisfied air proceeded to indulge in some trivial remarks. He then conferred with the viceroy, and remounting his horse, left at a gallop to concert measures with the other leaders of the *corps d armée* who were to co-operate in the attack.

In the meantime, Prince Eugene ordered Delzons' and Broussier's divisions to advance, the Italian Guard, left in the rear, being held in reserve. These two divisions had scarcely arrived on the plateau opposite that held by the enemy, when a heavy fusillade was opened on our right, between the skirmishers of Gerard's division and those of the enemy. At first our men advanced pretty close to the ravine which separated the two armies, but superior numbers obliged them to retire.

Towards our extreme right the Russians had a redoubt situated between two woods, from which a murderous fire carried consternation into our ranks. They had constructed it to strengthen their left wing, which was the weak part of their entrenchments. Napoleon saw this at once, and that there was nothing for it but to carry this redoubt. The honour was assigned to the soldiers of Compan's division (fifth division, first corps). These gallant fellows marched forward with a determination which guaranteed success. Prince Poniatowski meanwhile manoeuvred on our right with the cavalry to turn the position. When it had gained a convenient height Compan's division attacked the redoubt, and succeeded in taking it after an hour's struggle. The enemy, completely beaten abandoned the neighbouring woods, and fled in disorder towards the great plateau to rejoin the centre of his army.

Compan's division, while showing itself worthy of such an important enterprise, paid dearly for the honour. About a thousand of our soldiers fell in the attack, of which more than half were left dead in the entrenchments which they had so gloriously taken. On the morrow the emperor, reviewing the 61st Regiment, which had suffered most, asked the colonel what he had done with one of his battalions: "Sire," replied he, "*it is in the redoubt!*"

This affair was merely the prelude to a great battle. Before commencing it Napoleon attempted to manoeuvre and turn the Russian left wing; but in order to anticipate our attack they had placed the whole of Titschkoff's corps (third) and the Moscow militia in ambush behind dense brushwood, which covered their extreme left, while the second, fourth, and sixth corps of the enemy formed in the rear two lines of infantry protected by the works which connected the woods with the great redoubt, In spite of these obstacles our *voltigeurs* recommenced the combat with renewed desperation, and although the day was near its close, the firing on both sides continued with equal fury.

At the same time several villages set on fire upon the right, cast a lurid and frightful glare over the scene. The shouts of the combatants, the iron and flame belched from a hundred brazen mouths, spread death and destruction in all directions; the soldiers of our corps, all ranged in order of battle, were mown down by a murderous fire; and without flinching closed up their ranks when a shot destroyed some of their comrades.

The darkening of the night relaxed the fusillade without relaxing our ardour; but each of us, uncertain of the effect of his efforts, thought it better to reserve his strength and ammunition for the morrow. Hardly had firing ceased when the Russians, encamped as on an amphitheatre, lighted innumerable fires. This illumination, resplendent and almost symmetrical, gave to the hills an aspect of enchantment, and formed an extraordinary contrast to our bivouacs, where the soldiers, in the absence of firewood, lay in the midst of utter darkness, hearing nothing on all sides but the groans of the wounded.

Our headquarters were established on the spot where the Italian Guard was placed in reserve. Each man, with brushwood for his bed, sought repose after the fatigues of the day, and slept profoundly, in spite of a high wind and an extremely cold rain. Towards midnight I was awakened on a summons from the chief of our staff, who told me that the emperor wished to have the plan of the ground on which we were encamped. I handed the plan to the viceroy, who immediately sent it to the emperor. At dawn on the following day (6th September) the prince ordered me to correct this plan, by traversing the whole of our line, and endeavouring to approach the enemy as closely as possible, so as to discover the character of the ground upon which he was entrenched, and above all carefully to observe if there were any masked batteries or ravines which were unknown to us.

Armed with these instructions I set out, and ascertained that the Russian camp was situated behind the River Kologha, upon a very confined plateau; and that their left was much weakened by the loss of the redoubt which we had taken on the previous day. Facing us was the village of Borodino, a very strong position, situated at the junction of a rivulet with the Kologha. Upon the plateau were two large redoubts, separated from each other by a distance of about three thousand six hundred feet. The one in the centre had fired on us the previous evening; the one on the left was erected on the ruins of a hamlet which had been destroyed to make room for artillery. This last communicated with Borodino by three bridges thrown across the

Kologha, so that that village and the rivulet which separated it from us served as the enemy's first line.

On our extreme left the Italian cavalry had crossed this rivulet, but Borodino, situated on a height, remained guarded by a strong body of the enemy. The whole of this ground was exposed to the fire of their principal redoubts, as well as to that of several other smaller ones masked along the course of the river. As to our right, it will be understood that our success of the previous evening had enabled us to approach Kutusoff's extreme left, and to advance the greater part of our troops quite close to the plateau on which was situated the great redoubt.

We passed the rest of the day in carefully reconnoitring the Russian position. General Danthouard had fortifications reconstructed which seemed to him to have been placed too far back; upon the left there were also erected breastworks suitable for mounting batteries of guns. At last all was ready for commencing a decisive engagement, when towards evening the emperor sent a proclamation to the leader of each corps, with instructions to read it to the soldiers on the morrow, provided the battle then took place. For though the position was well chosen and of great strength, the enemy had so often eluded us, that it was to be feared that he might repeat the tactics adopted at Witepsk and Valontina. Here, however, the long marches and the separation from our reserves had at last equalised the forces of the two combatants; and, moreover, it was absolutely necessary for the Muscovites to fight if they wished to save their capital, from which we were now only twenty-six leagues distant.

The exhaustion of our soldiers and the reduction in the number of our horses promised the Russians an easy victory. We, on our side, were equally confident, as we found ourselves in a position where there was no alternative between victory or death, and the conviction gave us such desperate courage that in spite of the strength of the enemy and his seemingly impregnable entrenchments, each of us looked upon our speedy entry into Moscow as a foregone conclusion.

Our exertions, while crushing us with fatigue, oppressed us with the necessity for sleep; but there were men amongst us who, mad for glory, could take no repose in their excited state of mind. These remained awake, and as the gloom of night increased, and the camp-fires, burning low amidst the sleeping soldiers, threw a fitful gleam upon the piled arms, they thought over the marvels of our expedition, and upon the results of a battle which would decide the fate of two mighty Empires. They compared also the silence of the night with the tumult of the morrow. In their imagination they could almost see Death brooding over the slumbering thousands, but a murky darkness concealed those destined to be his victims. They themselves thought for a moment of their parents and their native land; and the uncertainty of ever seeing them again plunged them into melancholy. All at once, before daybreak, the sound of the drum was heard; officers shouted "To arms!" soldiers seized their muskets; and all, ranged in order of battle, awaited but the signal to commence. The colonels, then placing themselves in the midst of their regiments, sounded the roll-call, and each captain, surrounded by his company, read in a loud voice the following proclamation:

> Soldiers!—
> Behold the battle you have so ardently desired! Victory now depends on you; for us it is imperative; it will give us plenty, good winter quarters, and a speedy return to our native land. Bear yourselves as at Austerlitz, at Friedland, at Witepsk and at Smolensk, so that the most remote posterity will recall with pride your conduct on this day, and that it may be said of you— 'He took part in the great battle under the walls of Moscow.'

Each man was deeply impressed with this stirring address, and it was hailed with enthusiastic and long-continued acclamations. Some were exalted by a thirst for glory, others by anticipations of reward, but all were convinced that victory alone could save us from destruction. To the instinct of self-preservation were added the incentives of duty and courage. At these thoughts all hearts beat high, and each of us hoped that this memorable day would raise him to the ranks of those privileged beings born to excite the envy of their contemporaries and the admiration of posterity.

Drawn on the Spot by the Author on the 5th & 6th [...]

Labaume

Plan

OF THE

Field of Battle

of the

MOSKWA.

Sept. 7. 1812.

1. Russian Redoubt raised the 5th of September
2. Large Russian Redoubt of 24 Pieces of Cannon
3. Redoubt which the Russians[...] during the Battle
4. 24 Pieces in a masked Battery
5. Redoubt for to cover Mojaisk & the right of the position
6. Bivouac of Prince Ratinoff
7. Redoubts constructed by the 4th Corps
8. Russian Squadrons of Observation
9. French Troops of Observation

Distinctions between the French and Russian troops are

Cavalry   Infantry   Cavalry   Infantry

French Troops.   Russian Troops.

Russian Lines

Reserve of Cavalry

Corps of Prince Vice Roy

Corps of the Prince of Eckmuhl

Reserve of Cavalry

House of the Emperor
during the Battle

Imperial Guard of the Reserve

Borodino

Ambulance of the 1.st Corps.

Scale of English Yards.

Scale of French Metres.

CHAPTER 10

The Battle of Borodino Begins

Such was the spirit that animated the army, when suddenly from the midst of a dense fog we saw the sun that was to shine for the last time on so many of us, burst forth in radiant splendour. It is related that at this sight Napoleon exclaimed to those around him, "Behold the sun of Austerlitz!" The army hailed this happy omen with delight, and a thrill of emotion ran through it at the glorious recollection.

The grand manoeuvres carried out on our extreme right by the first and fifth corps under the Prince of Eckmühl showed clearly that the battle was about to take place. The two armies were face to face, the gunners at their pieces, and it only remained for the preconcerted signal to be given. At last, on the 7th September, at six o'clock in the morning precisely, a cannon-shot from one of Sorbier's batteries announced that the battle had begun. General Pernetti, with a battery of thirty guns, placed himself at the head of Compans' division, and skirting the wood, turned the enemy's entrenchments. At half-past six General Compans was wounded; at seven the Prince of Eckmühl had his horse killed under him. The Duke of Elchingen also carried out his movement and attacked the Russian centre under cover of sixty guns, which General Fouché had posted in battery the previous evening. He was supported by Latour-Maubourg's cavalry corps, which vigorously charged the enemy's masses, formed in square, around the great redoubt.

At the same time Delzons' division marched on Borodino, to which the enemy had already set fire. Our soldiers at once crossed the brook, and reached the village, which they captured at the point of the bayonet. They had been ordered to limit themselves to the occupation of the position, but, carried away by French *élan*, they rushed across the Kologha, and seized one of the bridges which connect the village with the plateau. It was at this juncture that General Plausonne, desiring to restrain the impetuosity of the 106th Regiment, was hastening to this point to prevent the advance, when a cannon-ball struck him in the middle of the body. It would be impossible to praise sufficiently the devotion of the 92nd on this occasion. Seeing that the 106th had placed itself in jeopardy, they crossed the bridge of Borodino and succeeded in bringing off that regiment, which would otherwise have been surrounded.

While Delzons' division was taking Borodino, Broussier's, crossing the Kologha below the plateau, succeeded in lodging itself in a ravine close to the great redoubt, from which the enemy was delivering a tremendous fire. On this day the Viceroy, besides the command of his own corps, had under his orders Morand's and Gerard's divisions (first and third of the first corps) together with General Grouchy's cavalry. Towards eight o'clock, Morand's division, which formed the extreme right of the fourth corps, was vigorously attacked just as it was getting ready to march on the redoubt, a movement which was to be supported by Gérard's division.

General Morand, while sustaining himself against the efforts of the enemy's lines, detached the 30th Regiment on his left to take the redoubt. By a marvellous display of bravery this position was captured, and our batteries then crowned the heights and secured the advantage which the Russians had enjoyed for more than two hours. The parapets, turned against us during the attack, now became favourable for us, and the battle was lost for the enemy when he believed it had only commenced. At this point part of his artillery was captured, the rest was abandoned in his last lines. In this extremity Prince Kutusoff saw that all was lost for Russia; eager to save her and preserve a reputation acquired during a career of half a century, he addressed the generals, reanimated the soldiers, and renewed the combat by attacking with his whole force the strong positions he had just lost. Three hundred French guns, posted on the heights, thundered upon these masses, and their vanquished soldiers died at the base of the ramparts which they had themselves raised, and which they regarded as the bulwarks of Moscow—the holy and sacred city!

But the 30th Regiment, assailed on all sides, could not maintain itself in the redoubt which it had occupied. In vain did the third division, only just entered into the battle, rush forward to support it—it was compelled to yield to superior forces. This brave regiment, led by General Bonnamy, having thus been surrounded on all sides, was compelled to retire without its leader, and rejoin its division, which, still upon the plateau, resisted, with that of General Gérard, all the most strenuous attacks of the Russians.

Encouraged by the success which he had just obtained, Kutusoff brought up his reserve to risk a last throw of the dice. The Imperial Guard took part in the move. With all these combined forces he fell upon our centre, upon which had pivoted our right. For a moment we feared we were broken, and would lose the redoubt captured on the previous evening; but General Friant, having hurried up with eighty guns, arrested and crushed the enemy's columns, which for two hours stood to be torn by grapeshot, neither daring to advance nor willing to retire. This state of uncertainty was at once seized by the King of Naples to snatch from them the victory which they thought to have secured. He ordered a charge by the corps of cavalry commanded by General Latour-Maubourg, who penetrated through the gap made by the grape in the serried masses of the Russians and in the squadrons of their cuirassiers, who, panic-stricken by this bold manoeuvre, broke and fled in all directions.

The viceroy seized this decisive moment, and flew towards his right to order a simultaneous attack upon the great redoubt by the first, thirteenth and fourteenth divisions. Having formed all three in order of battle, these troops advanced with the greatest deliberation; they had approached right up to the enemy's entrenchments, when a storm of grape burst from the whole of the guns, and carried death and consternation into our ranks. Our soldiers were at first shaken by this deadly reception, but the Prince, foreseeing this, revived their courage by reminding each regiment of the glory with which it had covered itself on so many previous occasions, saying to one, "Preserve the bravery which has won for you the title of invincible"; to another, "Remember that your reputation depends on this day."

Then, turning to the 9th of the line he said with emotion, "Brave soldiers, remember that at Wagram you were with me when we pierced the enemy's centre." By these words, but still more by his example, he inflamed their valour to such a degree that the whole of the troops, uttering shouts of joy, marched once more against the redoubt. The viceroy, passing along the line, directed the attack with complete *sang-froid*, and himself participated in it by animating Broussier's division; while General Nansouty, at the head of the first division of General Saint-Germain's heavy cavalry, vigorously charged the enemy to the right of the redoubt and swept the plain as far as the ravine. The brigade of *carbineers*, under the orders of Generals Paultre and Chouard, also marched forward, crushing all who dared to resist them. They covered themselves with glory, as did also General Pajol's *chasseurs*.

At this moment, a brigade of *cuirassiers* belonging to the corps under General Montbrun threw itself upon this same redoubt, and the scene which followed was terrible in its magnificence. The whole of the height which dominated our position appeared to be a moving mountain of steel; the glitter of arms, of helmets and *cuirasses*, under the rays of the sun, mingling with the flames from the guns which vomited death from all sides, gave to the redoubt the appearance of a volcano in the midst of an army.

The enemy's infantry, posted close by behind a ravine, delivered so destructive a volley upon our *cuirassiers* that it compelled them to retire; our infantry at once took their place. They were supported by the third cavalry corps, which, commanded by Generals Chastel, Thiery and Dommanget, charged and overthrew all that was in their way. The *aides-de-camp* Carbonel, Turenne and Grammont were wounded by the side of Count Grouchy, who was himself hit shortly afterwards; but he forgot the blood which flowed from his wound when he saw that the redoubt was ours. Our troops, on entering the entrenchments, perpetrated a horrible massacre of the Russians, which all our efforts failed to restrain.

In spite of the enemy's appalling fire, the Viceroy and his staff remained at the head of Broussier's division, followed by the 13th and 20th Regiments, and, rushing upon the redoubt, entered by the breach and massacred the gunners at the cannon they were serving. Kutusoff, struck with consternation at this attack, at once brought up the cuirassiers of the Noble Guard to endeavour to retake the position—it was the best cavalry in his army. The shock between these *cuirassiers* and ours was terrible, and the fury with which they fought may be realised when it is stated that the enemy, in abandoning the field of battle, left it covered with the dead of both sides.

It was in this sanguinary *mêlée*, for ever glorious for the staff of the fourth corps, that young Saint-Marcelin de Fontanes was wounded. He was one of the first to enter the redoubt, and received a severe sabre cut in the neck, which earned for him the Cross of the Legion of Honour, a distinction all the more flattering in that it had been gained upon the battlefield, and at an age when usually it could only have been hoped for at a later day.

The interior of the redoubt presented a frightful spectacle; corpses were piled one upon the other, and amongst them were many wounded, whose groans were heart-rending; arms of all kinds were scattered around; the breastworks were almost destroyed, and the embrasures could only be recognised by their guns, most of which, however, were overturned and detached from their shattered carriages. In the midst of this scene of ruin I noticed the body of a gunner who wore three orders on his tunic, and who still seemed to be breathing. In one hand he grasped a fragment of his sword, while the other clutched convulsively the gun which he had been serving so well.

The Russian soldiers entrusted with the defence of the redoubt died rather than surrender; and the general who commanded them would have suffered the same fate if his valour had not saved his life. This gallant officer had sworn to die at his post and he did all he could to keep his oath. The last remaining of all his force, he threw himself into our midst to meet his death, and would have been slaughtered, had not the honour of making such a distinguished prisoner stayed the fury of the soldiers. Brought before the viceroy, he was received with distinction; and the prince, desirous of honouring merit in misfortune, consigned him to Colonel Asselin with instructions to conduct him to the Emperor, who, during this memorable day, had remained constantly with the centre, directing the operations, on his extreme right, of the Poles and the first corps. The Prince of Eckmühl, by turning the Russian position at that point, facilitated the sanguinary and repeated attempts made by the third corps under the Duke of Elchingen to pierce the enemy's centre.

Upon the left, Bagration stubbornly opposed our efforts, and, reinforced by the grenadier divisions of Strogonoff and Woronsow, at first succeeded in checking the Poles; but the Duke of Elchingen, having strongly reinforced them by Westphalians, enabled them to resume the offensive, which they had temporarily lost. This marshal, linking Ledru's division with that of Generals Morand and Gérard, acted simultaneously with Prince Eugene and succeeded in penetrating into the midst of the Russian lines, preceded by numerous batteries which spread terror through the enemy's ranks. Such bravery and hardihood at last gave us the field, and secured for the Duke of Elchingen a glorious title, which connects his name with one of the most memorable of victories. (Ney was created Prince of the Moskwa for his distinguished services on this occasion.)

The attention of the viceroy was being devoted exclusively to his centre, when he was summoned to his left by a great movement of cavalry which the enemy was directing against that wing. General Delzons, who since morning had been menaced by this cavalry, formed his first brigade in squares to the left of Borodino. Several times he seemed on the point of being attacked, but the enemy, seeing that he could not be broken, transferred himself to our extreme left, and delivered a violent charge upon our light horse, commanded by Count Ornano, which for a moment was thrown into disorder. The prince, who happened then to be close to this point, placed himself in the centre of a square formed by the 84th Regiment, and was preparing to put it in motion, when the Cossacks were in their turn recalled, and taking to flight relieved our left, and order was completely restored.

The viceroy, however, rode along the line in all directions, exhorting the generals and colonels to do their duty, reminding them that on the result of this day would depend the glory of the French name; going to each battery, he ordered the guns to be advanced in proportion as he observed the Russians giving way, and, utterly indifferent to danger, pointed out to the gunners the direction in which they should fire. While thus visiting all the most perilous positions, his *aide-de-camp* Maurice Méjan was wounded in the leg; he himself General Gifflenga and the equerry Bellisomi, had their horses shot under them.

The prince, having stationed himself on the parapet of the great redoubt with his officers, surveyed the enemy's manoeuvres from the embrasures, entirely ignoring the shot which were raining upon him from every direction. Among those who formed his suite was Colonel Bourmont, whose great merit was only equalled by his rare modesty. This officer, like several others, had alighted, and was leaning on the neck of his horse, when General Guilleminot, having dropped a paper, the colonel stooped to pick it up. This movement saved his life, for at that instant a cannon-ball went through the breast of his charger.

Although the two redoubts had been taken, the enemy still held a third, situated upon another plateau separated by a ravine. From that quarter, the enemy, establishing batteries accurately served, delivered a terrific fire upon our regiments, some of which were under covered ways and others behind entrenchments. For several hours we remained inactive, quite persuaded that Kutusoff was beating a retreat; the artillery alone continued to vomit flames and death from all directions. It was at this juncture that General Huard, commanding the second brigade of the thirteenth division, was killed. Companion in arms of General Plausonne, they both perished on the same day; united during their lives, it was ordained that they should not be separated in death, and both were interred upon the battlefield which had witnessed their valour.

For more than ten hours the attacks of the enemy had been stubbornly resisted, and although the battle was by no means over, there was scarcely a division which had not suffered the loss of one or more of its leaders. The number of generals wounded reached a total of thirty, among whom were Grouchy, Nansouty, Latour-Maubourg, chiefs of army corps, and Friant, Rapp, Compans, Dessaix and Laboussaye, generals of division. The Russians, on their side, had some forty thousand men placed *hors de combat*, and fifty generals killed or wounded. Amongst the latter were Prince Bagration, who died a few days after from his wounds, and Charles of Mecklenburg; also Generals Tutschkoff, Rajewski, Gortschakoff, Kauvoitzen, Gregoff, Woronsow, Krapowitski, and the two Boekmetieffs.

Although victory was ours, the cannonade never ceased and each moment struck down new victims. Always untiring, and contemptuous of danger, the viceroy galloped over the battlefield amidst a continuous hail of grape and musketry. This torrent of fire never abated for an instant, and towards evening it was still so fierce that it was necessary to order the legion of the Vistula, under General Claparède, to kneel down behind the great redoubt. We had remained for more than an hour in this harassing position, when the Prince of Neuchatel having arrived, conferred with the viceroy until towards nightfall. Their conference having ended, Prince Eugene dispatched various orders to his divisions and ordered firing to cease. The enemy then became quieter, only firing a few shots at intervals, and the silence of his last redoubt showed beyond question that he was retiring by the road to Mojaisk.

The weather, which had been magnificent during the day, became cold and wet towards night, and the army encamped upon the field it had won. This bivouac was cruel: neither men nor horses had anything to eat, and the want of firewood subjected us to all the rigours of a rainy and icy night.

Chapter 11

Pursuit of Russians

Early next morning (8th September) we went again over the battlefield, and what had been predicted on the previous evening was found to be the fact. The enemy, in view of the audacity with which we had taken his redoubt, despaired of his position, and during the night decided to evacuate it. It was only then that, in traversing the plateau which had been the scene of the battle, we could realise the immensity of the losses which the Russians had sustained. Upon a space of about a square league, the ground was strewn with the dead and wounded. In some places bursting shells, in overturning a gun, had blown to pieces both men and horses. Similar discharges, continually repeated, had caused such destruction that the plain was covered with mountains of corpses. The few places where this was not the case, were littered with broken weapons; lances, helmets and *cuirasses*; or, with cannon-balls so innumerable that they seemed like hailstones after a violent storm.

The most appalling sight was the interior of the ravines. By a natural instinct, almost all the wounded had dragged themselves there to escape the fire, and these poor wretches, piled one on the other and weltering in their blood, uttered the most heartrending groans, and loudly invoking death, implored us to put an end to their frightful torments. The ambulances being quite insufficient, our fruitless pity was perforce restricted to deploring the suffering inseparable from so atrocious a war.

While the cavalry was pursuing the enemy, the viceroy ordered his engineers to demolish the redoubt, and as we still remained encamped on the battlefield, we presumed that we should there have to pass the next night. The prince had ordered his household to establish themselves in the church at Borodino, the only building which had escaped the general havoc, but it was full of wounded, upon whom the surgeons were busy with amputations. His *ménage* therefore proposed to betake themselves to the village of Novoë, near the road to Mojaisk, and situated on the banks of the Kologha. They were on the point of entering the château, when bands of Cossacks obliged them to beat a precipitate retreat.

In these circumstances, the viceroy, having learnt that the fifteenth division, just returned from Witepsk, had rejoined its *corps d'armée*, gave the order to move forward. On arriving at the village above which stood the redoubt abandoned by the enemy, we left on our right the main road to Mojaisk, which was that taken by the centre, and followed the course of the Kologha. During this march, we convinced ourselves that it would have been impossible to turn the Russian position on that side. Not only had they camps of reserve at this point, but several masked redoubts along the banks of the river. Half a league beyond the village of Krasnoë we found four others, which covered Mojaisk, and the extreme right of the entrenched camp of Borodino.

On quitting the battlefield we left as a guard a detachment formed of all the stray soldiers we could collect, and placed them under the command of Colonel Bourniout. This thankless mission was zealously carried out by that officer, who, after having destroyed the enemy's works, rejoined us some days later. During all that time he lived in the midst of the dead and dying, and was obliged to procure food from a distance of over five leagues.

The Château of Krasnoë, as well as the village of that name, where our corps halted, is situated on the Moskwa. The following day (9th September) we passed that river, and feigned to march upon Mojaisk by its right bank but the viceroy and his escort only advanced as far as the outskirts. From there we beheld several houses of this ill-fated village in flames, all the inhabitants having fled; but our dragoons, in searching the houses on our side of the river, took several prisoners. Some batteries posted upon a height situated behind Mojaisk, showed that we were masters of the town. We were told, in fact, that Napoleon had taken it after a glorious engagement; and that the enemy had only abandoned it after an obstinate defence, leaving it full of dead and wounded.

Our staff examined the environs of Mojaisk, while the troops, turning to the left, followed the main road running through woods, on emerging from which we found a good-sized village, and a little farther on another larger one called Vedenskoë in an enchanting situation, where there was a *château*, the furniture of which corresponded to the splendour of its exterior; but in an instant everything was destroyed, and nothing remained but some thousands of bottles of wine, which were seized by the soldiers.

Pursuing our route through the midst of brushwood, we arrived at a large village called Vrouinkovo, which we assumed was to be our headquarters. On entering the place we saw, a little farther on, upon rising ground, some fine houses and four belfries symmetrically constructed. We would have established ourselves in the village, where plenty seemed to reign, if we had not been informed that our corps was to proceed to the town whose belfries were in sight, and which was called Rouza. On leaving Vrouinkovo, we observed a number of peasants, with vehicles loaded with all their most precious belongings. Such a novel sight evoked general astonishment, and on my asking Colonel Asselin to explain the reason of this concourse of country people, he replied as follows:—

In proportion as our armies advance into the interior of Russia, the Emperor Alexander, in order to aid the intentions of the nobility, desires to follow the example of Spain and make this war a national struggle. In accordance with this plan, the nobles and the parish priests have, by means of their money and their exhortations, persuaded the peasants who were under their domination to rise against us. Of all the districts which have adopted this plan of defence, that of Rouza has shown itself most determined in its execution. The whole population, stimulated by the landowner, who has been the prime mover in the rising, has been organised on a military basis, and was ready to join the Russian army as soon as it received the order to do so.

As Rouza is five or six leagues from the main road, the inhabitants had entertained the hope that we would not pass through their town, and in this persuasion they lived contented and tranquil. What was their surprise, however, when by order of the prince I arrived before Rouza with a dozen Bavarian *chasseurs*. You would then have seen the terrified peasants rushing from their houses, harnessing their horses to the vehicles you observed, and driving them before them escaping in headlong flight.

The men, however, who had been selected to take part in the rising, having assembled at the call of their master, armed with staves, pikes or scythes, met on the *place* and in an instant advanced towards us; but this cowardly mob were quite unable to withstand a handful of soldiers inured to war, and immediately took to flight. The *seigneur* alone showed more courage. He awaited us on the *place*, and armed with a dagger menaced all those who summoned him to surrender. 'How can I survive the dishonour of my country?' cried he, foaming with rage; 'our altars are cast down, our empire is blasted. Kill me, for life has become hateful!' Efforts were made to calm him, and to deprive him of his dagger, but he only became more furious, and struck several of our soldiers, who thereupon, thinking of nothing but vengeance, ran him through with their bayonets.

This episode was scarcely ended, when our advance-guard entered Rouza. The peasants who had decamped with their effects and cattle, were promptly pursued and quickly overtaken, and those whom you see here are part of the fugitives. But go into the village and you will see much more.

As we approached, numbers of small vehicles escorted by horsemen were encountered, and it was touching to observe that they were filled with children and infirm old men. One's heart could not fail to be moved by the knowledge that those carts and horses, which constituted the whole fortune of those desolated families, would soon be divided among the soldiery.

At last we entered Rouza and found a crowd of soldiers looting the houses, without paying the least regard to the cries of the owners, or to the tears of a mother who, to soften the hearts of the conquerors, held up her infant on her bended knees. This rage for plunder might have been excusable for some who, dying of hunger, only sought to procure food; but most of them, under this pretext, simply sacked everything, and even stripped the clothes off the women and children.

The viceroy, who had arrived some hours previously, at Rouza, attended only by his staff, had left between that town and Vroumkovo the infantry divisions and the Royal Guard who were encamped in our rear. Every one, delighted to find himself in such an agreeable town as Rouza, gave himself up to the security or rather to the disorder which plenty engenders after long privations, when all at once, some Bavarian light horse, who had been out reconnoitring, returned at full gallop, with the news that the Cossacks, marching in squadrons, were advancing on the town. Imagine the sensation caused by this news! The tranquillity which we had been enjoying, contrasted with the imminence of the danger, was for us a plunge from joy into consternation.

"The Cossacks are upon us," cried one; "Here they are arriving," yelled another, in terror-stricken tones. "What have we to resist them?" was the general inquiry. "Nothing," was the reply; "there are only a few scoundrelly soldiers who have come here to plunder peasants." Nevertheless they were our only hope. They were promptly assembled on the *place*, and were found only to number sixty, all told, and of these quite one-half were unarmed.

The viceroy, informed of the cause of this commotion, mounted his horse and told his officers to follow him. We hastened out of the town, and entered upon the plain, but imagine our astonishment, when instead of finding several squadrons, we only saw a dozen or so of horsemen, at such a distance that they could hardly be distinguished. The Bavarian *chasseurs* whom we had with us, advanced to reconnoitre them, and reported that they actually *were* Cossacks. From their small number and their timid and cautious movements it was easy to see that they did not mean much mischief.

As these Cossacks might have been detached from a considerable body, the prince deemed it necessary to confirm the order already given to advance the troops; but he modified it, limiting the movement to two battalions instead of including in it the whole of the thirteenth division, as at first directed. These two battalions, having encamped beyond Rouza, dissipated our fears. All then tranquilly returned to their quarters, where a well-served table and exquisite wines soon enabled us to forget the alarm which had disturbed the close of the day.

We remained next day at Rouza. The viceroy profited by this rest to get a report drawn up by General Guilleminot, the chief of his staff, giving a very detailed account of the famous day of the 7th September, when the fourth corps had particularly distinguished itself.

While the thirteenth and fourteenth divisions submitted to the emperor the claims they had on his consideration, the fifteenth, not less trusty than the others, but deprived of the honour of fighting at the Battle of the Moskwa, could none the less ask for some reward in recompense for the hardships which it had endured during the expedition against Witepsk. This division, continually marching through swampy meadows, and villages either deserted or sacked, had been frequently without food, and constantly suffering the most frightful hardships in its endeavour to overtake an enemy who always fled at its approach. During a period of nearly twenty days it had done nothing but march through a country which we had ravaged, until at last, overcome by want, fatigue and disease, this unfortunate division only managed to arrive at Borodino on the morrow of the battle. Its fatigue, and above all its heavy losses, obliged the viceroy to leave it in reserve. It was the highest mark of his esteem that the prince could accord, to associate it with the veterans of the Royal Guard, the greater part of which had been recruited from this division.

On leaving Rouza, it was decided to retain that position, which was of all the more importance in that it still contained food in abundance, and that a kind of fortress, situated upon a mound and surrounded by wide ditches, could serve as a refuge for the garrison, and secure it from a *coup de main*. This honourable command was entrusted to Captain Simonet de Maison-Neuve, who did not betray the confidence reposed in him, for during the whole of his mission, this active and intelligent officer rendered himself as valuable to the army by his foresight as by the skill of his dispositions.

Chapter 12

March on Moscow

After the Battle of the Moskwa our victorious army marched in three columns on the capital of the Russian Empire. Napoleon, impatient to capture it, pursued the enemy with his accustomed impetuosity by the high road from Smolensk, while Prince Poniatowski, at the head of the fifth corps, followed that of Kaluga. The viceroy, with the fourth corps, continued to flank the left, and by the road through Zwenighorod, directed himself upon Moscow, where the whole army was to concentrate.

One could judge of the consternation which reigned in the capital by the terror which we inspired among the peasantry. Hardly had the news spread of our arrival at Rouza (9th September), and of the ruthless manner in which we had treated the population, when all the villages upon the road to Moscow were precipitately abandoned We created universal panic, and many of those who fled seized with a kind of despair, burnt their houses and their *châteaux*; and the wheat and other corps which had recently been harvested. The majority of these wretched people, cowed by the futile and fatal resistance of the militia at Rouza, threw down their pikes and fled hastily to conceal themselves, with their wives and children, in the dense forests which spread along our route.

It was hoped, however, that in the vicinity of Moscow, civilisation, which always has an enervating effect, and the instinct of property, so natural to the inhabitants of great cities, would have induced the people of the neighbourhood to remain in their dwellings, in the belief that the looting by our soldiers had been provoked by the deserted state of the villages. But the land around Moscow is not in the possession of individual owners among the inhabitants of the city; it belongs to the landowners who had declared against us; and their peasantry, quite as subservient and enslaved as those of the Dnieper and the Volga, obeyed the behests of their masters, who had ordered them, under pain of death, to flee on our approach, and to bury or conceal in the woods everything that could by any possibility be of use to us.

On entering the village of Apalchtchouima we beheld the execution of this fatal measure. Houses deserted, the château abandoned; furniture smashed to pieces, and provisions ruined, presented a scene of unparalleled desolation, which proved to us the extremities to which a people can resort when it is great enough to prefer its independence to its material welfare.

Close to Karinskoë, a village situated about halfway to Zwenighorod, for which we were bound, Cossacks were signalled. In accordance with their usual practice, they did not face our advance-guard, but limited themselves to watching us by moving on our left along a ridge of hills parallel with the high road. On the summit of these hills and beyond a dense birch wood, rose the grey walls and towers of an ancient abbey. At the foot of the hill was the small town of Zwenighorod, built on the banks of the Moskwa. There the Cossacks united, and forming into several groups, exchanged shots for some time with our *voltigeurs*; they were, however, gradually dislodged from the shelter they had chosen, and we took up our position around Zwenighorod.

Situated above this small town, the abbey surveys the course of the Moskwa. The battlemented walls, more than twenty feet high, and from five to six feet thick, are flanked at the four corners by great embrasured towers. This edifice, built in the thirteenth or fourteenth century, carries us back to the times when the Muscovites, full of veneration for their priests, permitted the sacerdotal power to surpass that of the noble; and when the *Czar* on holy days walked beside the Patriarch of Moscow, holding the bridle of his horse. But these monks, so powerful and arrogant before the reign of Peter the Great, were reduced to apostolic simplicity when that great monarch, in founding his empire, confiscated their property and reduced their number.

To obtain an idea of the changes effected by this reform, it suffices to enter the Abbey of Zwenighorod. At the sight of these lofty towers and frowning walls, we concluded that their interior would present spacious and commodious buildings, and that we should find among these religious, the plenty always associated with richly endowed abbeys. We were preparing to force an entry when an old man, whose long beard was as white as his habit, came to admit us. We immediately requested him to conduct us to the abbot. On entering the court, we were extremely surprised to see that this vast edifice by no means fulfilled the high expectations we had formed of it, and that our guide, instead of introducing us to the apartments of the superior, took us into a small chapel, where we found four monks prostrated before an altar constructed in the Greek manner. On approaching them, these venerable old men embraced our knees, imploring us, in the name of the God they worshipped, to respect the church and the tombs of the bishops of which they were the faithful guardians. They said, through an interpreter:—

> From our poverty you can see that we have no hidden treasures; and our food is so coarse that your soldiers would disdain to eat it. We have no other wealth than our relics and our altars; we beseech you to respect them in deference to our religion which so closely resembles your own.

We gave them the required promise, which was confirmed on the arrival of the viceroy, who, on taking up his quarters in the abbey, preserved the church and monastery from the pillage with which they were threatened.

While this retreat, formerly so tranquil, was the prey to the tumult inevitable in such circumstances, I noticed one of the pious monks, who, for the purpose of disrobing, retired to a cell which might be said to be almost subterranean, and the austere simplicity of which had enabled it to escape from our inquisitiveness. This religious, aware of my friendly attitude, showed his gratitude by admitting that he spoke French, and that it would afford him great pleasure to have a chat with me. Touched by his frankness, I availed myself of it to learn from his conversation everything I could with respect to the feelings of the people, and the character of a nation whose territory we had overrun for more than two hundred and fifty leagues without being able to learn anything about it. When I mentioned Moscow, he said it was his birthplace, and I noticed that a deep sigh accompanied the statement. By his silent grief, I gathered that he lamented the misfortunes to which the capital was exposed. I sympathised with him; but, anxious to know what was passing there, when we were about to enter it, I ventured to ask him the news. Replied he:—

> The French have invaded Russia with a great army; they ravage our beloved country, and they are advancing even towards this holy city, the centre of the Empire and the source of our

prosperity. But, ignorant of our customs and our character, they think that we will submit to the yoke, and that, forced to choose between our hearths and our independence, we shall follow the example of others, and elect to languish in chains and abdicate that pride of nationality which constitutes the power of a people. No! Napoleon deludes himself; too enlightened to submit to his tyranny, we are not sufficiently degenerate to prefer slavery to freedom. Vainly does he hope by his innumerable armies to compel us to sue for peace. Here again he deceives himself. Our nation is a nation of nomads; and the nobles of our Empire, being able at their will to cause the migration of a whole population, will order their peasantry to flee into the wilderness to escape the invaders, and even if necessary to destroy town and country rather than allow them to fall into the hands of a ruthless barbarian, whose oppression is far more cruel to us than death.

We know, also, that Napoleon counts upon the dissensions which in former times broke out between the sovereign and the nobility; but patriotism stifles all these ancient discords. He flatters himself, again, that he can arm the People against the nobility. Vain effort! The people, taught by religion, submit themselves to their superiors, and believe none of the specious promises of him who burns their cottages, slaughters their children, devastates our countryside, and overturns our altars. Besides, has not all Europe before her eyes the most convincing proofs of his perfidy? Is he not the scourge of Germany, of which he arrogates to himself the title of protector? Spain through having believed in the sincerity of his alliance is the prey to the most frightful misfortunes. The *pontiff* who crowned him, and who thus raised him from obscurity to be the most powerful monarch in the world,—what has he received as his reward for placing on his head this brilliant diadem? A bitter captivity! And your own country which from a frenzy of democracy has voluntarily passed under the yoke of depotism, what has it gained by its submission?

New taxes without intermission to maintain a set of useless courtiers, or to satisfy the luxury of a family insatiable in the pursuit of pleasure. More than that, you have proscriptions without number; secret executions; thought enchained; whole generations devoured until at last your very mothers deplore their fecundity. Such is the position to which your tyrant has reduced you; a tyrant all the more contemptible and odious in that, having been nurtured in obscurity with hardly a servant to attend on him, he now demands that the whole universe shall grovel at his feet and that kings themselves shall dangle in his antechamber. Ah! if I did not shrink from defiling the majesty of the monarch whom we love as he loves us, I would compare your Emperor with ours—but such a comparison would be revolting, as a contrast between vice and virtue.

Struck by the energy of this religious, whose mental power had been in no wise diminished by age, I was reduced to silence, while at the same time charmed by his sincerity. Touched by the confidence he had reposed in me, I thought myself justified in opening my mind to him, so as to obtain from him information that might be useful to me. "As you have mentioned the Emperor Alexander," I replied, "do you know what has become of him? Since leaving Wilna we have heard nothing of him; and at Witepsk Napoleon, in a public audience, announced that this monarch had ended like his father, having fallen a victim at Waliki-Luki to the treachery of his courtiers."

"A man must have very little nobility of soul," replied the old man with a sad smile, "who makes the death of one of his enemies a subject for triumph. But in order to prove to you the falsity of this report, and to make you understand what complete harmony reigns at this critical moment between all classes, and their devotion to their sovereign, I will read to you an authentic letter which was sent to me from Moscow a few days after Alexander, quitting the army, arrived in his capital."

At these words he read me the following letter, translating it as he went along:—

Moscow, 27th July 1812.

This will be another red-letter day in our calendar, and the recollection of it will be transmitted to the most remote posterity. In accordance with a public announcement on the previous evening, the order of the nobility and the guild of merchants assembled at eight in the morning in the halls of the Slobode palace, there to await the arrival of our gracious sovereign. Although the object of the assemblies had not been notified in advance, all those who attended them were full of the sentiments aroused in every heart by the appeal of the Father of their country to his children of the ancient capital. The very silence which pervaded the large gatherings unmistakably proclaimed their unity of feeling, and their readiness to make any sacrifice which the crisis might require.

After the manifesto of His Imperial Majesty, summoning all to the defence of the fatherland, had been read, the nobles announced their eagerness to sacrifice their fortunes, and even their lives, for the country, and undertook to raise, equip and maintain a force for the defence of Moscow. The manifesto was next read to the assembly of the merchants, and this body, imbued with the general enthusiasm, decided to levy upon its members a sum proportionate to the capital of each to meet the cost of this army of the interior. Not content with this, the majority expressed themselves desirous of making special sacrifices, and asked permission to open a voluntary subscription before separating. This was at once taken in hand, and in less than an hour more than a million and a half of roubles were subscribed.

Such was the feeling of the two bodies, when His Majesty, after having attended Divine service in the palace chapel, entered the assembly of the nobles. The emperor, in the course of a short address, said that he regarded the zeal of the nobility as the surest support of the throne; and that their order had shown itself in every age and in all circumstances the guardian and faithful defender of the integrity and glory of their beloved fatherland. He then deigned to give them a summary of the military position, which demanded exceptional measures of defence. On being informed of the resolutions that had been passed, the emperor hailed with extreme satisfaction this new proof of devotion to his person and love of country; and in the fullness of his heart exclaimed, 'I expected no less; you have fully confirmed the opinion I had of you!'

His Majesty next proceeded to the hall where the merchants were assembled, and as soon as he was informed of the zeal which they had displayed in resolving to levy a contribution upon their whole body, the Emperor signified his satisfaction in words which were received with unanimous acclamations. To do it justice, the scene of this morning would require the pen of another Tacitus, and the brush of a new Apelles. It presented the picture of a monarch, the father of his country, overflowing with goodness, receiving from his children, massed around him, the sacrifices which they came to offer upon the altar of the fatherland.

May all this reach the ears of our enemy! Of that vainglorious man who sports with the destinies of his subjects. May he learn it and tremble! United, we march against him; we are inspired by religion; by an unalterable love for our sovereign and our country. Together we will perish or triumph.

After reading this letter, the worthy ecclesiastic informed me that the Archimandrite Platon, Metropolitan of Moscow, though advanced in age and very feeble, kept vigil of prayer for the safety of the sovereign and the Empire, and that he had just sent to His Majesty the precious statue of St. Sergius, Bishop of Radouegar. Added he:—

The monarch in accepting this sacred relic, presented it to the army of Moscow, in the hope that it would secure them the protection of this saint, who, by his benediction in olden times prepared Dimitri Douskoi for his combat with the cruel Maimai.

The following is the letter of His Eminence Platon, dated from the Abbey of Troitsa, 26th July 1812:—

The City of Moscow, first capital of the Empire of the New Jerusalem, receives her Christ like a mother in the arms of her zealous sons, and through the mists which spread around, foreseeing the resplendent glory of her power, she chants in ecstasy, 'Hosanna! blessed is he that cometh!' What though the arrogant, boastful Goliath brings from the utmost limits of France his mortal terrors to the confines of Russia! the religion of peace, that sling of the Russian David, will swiftly beat down the head of his bloody pride. This image of St. Sergius, of old the champion of our country's welfare, we humbly offer to your Imperial Majesty.

Astonished at a spirit so far removed from ours, I asked if it was really the fact that the Emperor Alexander had given this emblem to his soldiers. Replied the monk:—

I am so certain of it, that to doubt it were sacrilege. The news from Moscow is to the effect that Bishop Augustin, vicar of the capital, having assembled all the troops who were in the city, chanted a *Te Deum*, and presenting them with the statue of St. Sergius, delivered a discourse which drew tears from every eye. We ourselves have seen the soldiers passing under the walls of this abbey to take part in the Battle of the Moskwa. Full of veneration for this sacred banner, they marched to the combat like true Christian warriors, devoted to their religion, to their country and to their prince. These feelings were revealed on every face; the celestial joy of fighting the common foe glowed in their flashing eyes; each soldier, although only just enrolled in the ranks, burning with the courage of a veteran, displayed an unbounded obedience to his leaders, and maintained that absolute discipline which is the sure sign of a good soldier. Wherever they passed the country people earnestly invoked the protection of Heaven for these heroes, issuing from the ancient capital of Russia, which had by her own might chastised in former times the insolent enemies who, in their blindness, had thought to destroy her.

Alas! Fortune did not smile upon their efforts. You vanquished them at Borodino, and ever since that fatal day consternation has reigned supreme through the land. The highways are covered with fugitives, who fly to seek safety on the frontiers of Asia; we alone are left, and you may imagine our alarm, when yesterday at nightfall your arrival was signalled by the fires of your bivouacs which covered the neighbouring hills, and above all by the burning villages, the flames of which lit up the midnight sky.

Astonished beyond measure at the extraordinary things this worthy old man had told me, I was at the same time filled with respect for a nation, so great amidst misfortune, and said to myself, "That people is invincible which, unshaken in its fortitude, remains unmoved in the presence of danger and risks its existence for the preservation of its independence."

CHAPTER 13

The Fourth Corps Enters Moscow

We quitted this abbey on the following day. In leaving it I looked back, and saw the first beams of the rising sun tinting the summits of those lofty walls, raised to be the home of peace, but which after our departure became a scene of riot and disorder. I shook off these harrowing thoughts, however, and, taking the road that runs parallel with the Moskwa, I observed that in front of Zwenighorod bridges had been constructed across the river, doubtless to establish communication with the Grand Army which was marching upon Moscow by the opposite bank. We were still advancing when the Cossacks again appeared, manoeuvring as on the previous evening. Below Aksinimo, they attempted for a moment to arrest the progress of the Bavarian light horse; but having had some men wounded, they took to flight, and retired across the river, which we crossed below the village of Spaskoe.

At this point the Moskwa, not being very deep, was easily forded both by men and horses. The Cossacks, who awaited us at the entry to a wood, scattered on observing that we had cleared the barrier which had separated us. Thence we continued our march as far as Buzaievo, where there was nothing but the post office, and on the top of a very steep hill a wooden *château*, where Prince Eugene took up his quarters.

On the following day, eager to get to Moscow, we started betimes, and encountered nothing but deserted villages. Upon our left were to be seen on the banks of the Moskwa several splendid *châteaux*, which the Tartars had gutted, to deprive us of the supplies they contained; for the harvest, ready for the sickle, had been trodden down or eaten by the horses, and the hayricks which covered the country, having been delivered to the flames, filled the air with a dense smoke. On arriving at the village of Techerepkova, while our cavalry moved onward, the viceroy ascended a hill to our right, and for a long time endeavoured by careful examination of the surrounding country to catch a glimpse of Moscow, which was the object of all our desires, since it was regarded as the end of our fatigue, and the limit of our expedition. Several hills intervened to conceal it still from our eyes; we saw nothing but great clouds of dust, which, moving parallel with our route, indicated the march of the Grand Army. Some cannon-shots fired a long way off and at long intervals, led us to conclude that our troops were approaching Moscow without experiencing much resistance.

On descending from this rising ground, we heard the most alarming yells; they proceeded from several "*pulsks*" of Cossacks who issued from a neighbouring wood, and charging our chasseurs in their usual fashion, tried to stop our advance-guard. Our men, far from being disconcerted at this unexpected attack, received with perfect coolness the futile efforts of this rabble to check our entry into the capital. As a matter of fact this attempt was the last we experienced, and the Russians defeated and dispersed, found themselves obliged to seek refuge under the walls of the Kremlin.

At a great distance, and through the clouds of dust, long columns of the enemy's cavalry could be distinguished, all marching upon Moscow, and retiring in good order behind the city in proportion as we approached it. The staff, while waiting for a bridge to be thrown across the Moskwa, took station at about eleven o'clock upon a high hill, whence we perceived in a brilliant light a thousand gilded domes, which, glittering in the rays of the sun, resembled in the distance so many luminous globes. These globes, placed on the summit of columns or obelisks, gave one the impression of balloons suspended in mid-air. We were transported with astonishment at such a magnificent vista; all the more so after the awful scenes we had recently witnessed. No one could now contain his delight, and by a spontaneous impulse there was a universal cry of "Moscow! Moscow!"

At this name of a city so long desired, every one made a rush for the hill, and each moment the scene revealed fresh marvels. One would admire a magnificent *château* situated to our left, the architecture of which suggested the Orient; another directed his attention to a palace, or a church, but all were struck by the superb panorama presented by this great city, situated in the midst of a fertile plain, with the Moskwa winding through smiling pastures till it is lost in the distance. After having fertilised the surrounding country, this river passes through the centre of the capital, and divides an immense mass of houses built of wood, stone or brick, which present a curious mixture of the architecture of the East and West. Walls variously coloured, cupolas either gilded or covered with lead or slate, displayed the most striking variety; while the terraces of the palace, the obelisks at the city gates, and above all the turrets constructed in the form of minarets, brought actually before our eyes one of those famous cities of Asia, which until then had seemed to us to exist only in the fertile imagination of Arabian poets.

We were absorbed in the contemplation of this magnificent view, when we observed a well-dressed man coming from the direction of Moscow, and advancing towards us. We at once hastened to meet him, and our suspicious minds already suggested the idea of making him pay dearly for his indiscreet curiosity. But the calmness with which he accosted us, the ease with which he spoke our language, and above all the impatience which we experienced to hear the latest news, constrained us to listen to what he had to say.

I have not come here to spy out your movements, nor to give you false information. I am an unfortunate merchant, utterly ignorant of all that relates to the war; and although I am one of its victims, I have not tried to fathom the motives which have induced our sovereigns to engage in it. Today at noon your emperor entered Moscow at the head of his invincible legions, after having received an envoy who implored him to spare the city, which was about to be evacuated. But he has found the streets deserted; a few escaped criminals, some abandoned prostitutes, are the only beings who break the solitude. Hasten, if you can, to put a stop to their excesses, for they have been set at large in the hope that all the crimes which they commit will be ascribed to the French Army.

Foreseeing the misfortunes with which we are threatened, I have come to see if I can find among you a man sufficiently humane to protect my family, for, notwithstanding the orders of our governor, I cannot consent to abandon my house to drag out a life of wandering and wretchedness in the wilderness. I prefer to appeal to French generosity, and to seek a protector among those who have been represented to us as our cruellest enemies. The nobles of our empire, committed to a barbarous and destructive policy, aim doubtless at exasperating you by the emigration of an entire population, and only leaving you a deserted city in order to deliver it in due course to the flames.

At these words everyone exclaimed that it was impossible that a people could be mad enough to accomplish its own ruin with the doubtful expectation of thereby precipitating the ruin of its enemy. Replied he:—

It is only too true that this resolution has been taken, and if you still doubt it, know that Count Rostopchin, our governor, left this morning some hours before the entry of the French. The police followed him, taking with them the pumps and all that could be of any service in extinguishing fires. In quitting the city, he confided to the lowest scum of humanity the duty of seconding his design. I cannot say to what extremes he may go, but I shudder when I think that he has frequently threatened to burn Moscow to the ground if the French approached it. Such an act of barbarism would appear atrocious to you and even incredible, if you were not aware of the intensity of the hatred with which your unparalleled victories have filled the nobility. They know that the whole of Europe is under your domination, and rather than share the same fate, they prefer to annihilate their country.

Ah! if our nobles, humiliated with their defeats, have not resolved upon the destruction of the capital, why have they fled with all their wealth? Why have the merchants been compelled to follow them, taking with them their merchandise and money? Why, in fine is there not left in this doomed city a single magistrate to implore the mercy of the conqueror? All have fled, as if by that course to incite your troops to universal plunder, since the constituted authorities, our only protection, in abandoning their posts have abandoned everything to them.

We endeavoured to comfort him by promising him protection and trying to reassure him as to the fate of his country. Seeing that he gradually grew calmer, and that he was secretly flattered by the admiration we expressed of the magnificent appearance of the city and its environs, I asked him presently to give me some detailed information regarding it, with which request he readily complied, and we parted with expressions of mutual esteem.

Although the bridge in course of construction over the Moskwa was not yet completed, the viceroy ordered his corps to pass the river.

The cavalry had already crossed and had taken up a position beyond the village of Khorechevo; and there we heard officially of the entry of our troops into Moscow. The fourth corps received orders to halt until next day, when the hour would be fixed for our entry into the capital of the Russian empire.

On the 15th of September, our corps left the village at daybreak, and marched upon Moscow. On approaching the city we noticed that it was not surrounded by walls, and that a simple parapet of earth alone marked its boundary. So far there had been nothing to show that the capital was inhabited, and the suburb by which we arrived was so deserted, that not only was there no Muscovite to be seen, but not even a French soldier. Not a sound was heard in the midst of this awful solitude A vague apprehension oppressed every mind, and increased when we perceived dense smoke rising in a great column in the very centre of the city. It was at first supposed that this only proceeded from some magazines which the Russians had, in accordance with their invariable practice, set on fire previous to their retreat. Nevertheless, remembering the statement of the fugitive from Moscow, we felt great uneasiness, lest his prediction was about to be fulfilled. Eager to ascertain the cause of this fire, we sought in vain for some one to satisfy our anxious curiosity; and the impossibility of doing so redoubled our impatience and greatly increased our alarm.

We did not make our entry by the first barrier at which we arrived, but, turning to our left, continued to march round the outskirts of the city. At last, by order of Prince Eugene, I placed our troops in position to guard the high road to St. Petersburg. While the thirteenth and fifteenth divisions encamped around the Château of Peterskoe, the fourteenth established itself in the village situated between Moscow and the *château*, and the Bavarian light horse, under the orders of Count Ornano, were a league in advance of that village.

These positions having been occupied, the Viceroy entered Moscow, and took up his quarters in the palace of Prince Memonoff in the street St. Petersburg. This quarter, assigned to our corps, was one of the finest in the city, formed entirely of splendid edifices, and of houses which, although built of wood, appeared to us to be of an astonishing wealth and grandeur. The magistrates having abandoned their post, every one was at liberty to establish himself in one of their palaces, so that the obscurest officer found himself lodged in the midst of vast and richly decorated apartments, of which he might look upon himself as the owner, seeing that the only person to be found in the place was an obsequious porter, who, with trembling hand, delivered to him all the keys of the house.

Since the previous evening Moscow had been in the possession of our troops, and yet throughout the quarter in which we were established neither resident nor soldier was to be seen, to such an extent had the city been depopulated. A mournful silence brooded over these deserted quarters, and even the most intrepid hearts were depressed by this awful isolation. The length of the streets was such that horsemen at one end could not recognise those at the other. Uncertain whether they were friends or enemies, they would mutually approach, and then, suddenly panic-stricken, they would turn and flee.

Whenever a new quarter was occupied, pioneers were sent in advance to reconnoitre, who carefully examined all the mansions and churches; but only children, old men and wounded Russian officers were discovered in the former; while in the churches the altars were found to be adorned as for a *fête* day, and a thousand lighted candles, blazing in honour of the patron saint of the country, showed that the pious Muscovites had not ceased to invoke his protection. This imposing manifestation of religious fervour proved the devotion and steadfastness of the people we had vanquished, and roused within us those terrors of conscience inseparable from the commission of a great crime. Henceforth we only dared to march with fearful steps in the midst of this awful solitude; often stopping to look behind us; sometimes listening with anxious ear; for the terrifying immensity of our conquest made us imagine snares in every direction, and at the slightest noise, our nervous tension magnified it into the clash of arms, and the shouts of combatants.

CHAPTER 14

Napoleon Leaves the Kremlin

On approaching the centre of the city, and especially the vicinity of the bazaar, we began to see a few of the inhabitants gathered round the Kremlin. These unfortunates, misled by a deceptive tradition, believing that this citadel was inviolable, had attempted on the previous evening to dispute its possession with our advance-guard, commanded by the King of Naples. The valour of our troops soon undeceived them. Cowed by their defeat, they regarded with moistened eyes those lofty towers which they had hitherto believed to be the palladium of their city. Advancing farther, we saw a mob of soldiers publicly selling and bartering a large quantity of movables they had looted; for it was only before the great stores of food that the Imperial Guard had placed sentries. The number of soldiers increased as we proceeded, carrying on their backs pieces of cloth, loaves of sugar, and whole cases of merchandise. We were puzzled as to the cause of all this disorder, when some fusiliers of the Guard told us that the smoke we had seen on entering the city proceeded from a large building full of merchandise called the Bourse, and that the Russians had set it on fire before retiring. These soldiers said:—

> Yesterday we entered Moscow at about noon, and this morning the fire broke out; at first we tried to extinguish it, persuaded that it was caused by the carelessness of our bivouacs, but we have abandoned the attempt, as we have been informed that the governor gave instructions to burn down the city, and to remove all the pumps, so as to prevent the fire being put out; hoping by this desperate expedient to destroy our discipline and ruin the merchants, who strongly opposed the abandonment of Moscow.

A natural curiosity urged me forward. The farther I advanced the more were the streets leading to the Bourse obstructed by soldiers and beggars, carrying with them all kinds of effects; the least valuable of which they threw away, and the streets were thus soon littered with immense quantities of merchandise. At last I succeeded in penetrating into the interior of the building; but alas! it was no longer the edifice once so famed for its magnificence; it was rather a vast furnace from which burning rafters were falling on all sides. The only place where it was possible to remain was under the portico, where there were still a number of shops; and there soldiers were breaking open cases, and dividing a booty which exceeded their utmost expectations. No shouts, no tumult were heard amidst this horrible scene, so intent was each upon satisfying his rapacity.

Nothing was heard but the crackling of the flames, the din of the smashing in of doors, and then suddenly the appalling crash of a collapsing arch. Cottons, muslins, silks—in fact all kinds of the richest stuffs of Europe and Asia, were being rapidly consumed. Sugar had been piled up in the cellars, with oils, rosin, and vitriol—and all these, burning together in the subterranean magazines, vomited torrents of flame through thick iron gratings. It was a terrifying sight, as such a fearful catastrophe forced upon the most callous mind the conviction that divine justice would one day exact a terrible retribution from those who were the cause of this frightful devastation.

The information which I tried to procure as to the cause of this fire, by no means satisfied me; but that evening, on entering the palace where our staff was quartered, I met a Frenchman, formerly tutor to the children of a Russian prince. This man possessed considerable knowledge, combined with very sound and sane political views, all the more valuable inasmuch as, having long associated with the *haute noblesse*, he was intimately acquainted with their sentiments. Moreover, he had personally witnessed the events which had occurred in Moscow since the Battle of the Moskwa; and in spite of his being a Frenchman, was one of the few who, by their discretion and abilities, had always been on intimate terms with Rostopchin. This meeting seemed to afford me an opportunity of learning what I was so anxious to know, especially the character of this governor, who, in spite of the blackest calumnies, will be venerated by his fellow-countrymen and held up as a model of courage and patriotism in all future ages. He said:—

Although the French after the Battle of Borodino marched in three columns upon Moscow, it was only the nobility and government authorities who were informed of the disaster with which the city was threatened. Count Rostopchin, deeming it prudent to conceal the truth from the people, caused it to be announced that the French had been defeated. This artifice served to prolong their illusion, but when the Russian Army appeared within the walls, preceded by some twenty thousand wounded, and bringing with it the whole population of the countryside, the citizens abandoned their usual occupations, and gave way to the wildest excitement. Associations were dissolved, the public buildings deserted, the very artisans ceased the labour which provided for their families, and sharing in the general gloom thronged the streets in vast crowds, and repaired to the governor to ask whether they were to remain in the city or abandon it.

In this critical and distressing situation, Count Rostopchin proclaimed that he was about to march against the French at the head of a hundred thousand men, and ordered the construction of redoubts to protect the city. He also caused lances and sabres to be forged, and distributed arms among the citizens who applied for them. It was also stated that an English expert was secretly engaged in his Château of Voronovo in preparing fuses and explosives, while he announced to the people that he was working at a new kind of balloon by means of which all the leaders of the French Army would be exterminated.

At last the governor having convoked all the most illustrious of the nobility, and the most wealthy and respected among the merchants, reminded these good citizens of their solemn promises to their emperor, and of the touching scene when the sovereign, the father of his country, received from his children the offering of their fortunes and their lives. At this recital, Count Rostopchin, overcome by excess of emotion, found himself unable to proceed. This pathetic silence lasted for several minutes, and drew forth more tears than the most eloquent oration could have done.

But the recollection of the national danger overcame this natural emotion, and one of the nobles present, who by his diplomatic connections understood the motives of this disastrous war, took the governor's place, and addressed the assembly in an eloquent speech, in which he enlarged upon the sufferings endured by the emperor in witnessing the misfortunes which had befallen the country; his earnest efforts to preserve peace; the increasing arrogance displayed by Napoleon at each fresh concession; the iniquitous and unprovoked aggression of which he had been guilty by invading Russia; the hollowness of his pretension that he represented civilised Europe against Northern barbarism, and the wanton atrocities which had marked the devastating progress of his army through Russia. At the conclusion of this oration Count Rostopchin again rose, and discarding the popular eloquence of his proclamations, profited by the profound impression which the speech had produced upon the audience, to address it in the following terms:—

Brave Muscovites!—Our enemy advances, and already his thunder may be heard at our very gates. The tyrant aims at overturning a throne, the brilliancy of which eclipses his own. We have yielded territory, but we have not been vanquished. You well know that our Empire, following the traditions of our forefathers, is to be found in our camp. Our armies are almost intact and are daily increased by new levies; that of the perfidious invader, on the contrary, arrives diminished and exhausted. Madman! he imagined that his victorious eagle, after having flown from the banks of the Tagus to the sources of the Volga, could destroy that other which, nourished in the bosom of the Kremlin, has soared with lightning flight, until hovering above us he extends his pinions from the pole to beyond the Bosphorus.

Let us only be firm, and I promise you that the country will rise once more from its ruins, greater and more majestic than before. To achieve this great result, remember, friends, that great sacrifices must be made, and the dearest ties of affection ruptured. But to obtain victory no sacrifice can be too great, since defeat means dishonour, and the loss of fortune and independence. If it be the will of Heaven that crime shall for the moment triumph, remember that it is your most sacred duty to flee into the deserts, and abandon a country which can be yours no longer, since it will have been polluted by the obscene presence of our oppressors.

The inhabitants of Saragossa, having continually before their eyes the immortal courage of their ancestors, perished under the ruins of their town rather than bend the knee to injustice. Today the same tyranny threatens to crush us. Be it so! show the whole world that the memorable example of Spain has not been lost on Russia!

To this discourse succeeded the most violent agitation. All the senators hailed it with transports of delight; and all except seven voted that it was absolutely imperative to lay Moscow in ashes. As soon as the populace learnt of this resolution, they thronged into the principal streets; and, urged by the nobility, cried that it would be better to perish than survive the destruction of their country and religion. Those who had not been endowed with courage by Nature, rushed home to withdraw their families from danger. Some taking to flight retired into the woods to face the horrors of famine and the rigours of death; others, on the contrary, swore to defend the city, or to join the army which was in retreat. The remainder of the population, taking arms, sought refuge in the Kremlin, while the most exasperated, seizing torches, rushed to set fire to the Bourse, which, as you know, contained immense wealth, and where the French army might have found supplies to last them through the whole winter.

Such was the narrative related to me by this tutor. We deplored such awful misfortunes, but as everything remained quiet, we still hoped that the destruction of the Bourse would prove to be the limit of the evil. At daybreak on the morrow, however, what was our consternation when we saw that the fire was raging at the four corners of the city, and that a violent wind was whirling the sparks in all directions.

The spectacle which I then beheld was the most appalling that imagination could conceive, exceeding in horror the most harrowing catastrophes recorded in history. A large part of the population of Moscow, terror-stricken by our arrival, had remained concealed in the recesses of their habitations, from which they were now driven by the flames. They crept out pale and trembling, not daring even to utter a muttered curse on the authors of their misery, to such an extent had they been struck dumb by terror. From their hiding-places they carried with them their most valuable effects, but those among them who were most susceptible to natural affection only thought of saving their families; on one hand could be seen a son supporting his infirm father; on another women who wept bitterly over the infants whom they carried in their arms; and who were followed by others a little older hurrying on for fear of being left behind, and calling in piteous tones to their mothers. The old men, more crushed by the weight of misfortune than by years, could seldom follow their families, and many lay down to die before their ruined homes. The streets and public buildings, and especially the churches, were filled with these unfortunates, who, lying amidst the remnants of their household goods, gave themselves up to hopeless despair.

The fire, continuing its ravages, soon reached the finest quarters of the city. In a moment all those palaces which we had admired for the elegance of their architecture and the taste of their furniture were enveloped in sheets of flame. Their superb *façades*, decorated with *bas-reliefs* and statues, fell with a crash upon the *débris* of the supporting columns. The churches, although roofed with sheet-iron and lead, fell also, and with them those superb domes which we had seen the previous evening, glittering in gold and silver. The hospitals, which contained upwards of twelve thousand wounded, were also soon alight, and the horrors which followed were such as to freeze the blood in one's veins. Nearly all of these wretched creatures perished, and those who survived might be seen dragging their half-burnt bodies over the smoking ashes, in an almost hopeless effort to escape.

How shall I describe the frightful disorder which broke out when licence was granted to pillage every part of this immense city? Soldiers, *vivandiers*, convicts, prostitutes thronged the streets, entered the deserted palaces, and dragged out everything that excited their cupidity. Some covered themselves with cloth of gold or rich silks; others threw over their shoulders priceless furs; many decked themselves with women's and children's pelisses, and even the escaped convicts hid their rags under court robes! The remainder, rushing in a mob to the cellars, forced the doors, and, after getting drunk on the most costly wines, staggered off with their immense booty.

This frightful looting was not limited to deserted houses; the confusion throughout the city and the rapacity of the mob reacted one on the other, and led to a destruction almost as disastrous as the fire itself. Every house was ransacked by the maddened soldiery. Those with whom officers were lodging hoped to escape the common ruin. Vain delusion! The flames swiftly advancing soon destroyed all their hopes.

Towards evening, Napoleon, no longer feeling safe in a city which appeared doomed to complete destruction, abandoned the Kremlin, and with his suite established himself at the Château of Peterskoë. On seeing him pass, I could not behold without a shudder the leader of this barbarous expedition, who, to avoid the public indignation, sought out the darkest streets by which to make his escape. But it was all in vain; the flames seemed to pursue him, and as I saw their lurid glow light up his pallid face, I thought of the torches of the Eumenides pursuing criminals consigned to the Furies.

The generals also received orders to quit Moscow. At once licence assumed the frenzy of madness; the troops, no longer restrained by the presence of their leaders, gave themselves up to the wildest excesses; no retreat was safe, no place sufficiently sacred to ensure protection from their bestial passions. Nothing, however, excited their cupidity more than the Church of St. Michael, which contained the tombs of the emperors of Russia. An unfounded tradition had led to the belief that this edifice concealed immense treasure, and under this delusion soldiers carrying torches descended into the vast subterranean chambers beneath the church to disturb the repose and silence of the dead. Instead of treasure they found only stone coffins covered in purple velvet, and bearing thin plates of silver, upon which were inscribed the names of the *Czars*, and the dates of their births and deaths.

Disgusted at finding their hopes disappointed, they broke the coffins to pieces, and tore off the pious offerings whose only value consisted in the devotion of those who had deposited them there. To all these excesses of cupidity was added an orgy of lust; neither gentle blood nor the innocence of youth, nor the tears of beauty were respected: a savage licence, the inevitable accompaniment of such a monstrous war, where sixteen allied nations, widely differing in customs and language, acted as though their crimes could never be brought home to any one of them.

Horror-struck by such calamities, I still hoped that the darkness of night would blot out the frightful picture; but, on the contrary, it only served to make the conflagration more terrible. The violence of the flames increased; they now extended from north to south, and, fanned by the wind, seemed to ascend to heaven. We could see the burning fuses that the malefactors were throwing from the summits of the towers; they left trails of fire, and from a distance resembled falling stars. The terror that froze every heart was intensified by the ghastly shrieks of the victims of murder, or the cries for mercy of women struggling desperately with their ravishers, whose rage was only inflamed by resistance. To these frightful sounds was added the agonised howling of innumerable dogs, chained, as is customary in Moscow, to the doors of the palaces, and unable to escape from the flames by which they were encompassed.

I attempted to seek relief in sleep, but the recollection of the horrors I had witnessed came crowding upon me, and it was long before my wearied senses found oblivion. Scarcely had I closed my eyes, when the glare of this vast conflagration awoke me with a start, and at first I was under the impression that it was broad daylight. Then, quickly recalling the events of the evening, it flashed upon me that my room was itself on the point of falling a prey to the flames. Nor was this a dream; on rushing to the window I saw that our quarter was on fire, and the house in which I was, in imminent danger. Sparks were falling in our courtyard and upon the wooden roof of our stables. I hastened immediately to my hosts, who, realising the full extent of their danger, had abandoned their usual habitation and had sought refuge in an underground apartment which afforded greater security. I found them there, sleeping with their domestics. They refused to leave, dreading the soldiers, as they said, more than the fire, and it was only by resorting to force that I succeeded in removing them.

To avoid prolonging the narrative of this horrifying catastrophe, to which history affords no parallel, I will pass over a crowd of harrowing episodes, and limit myself to describing the appalling confusion which reigned in our army when the flames had enveloped the entire city, and Moscow had become one vast funeral pyre.

A few stone pillars, calcined and blackened, were all that was left of the once stately buildings. The violent wind, roaring like the waves of a stormy sea, brought down with a terrific crash the huge sheets of iron which covered the palaces. The fire spread as if impelled by some occult power; whole quarters of the city became ignited, burnt and disappeared together.

Through the dense smoke long trains of vehicles could be seen, laden with booty and hardly able to force their way through the encumbered streets. The air rang with the shouts of their drivers, who, fearing to be burnt alive, frantically endeavoured to advance, pouring out a torrent of the most frightful imprecations. On every side armed soldiers were occupied in breaking open doors in search of fresh plunder, and if the new spoil proved preferable to that which they had already seized, the latter was thrown away to make room for the former. There were many who, having piled up their vehicles with loot, carried on their shoulders the rest of their plunder, but the fire having blocked the principal thoroughfares, compelled them to retrace their steps; and they wandered aimlessly from one quarter to another, striving to discover amidst this vast city, with which they were entirely unacquainted, some exit from the labyrinth of fire.

A great number thus fell victims to their own cupidity, which nevertheless nerved them to brave all dangers, and the soldiers, carried away by the madness of pillage, threw themselves into the midst of the burning vapours, trampling over corpses, while the falling ruins threatened them with destruction. All would certainly have perished had not the insupportable heat at last forced them to find safety in flight.

The fourth corps having been ordered to leave Moscow, we set out on the 17th September for Peterskoë, where our divisions were encamped. It was just about daybreak when we started, and the scene which met my view was at once terrible and pathetic. A crowd of the wretched inhabitants were dragging along in tumbledown vehicles all the effects which they had been able to save from their ruined homes; and as the soldiers had seized all their horses, I saw men and even women harnessed to these carts, in which could be seen, here an infirm mother of a family, and there a paralysed old man. Half-naked children followed these pathetic groups; extreme depression, so out of keeping with their age, was imprinted upon every face; and if any of the soldiers approached them, they ran weeping to the arms of their mothers. Without shelter, without succour, these miserable beings wandered about the country, seeking refuge in the forests, but finding on every hand the conquerors of Moscow, who frequently maltreated them, and sold under the very eyes of these poor wretches the effects stolen from their houses.

CHAPTER 15

Disastrous Results of Napoleon's Mad Ambition

The arrival of a victorious French army in the ancient capital of the *Czars*—the wealthiest and most central city of Russia, which the Russians regarded with veneration as holy and inviolable, was one of the most extraordinary events in modern history. It is true that our previous conquests had for many years accustomed Europe to look upon the success of our campaigns, however vast and astonishing, as a foregone conclusion But this expedition exceeded in colossal grandeur all those which had preceded it, and nothing recorded in history of the Persians, the Greeks and the Romans, surpassed it either in the daring of its conception or the difficulty of its execution. The distance from Paris to Moscow, almost equal to that which separated the capitals of Alexander and Darius; the character of the country and climate, which were deemed inaccessible to the armies of Europe; the fate of Charles XII. who, in attempting a similar project, had not dared to advance beyond Smolensk; the terror of the Asiatic nations, dismayed to see arriving in their midst the peoples who fled before our arms—all these circumstances combined to give to the exploits of the Grand Army an air of the marvellous, which recalled the most astounding episodes of antiquity.

Such was the glamour of our conquests when they were seen in the full blaze of success; but when cold reason compelled us to gauge the future, the picture became dark and gloomy in the extreme. The frightful extremities to which the Muscovites had been reduced proved to us that it was useless to negotiate with a people determined to make such enormous sacrifices; and that the empty glory of signing a treaty in Moscow had ignited a conflagration, the ravages of which would extend to all Europe, and give this war so envenomed a character that it could only end, either in the ruin of a doomed people, or in the downfall of the evil genius, whom God in His wrath appeared to have created to be a chastisement to men, and a new destroying angel. Moreover, no one with the least discretion or endowed with the slightest judgment could view without alarm the destruction of a city which for five days had been a prey to the flames, the glare of which still illumined our camp when darkness set in. What was to be the limit of our conquests? After Moscow, was it to be St. Petersburg? And after we had conquered the whole of Russia, had it not been rumoured that we were to march upon the Euphrates and the Ganges? So that our very success was only to prolong the ills of our country, by suggesting fresh ideas of aggrandisement to an ambition which knew no bounds.

Although the destruction of Moscow was a great disaster for the Russians, it was a greater still for us, as it assured the success of their plan to call in the rigours of winter to deprive us of all the fruits of our conquest. It was futile to argue that the burning of the capital was useless, and that the French Army should welcome it as ridding them of an immense population whose excitability and fanaticism, would goad them into insurrection. After much reflection, I am convinced that in view of the capacity of our leader for cunning and corruption, it was the Russian Government that had to fear lest this population should become an instrument for our designs, and that the majority of the upper classes, seduced by the dangerous example, or led away by brilliant promises, might desert the interests of the country, to lend themselves to all that Napoleon's ambition required of them.

It was beyond doubt to avert this calamity that Count Rostopchin sacrificed his whole fortune in the burning of Moscow, knowing that this great example was the only way to rouse the energy of the nobility, and instil into the nation that violent hatred which sustained it by making us the object of its execration. Moreover, the city having been provisioned for eight months, the French army by occupying it could have awaited the return of spring, and then resumed the campaign, reinforced by the army of reserve which was encamped at Smolensk and on the Niemen; while by the destruction of Moscow we were forced, on the contrary, to beat a precipitate retreat in the depth of winter. The hopes of the Russians founded on this result appeared certain of fulfilment; for our formidable army, in spite of making its advance during the finest season of the year, had lost a third of its strength merely by the rapidity of its marching. [1]

Nor was it possible to go into quarters elsewhere, for we had made a desert of all our conquests, and our leader had entirely neglected to take measures to facilitate our return. In order to understand our distress in the midst of our nominal victory, it suffices to say that we were deadbeat with marching, and utterly discouraged by the stubbornness of the Russians. The cavalry was nearing its ruin, and the artillery horses, reduced to skeletons through bad fodder, could barely drag the guns. Moreover, although we had been the unfortunate victims of the burning of Moscow, we could not but admire this unselfish devotion, and render justice to the inhabitants of the city, who, following the example of the Spaniards, have raised themselves by their courage and persistency to that height of true glory which makes the greatness of a nation.

When one recalls the sufferings we had endured, and the losses which fatigue alone had inflicted on us before arriving at Moscow, at a period, too, when the land, covered with its produce, afforded us abundant supplies, one cannot imagine how Napoleon could be so blind or so obstinate as not to return at once to Smolensk, particularly when he saw that the capital on which he had counted no longer existed, and that winter was approaching. It must have been that, determined to punish his overweening pride, Divine Providence had given him over to infatuation, since he turned his back on such evidence, and was fool enough to imagine that the men who had had the courage to destroy their country, would immediately afterwards display the weakness of accepting his oppressive conditions, and sign a peace upon the smoking ruins of their city. Even the least foreseeing predicted our coming disasters, and on passing the walls of the Kremlin could almost imagine they heard the prophetic words pronounced by a Divine voice against Nebuchadnezzar at the height of his prosperity:—

Thine empire shall pass into other hands; thou shalt be driven from the society of men; thou shalt live in exile and debasement, until thou recognisest that the Most High rules over kingdoms and bestows them on whomsoever He thinks fit.

1. The fourth corps, on leaving Glogau, consisted of about fifty thousand men, and when we issued from Moscow there only remained twenty thousand infantry and two thousand horse. The fifteenth division, which numbered thirteen thousand at the opening of the campaign, and which had very little fighting, was then reduced to four thousand.

The day on which we entered Moscow the Russians retired upon the high road to Wladimir; the main body of their army then returned and followed the course of the Moskwa to gain Kolomna, where it took up a position along the river. This army, accompanied by the fugitive population, passed under the walls of Moscow two days after our arrival, while the city was still burning, and was lighted on its way by the flames. The wind, which was blowing with violence, carried into its very ranks the *débris* of the fatherland reduced to ashes, and announced to the inhabitants that they had homes no longer. In spite of all these disasters, this body preserved the greatest order and maintained a profound silence, a resignation, in face of such misfortunes, which gave to their march the solemnity of a religious procession.

During the four days (17th, 18th, 19th and 20th September) on which we remained near Peterskoë, Moscow never ceased burning. The rain fell in torrents, and the few houses which were in the vicinity of this palace, combined with the multitude encamped there, made it very difficult to find shelter, so that men, horses and vehicles had to bivouac in the middle of the fields. The staff, placed around the *châteaux* where the generals were lodged, were established in the English gardens, in grottos, Chinese pavilions, kiosks or arbours, while the horses, tethered under acacias or limes, were separated from each other by hedges or flower-beds. This camp, which in itself was extremely picturesque, was rendered more so by the new costumes adopted by the soldiers; most of whom, to protect themselves from the inclemency of the weather, had donned the garments in which we had seen them decked out in Moscow. There were thus to be seen in our camp soldiers attired like Tartars, Cossacks and Chinamen. Some wore Polish caps, others the tall hats of the Persians, Baskirs or Calmucks. Our army, in fact, at this period presented the appearance of a carnival, which gave rise to the saying that our retreat having begun with a masquerade had ended with a funeral.

The abundance, however, which the army was enjoying made us forget our troubles; the good cheer which resulted from the sale of the loot brought from Moscow consoled us for having to endure rain above and mud below. For although forbidden to enter the city, the soldiers, attracted thither by the lust for gain, eluded the passwords, and continually returned loaded with food and merchandise. Under the pretence of foraging, they returned to the neighbourhood of the Kremlin, and groping under the ruins and ashes discovered *dépôts* which had escaped the fire, from which they extracted a profusion of all sorts of goods. Our camp thus no longer resembled an army, but rather a great fair, where each soldier, transformed into a merchant, sold the most costly things at the most absurd prices. Although encamped in the fields, and exposed to the rigours of the weather, they ate, by way of contrast, off porcelain plates, drank out of silver goblets, and possessed, in fact, everything that luxury could imagine for the enjoyment of life.

Our sojourn at Peterskoë and its gardens, becoming as unhealthy as it was inconvenient, Napoleon returned to the Kremlin, which had entirely escaped the fire, and the guard and general staff received orders to re-enter the city (20th and 21st September). On an estimate made by our engineers, one-tenth part of the houses were still standing; and they were distributed among each of the corps of the Grand Army. We were assigned the same quarters as before, namely, the suburb of Petersburg.

Chapter 16

Futile Negotiations

On our return to Moscow we were not puzzled as to the selection of our lodgings. On re-entering the city our hearts sank when we saw that not a vestige remained of the handsome mansions which we had occupied; they had all disappeared, and their still smoking ruins gave forth vapours which, hanging suspended in the atmosphere, obscured the light of the sun, and gave its disk a red and bloody hue. The course of the streets was no longer distinguishable, and it was only the edifices built of stone that preserved traces of what they once had been. Isolated among piles of ashes, and blackened by smoke, these *débris* of a modern city resembled the remains of antiquity.

It was seldom possible to quarter the troops together, and some companies had to occupy a vast extent of ground, where there were only to be found detached houses standing at long distances apart. The churches being less inflammable than the other buildings, had still preserved their roofs, and were transformed into barracks and stables. Thus the neighing of horses and the horrible blasphemies of the soldiery replaced the sacred harmonies of the hymns which formerly re-echoed through those consecrated aisles.

Curious to see the state of the house where I had previously lodged, I searched for it in vain; a neighbouring church which was yet standing at last enabled me to find it; but in its present state I could hardly recognise it. It was entirely burnt; nothing was left but the four walls, all cracked by the violence of the fire. I was looking with horror on such destruction when the unfortunate servants of this ill-fated house issued from the depths of a cellar. Worn to skeletons by hunger, I should have found their features deplorably altered, had not the ashes and the smoke made them utterly unrecognisable; and they seemed to me spectres rather than living creatures.

But imagine the shock I sustained in recognising among those miserable wretches, my host, scantily clad in rags lent him by his servants. He now had to live like them, to such an extent had misfortune equalised their condition. On seeing me he could not restrain his tears, especially on showing me his children, half-naked and dying of hunger. His speechless grief made a most profound impression on me, and by signs this unhappy man gave me to understand that the soldiers, after having looted his house while it was burning, had actually stripped him of his clothes. The sight of this distressing picture tore my heart-strings, and while seeking to assuage his misery, I fear I was able to give him very barren consolation; and the same man who a few days before had entertained me at a sumptuous repast now gratefully accepted a piece of bread at my hands.

Although the population of Moscow had almost entirely disappeared, there still remained in the city many of those unhappy beings whom misery has rendered indifferent to every event. These thronged the streets with the soldiers, served them as domestics, and thought themselves very lucky to receive as recompense the trifles which the soldiers threw away. A great many women of the town were also to be seen. This class was the only one that derived any advantage from the sack of Moscow; for every soldier desirous of acquiring a partner received these women with delight. They were introduced into the houses, of which they at once became the mistresses, wasting and destroying all that the flames had spared. There were others who really deserved pity for their misfortunes, for hunger and misery often compelled their mothers to offer them to us.

There was also in Moscow a class of men who were the most criminal of all, as they atoned for their crimes by the commission of still greater ones. These were the convicts. As long as the burning of the capital continued, they distinguished themselves by the audacity with which they carried out the orders they had received. Armed with phosphorus matches, they relighted the conflagration wherever it gave signs of dying out; and crept furtively into inhabited dwellings, to set them on fire. Many of these abject wretches were caught red-handed; but their prompt execution produced but little effect. The populace, who always hate their conquerors, merely regarded these executions as part of our policy. The victims were, as a matter of fact, too obscure adequately to expiate so heinous a crime. The rough-and-ready methods by which they were tried threw no light upon the causes of the great catastrophe, and did not of course serve to vindicate us in the eyes of those who persisted in believing that we were its authors.

A considerable number of Muscovites, who had concealed themselves in the neighbouring forests, seeing that the fire had ceased, believed they had no longer anything to fear and re-entered the city. Some looked for their houses and found they had ceased to exist; others, hoping to find sanctuary in the temples of their God found that they had been desecrated. The thoroughfares presented a revolting spectacle; at each step were to be seen dead bodies, and on many half-burnt trees swung the corpses of incendiaries. In the midst of these horrors the unfortunate inhabitants could be seen collecting the iron sheets which had covered the roofs to construct huts, which they erected in distant parts of the town or in the ruined gardens. Having nothing to eat, they scraped up the earth to find the roots of the vegetables which our soldiers had gathered; or wandering among the *débris* they searched the ashes to find fragments which the fire had not entirely consumed. Pallid, emaciated and almost naked, the slowness of their movements showed the extremity of their sufferings. Some also recollecting that several boats loaded with grain had been sunk, plunged into the river to allay their hunger with putrefying wheat, the stench of which was perfectly sickening.

To soften the effect of such a recital, let me record the action of a French soldier who found in a cemetery an unhappy woman who had recently given birth to a child. As she was absolutely without assistance and food, this worthy man, touched with the cruel situation of the poor creature, bestowed on her the most tender care, and for several days shared with her the scanty fare which he had been able to procure for himself.

While the bulk of the Russian Army took up different positions, the *seigneurs* of the provinces in the vicinity of Moscow took advantage of the exasperation felt by the people at the sufferings inflicted on them by the war, to raise and arm them against us. Many made levies at their own expense, and placed themselves at the head of their insurgent peasantry. These irregular forces united themselves with the Cossacks, and intercepted our convoys arriving by the great highways. But the main object of these bands was to harass our foragers, and particularly to prevent access to the villages where supplies could be found. As to our various *corps d'armée*, they were distributed over an immense plain, covered with woods, so that it was impossible for them successfully to cope with a method of warfare which foreshadowed disaster for us in the future.

In trampling over the ruins of Moscow, magazines of sugar, wine and brandy were often found. These discoveries, which might have been valuable under happier circumstances, were of little use to an army which had devoured all the produce of the fields, and which now saw itself almost without bread or meat. The want of fodder was destroying our horses, and in order to procure it we had to engage in daily combats which, for us, were disastrous; for at such a vast distance from our base the smallest losses became of the utmost importance.

Our real want was hidden under an apparent plenty.

We had neither bread nor meat, but our tables were covered with confectionery and sweetmeats. Tea, liqueurs and wines of all kinds, served in rare china, or crystal goblets, made it evident that luxury with us was the neighbour of want. The extent of our needs made money of no value, and led to a system of exchange; those who had cloth bartered it for wine, and those who had a *pelisse* could procure with it much sugar and coffee.

Napoleon still deluded himself with the ridiculous idea of inducing those who had fled from his intolerable yoke to return to the city, by issuing proclamations full of soothing phrases. With the object of inspiring them with some degree of confidence, he had divided the remains of the city into quarters, appointed governors for each of them; and installed magistrates entrusted with the administration of justice among the few people who remained. The consul-general, Lesseps, who was appointed Governor of Moscow, published a proclamation announcing to the inhabitants the "paternal intentions" of Napoleon; but these "generous and benevolent" promises scarcely ever reached the Muscovites; and when they did, the actualities of the situation caused them to be regarded as bloodstained irony. The greater part of the inhabitants had fled behind the Volga, and the rest having sought refuge with the Russian Army, and being animated by the bitterest hatred, only nourished thoughts of a terrible vengeance.

Meanwhile Prince Kutusoff, having removed his army to Lectask-ova, between Moscow and Kaluga, in order to cover the southern provinces, closely hemmed in Napoleon; so successfully, indeed, that the latter, in spite of his various manoeuvres, could not extricate himself from his disastrous position, and found himself continually obliged to close in his forces. It was impossible for him to advance upon St. Petersburg without having the Russian Army on his rear, and compromising our safety by abandoning all communication with Poland. Neither could he march upon the Volga, for an advance in that direction would only have separated him farther from his base. Nothing, consequently, could be more critical than the situation of the French Army, seeing that it was forced to remain in Moscow surrounded on all sides, having hardly any cavalry, and compelled to confront a hostile line forming a circle of about one hundred leagues in circumference.

Besides all this, the capital, once so magnificent, now only offered a pestilential refuge in the midst of ruins, and the surrounding country was a desert without inhabitants. The Cossacks, who swarmed everywhere, captured our transports, made prisoners of our messengers and slaughtered our foragers; in fact, inflicted on us irreparable losses. Our condition, therefore, became every day more calamitous. Want and discontent eventually increased among the soldiery; and as the crown of all our misfortunes, peace was recognised by every thinking man as beyond the range of all probability.

In these circumstances it is interesting to note the harebrained schemes that were discussed in the army. Some talked of advancing into the Ukraine, others of marching on St. Petersburg, but the most intelligent foresaw that ere long there would be no alternative but to return to Wilna. Napoleon, who always grew more obstinate as difficulties increased, and who had a passion for the supernatural, persisted in remaining in a desert for the sole reason that it was sought to drive him out of it, and believed he could compel the enemy to sue for peace by pretending to pass the winter in Moscow. To assure the success of this subterfuge, he entertained the idea of fortifying the Kremlin, and making a citadel of the massive building in the Petersburg quarter, called by the Russians *Ostrog*, but to which we had given the name of *Maison Carrée*. At last, when everything was exhausted and we had no means of subsistence left, he ordered us to lay in provisions for two months.

6th October.—While we gave ourselves to meditating on all these things, and particularly on the problem of filling stores without anything to put into them, rumours of peace, only credited because we wished them to be true, filled our hearts with joy, and inspired us with the hope that it would not now be necessary to attempt impossibilities. This rumour gained credence from the harmony which reigned between the Cossacks and the advance-guard of the King of Naples. This was taken to indicate that there was a prospect of an understanding between the two emperors. Moreover, it was known that General Lauriston had been sent to the headquarters of Prince Kutusoff, and that as a result of their interview a courier had been dispatched to St. Petersburg to decide the question of peace or war.

Meanwhile Napoleon, instead of visiting the *corps d'armée* and so making himself acquainted with their critical position, and particularly with their dwindling strength, remained shut up in the Kremlin, doing nothing but review the troops of the garrison. By vigilant supervision he obliged the colonels to maintain their regiments in the highest efficiency, hoping by their brilliant appearance to overawe the Russians and force them to submit to his conditions. Much to our surprise the weather continued magnificent, and contributed greatly to the impressiveness of these reviews. This extraordinary weather struck the Muscovites with astonishment, accustomed as they were to the advent of snow in the month of October.

The people who were superstitious by nature, and had long looked forward to winter as their avenger, began to think themselves abandoned by Providence, and to regard such a marvel as the result of Divine interposition on behalf of Napoleon. But this apparent favour was the actual cause of our destruction, by blinding him to such an extent that he began to believe that the climate of Moscow resembled that of Paris. [1] In his insane vanity, he hoped to control the seasons as he governed men, and by a gross abuse of his lucky star he imagined that "the sun of Austerlitz" would shine upon him to the pole, or that, like another Joshua, he could arrest the luminary in its course to guide him on his wanderings.

While negotiations were in progress, everything was being got ready for a renewal of the war, but nothing was done to prepare for the rigours of winter. And yet the outlook was appalling; the longer we remained in Moscow, the worse our situation became. In proportion as we exhausted the neighbouring villages, we were obliged to resort for supplies to places farther and farther away. The distances made our efforts as dangerous as they were exhausting; leaving at dawn, our foragers rarely returned before nightfall. Such exertions recurring day after day, wore out the men and exterminated the horses, and more especially the artillery teams. The strongest regiments had less than one hundred horses, and nothing was left to feed the soldiers but the flesh of these animals. In the midst of these torments the audacity of the Cossacks redoubled in proportion as our confidence diminished.

Of this they gave a proof by attacking the village near Moscow

---

1. 22nd, 23rd and 24th Bulletins: "The weather is superb, like that of France in October, perhaps a little warmer. Everything points to our going into winter quarters."

where the dragoons of the Guard were cantoned. These, although attacked by superior numbers, defended themselves with great bravery, and the affair would have been glorious for them had not Major Marthod, after being wounded, fallen into the hands of the Russians with fifty of his men. Some days after, the enemy also captured a convoy of artillery coming from Viazma, commanded by two majors. Napoleon considered these officers to blame, and ordered a commission of inquiry into their conduct. One of them blew out his brains, more, doubtless, from despair at having lost his guns than from consciousness of guilt.

To avert similar losses Broussier's division, with the light horse, commanded by Count Ornano, was ordered to quarter itself in the Château of Galitzin between Mojaisk and Moscow. These troops cleared the surrounding country of Cossacks, who always shunned encountering them, but the slightest gap left by our troops was at once filled by these hordes of Tartars, who availed themselves of every advantage offered by the ground to attempt feats of the greatest daring.

They renewed their operations by attacking another convoy of artillery, which had come from Italy under Major Vives. With regard to this affair, the escort having taken to flight, abandoned the whole of their guns to the Cossacks, who promptly carried them off; but Count Ornano, having been informed of the disaster, pursued the enemy, and overtook them in the midst of a wood. At the sight of our cavalry the Cossacks fled, abandoning without resistance all the fruits of their victory. Major Vives would have been tried by court-martial, if our retreat and subsequent disasters had not forced Napoleon to relax his severity.

While the fourteenth division secured the road to Viazma, the thirteenth was upon that of Tver. The latter was resting quietly in its cantonments, when information was received that Count Soltikoff, a favourite of the emperor Alexander, and *seigneur* of the village of Marfino, near Dimitrow, had armed all his peasants and assembled in his *château* several other *seigneurs* with the object of planning a general uprising. To nip this dangerous scheme in the bud a brigade of the thirteenth division was ordered to proceed to the Château of Marfino. The general in command made the most careful investigation as to the assembly having taken place, but utterly without result. Obliged, however, to carry out his orders, he committed to the flames a palace justly renowned as one of the finest in Russia. This allegation of conspiracy gave rise to the belief that in ordering this act of vandalism Napoleon had been prompted by personal spite against Count Soltikoff for having clung with unalterable fidelity to his sovereign.

15th October.—The attacks to which the *corps d'armée* were in turn subjected demonstrated the impossibility of our remaining longer in our present position. Everything pointed to our speedy departure, and this became a certainty in view of the removal of the hospitals towards Minsk and Wilna, and the fact that the majority of the wounded generals were being conveyed thither, escorted by about one thousand infantry. We also learnt that the cavalry of the Italian Guard were leaving their cantonments in the vicinity of Dimitrow, to return to Moscow, thence to occupy the position of Charapovo, a small village situated upon the road to Borovsk, about six leagues from the capital. At the same time the viceroy recalled the thirteenth division, and advanced the fourteenth and General Ornano's cavalry, towards Fominskoe, where the whole of the fourth corps were to rendezvous. Informed of this movement, the Cossacks watched for the moment when the baggage of our light horse was weakly guarded, to attack the convoy in the neighbourhood of Osighovo, but on the arrival of Broussier's division they abandoned part of their booty, and under cover of the woods, eluded pursuit.

The return of the courier from St. Petersburg was being looked for with the greatest anxiety, when General Lauriston, left again to wait upon Kutusoff, and with such extreme haste that he was obliged to avail himself of the relays of horses reserved for the emperor. In the conviction that all these conferences would have a favourable result, our army relaxed its vigilance and lulled itself into a false security. The enemy profited by this blunder to attack the cavalry of the King of Naples at Winkovo, near Tarontina, on the 18th of October, and captured from General Sebastiani a park of twenty guns, which were carried off, along with several waggons filled with baggage. This attack, which was made when our cavalry were out foraging, would have been fatal to that arm, which was already in a deplorable condition, had not the King of Naples, who was at the time on foot, mounted his horse and galloped with his staff into the thick of the fray, which he directed with heroic courage, while our cavalry was getting into order of battle.

The Cossacks were routed and abandoned the guns; the Russian infantry advanced to their support, and the action became general, both sides displaying great ferocity. Generals Bagawout and Muller were killed, and General Beningsen was wounded. On our side, more than two thousand men were *hors de combat*, and we had especially to deplore the death of Generals Fischer and Déry, the latter *aide-de-camp* to the King of Naples.

The emperor was at the Kremlin, indulging in his usual occupation of reviewing the troops, when he received this unexpected news. He was furious, and in the transports of his rage he charged the enemy with treason and infamy for having attacked the King of Naples in defiance of all the rules of war. [2] The parade was countermanded on the spot; all hope of peace vanished, and the order was given to evacuate Moscow that very evening. All the corps were directed to take the high road to Kaluga. It was hoped that we were about to advance into the Ukraine, to seek, under milder skies, countries less devastated and much more fertile. But the best informed alleged that our movement on Kaluga was but a feint to conceal from the enemy our intention to retreat upon Smolensk and Witepsk by a new route.

---

2. There had never been any truce between the two armies except that the outposts of Milloradowitch had suspended hostilities for some days, and expressed to those of the King of Naples the desire they had for peace.

CHAPTER 17

Blowing Up of the Kremlin

As it was very late when we started, we were obliged to halt at a miserable village only one league from Moscow. The cavalry of the Italian Guard, which was still at Charopovo, left that place on the following day (19th October) and rejoined us at Batoutinka, not far from the Château of Troitskoe. where Napoleon had established his headquarters. Almost the whole army was concentrated at this point, with the exception of the cavalry, which was in advance, and of the Young Guard, which had remained in Moscow to cover our retreat.

On the morrow the cavalry of the Royal Guard was to have directed itself towards Charopovo, followed by the whole of the fourth corps. At the moment, however, when it was about to start, it was recalled, and the Prince ordered these troops to continue their march along the same road which we had traversed on the previous evening. We crossed the Pakra near Gorki. This pretty village had ceased to exist, and the river, choked up with the *débris* of the burnt houses, rolled sluggishly along, a muddy and blackened stream. Higher up was the fine Château of Krasnoë, completely sacked; but the elegance of the building was still conspicuous in contrast with the wild hills upon which it stood. Here we halted, and an hour later we quitted the high road to seek on our right a track which would lead us to Fominskoe, where General Broussier and our cavalry had found themselves for four or five days in presence of the enemy.

Our march by this unfrequented road was extremely laborious, but we were fortunate enough to find some villages which, although deserted, were less ransacked than those on the highway. We passed the night at Inatowo, where there was a *château* situated on an eminence which commanded the country by which we had arrived.

Continuing our march, still with the intention of rejoining the

Charopovo road, we arrived at a village called Bouikasovo. We had no proper maps, had no guides, and were unable even to pronounce the names of the villages which were marked on such maps as we possessed. Having captured a peasant, we kept him with us for two days; but he was so hopelessly stupid that we could not even get out of him the name of his village. However, this march was of great importance to the emperor who, with the main body of the army, was to follow us. The prince each day made me draw a plan of the itinerary for the information of the major-general.

All obstacles having been surmounted, we at last rejoined the Kaluga road, and an hour later arrived at Fominskoe. Broussier's division was encamped in the environs of this village, and the cavalry, posted in advance, was drawn out by the viceroy, who at once proceeded to reconnoitre the plateau occupied by the Cossacks. On seeing us, however, they retired and abandoned the ground upon which we had prepared to attack them.

From the military point of view the position of Fominskoe would have been advantageous for the Russians had they resolved to defend it. Through the centre of the village, which was commanded by a hill, ran the River Nara, which at this point is confined by the narrowing of the valley, and forms a small lake, the shores of which are exceedingly marshy. In spite of this, the whole army had to pass through the defile, where there was only one bridge, which appeared quite insufficient. It was reserved for the vehicles, and another was constructed for the sole use of the infantry.

One day was devoted to this work and to the passage of a portion of the troops (22nd October). In this interval the Poles under Prince Poniatowski marched upon Vereia, where the Hetman Platow was posted with his Cossacks. Presently Napoleon arrived with his usual escort. In a moment the village was crowded with men, horses and vehicles; but thanks to the skilful arrangements which had been made, the whole passed without confusion, which was not a little surprising, for the legions of Xerxes were not more encumbered with baggage than we were.

The same day Captain Evrard, who had been sent on a mission to Charopovo, informed us that he had heard a terrific explosion in the direction of Moscow, and we afterwards learnt that it was caused by the blowing up of the Kremlin. The destruction of that famous citadel and of the splendid buildings which it contained was effected by the Young Imperial Guard commanded by the Duke of Treviso. That

Plan
OF THE
Field of Battle,
of
MALO-JAROSLAVETZ.
24 Oct.ʳ 1812.

11.1. *Enemies Redoubts defended by 15 or 20 pieces of Cannon.*

12 *13ᵗʰ Division Delzons.*

12 1 *14ᵗʰ Division Broussier.*

3 *12ᵗʰ Division Pino.*

4 *Grenadiers & Chasseurs of the Royal Guard.*

5 *3ʳᵈ Division Gerard.*
6 *3ᵗʰ Division Compans.* } *1ˢᵗ Corps.*

7 *Light Troops of the Royal Guard in Reserve.*

8 *Light Cavalry of the 4ᵗʰ Corps in Reserve.*

9 *Cavalry of the Royal Guard.*

10 *Baggage of the 4ᵗʰ Corps.*

11 *French Troops of Observation.*

12 *Russian Divisions coming from the Camp of Lætaskova.*

13 *Russian Divisions retiring upon Kaluga.*

14 *Advanced Guard of the Enemy approaching Medenin.*

River Lonja

Distinctives between the French and Russian Troops are

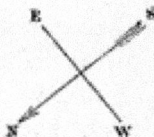

Cavalry	Infantry		Cavalry	Infantry

French Troops.   **Russian Troops.**

Scale of English Yards.

Road from Juchnu Kroga

Road from Kaluga

13

Russian   Infantry

1

MALO-JAROSLAVETZ

4

6

5   New Road from Medenin

14

12

River   Louja

Route from Moscow to Kaluga

Drawn on the lines by the Author 24th of Oct. 1812.

Labaume

19

Scale of French Metres.

marshal, on quitting Moscow, received a formal order to raze to the ground all that the flames had spared. Thus ended this famous city, founded by the Tartars and destroyed by the French. Crowned with all the favours of Fortune, its fall presented a picture of the extreme vicissitudes of human affairs; and history will record that the very man who professed to sacrifice us on the altar of progress, boasted in his bulletins that he had put back Russia a hundred years.

Moscow was not retaken by the Russians. It was evacuated by the Young Guard as part of our plan of campaign. General Winzingerode, who commanded the army of observation during our occupation, having advanced to a street in the neighbourhood of the Kremlin, with young Narishkin, his *aide-de-camp* and several horsemen, suddenly found himself face to face with a picket of the 5th Regiment of Voltigeurs of the Young Guard, commanded by Lieutenant Leleu de Maupertuis, who promptly seized the general's bridle and declared him his prisoner.

Part of the army having crossed the Nara, the fourth corps followed at about five in the morning (23rd October) and took the road to Borovsk. The enemy did not show himself, no doubt in order to inform the commander-in-chief that we had outwitted his vigilance, by leaving him on the new road to Kaluga to follow the old through Borovsk.

Informed of our march, Kutusoff immediately abandoned his entrenched camp at Lectaskova, but he left us in doubt as to whether he would debouch by Borovsk or by Malo-Jaroslavetz. Napoleon occupied the former town, situated on a hill, under which flows the Protva in a very deep bed.

Prince Eugene, who had encamped half a league beyond Borovsk, in a small village to the right of the road, sent Delzons' division towards Malo-Jaroslavetz with instructions to occupy it before the Russians could seize it. The general, having found the town undefended, took peaceable possession with only two battalions, leaving the rest in the plain. The position was thus believed to be secure, when on the morrow (24th October) at daybreak we heard a heavy cannonade on our front. The viceroy, suspecting the cause, immediately mounted his horse, and with his staff went full gallop towards Malo-Jaroslavetz. As we approached, the thunder of the guns redoubled in intensity; the fire of the skirmishers was heard on all sides, and at last we saw distinctly the Russian columns, coming by the new road to Kaluga to take a position opposite that which we occupied.

The base of the plateau of Malo-Jaroslavetz had been reached, when General Delzons hastened towards us and addressing the Prince, stated that the previous evening he had seized the position, which seemed to him perfectly safe from attack, when towards four in the morning, he had been assailed by a strong body of infantry; the two battalions had been overpowered by greatly superior forces, and had been obliged to abandon Malo-Jaroslavetz. The viceroy recognising the serious nature of this loss, at once resolved to repair it, and instructed the general to attack the position with his whole division. An obstinate engagement ensued; fresh troops having arrived in support of the Russians, our troops for the moment gave way; but General Delzons hastened into the thick of the fight to rally them. At the moment when he was stubbornly defending the approaches to the town the enemy's skirmishers delivered a volley and the general fell dead with a bullet through his forehead.

The prince was much affected by the loss of so distinguished and able an officer, but immediately appointed General Guilleminot to replace him That general, by his bravery and skill, rallied the division, which had been disheartened by the death of its leader. The fight was continuing with great fury in the streets of the town, when Broussier's division came up in support but fresh Russian columns, constantly arriving by the Lectaskova road, succeeded in overthrowing our troops, whom we saw, crushed by numbers and driven pell-mell down the hill, making for the bridge so as to escape across the Louja. They were promptly rallied, however, by Colonel Forestier, and resuming their accustomed coolness, returned to the position, which they captured with great intrepidity. But in view of the great number of wounded, and the difficulty of maintaining ourselves in Malo-Jaroslavetz, the Viceroy saw the absolute necessity of bringing more troops into action to counterbalance the reinforcements which the enemy was constantly receiving.

Pino's division, which throughout the campaign had always been eager for action, hailed the order to advance with enthusiasm. Led by several officers of the staff, they rushed up the hill at the double, and with exulting shouts succeeded in establishing themselves in the positions from which the enemy was driven. This success was, however, dearly bought; a great number of the gallant Italians having perished in their emulation of French valour. General Levié, who had only enjoyed his superior rank for eight days, was killed, and General Pino was badly wounded. In spite, however, of the pain of his wound, he was less regardful of that, than stricken with grief at the death of his brother, who was killed by his side.

The *chasseurs* of the Royal Guard, commanded by Colonel Peraldi, had joined in this movement. But the fifteenth division having been repulsed, they advanced to support it at the moment when the enemy were making rapid progress; and, marching towards the bridge, threatened to hurl the troops which had crossed it into the river. Seeing that there was not a moment to lose, they attacked the Russians, and recaptured the position from which the Italian division had been driven. The fight was being sustained on both sides with extreme fury, when the Russians, having unmasked two large redoubts, fired several rounds of grape, which almost annihilated the *chasseurs*.

Those that remained wavered for a moment, but Colonel Peraldi having reminded his troops of the dishonour which would cover them if they did not die at their posts, had the satisfaction of seeing those veterans supply themselves with cartridges (their own being exhausted) out of the boxes of their dead comrades; and with heads down they charged the Russians, who, dumbfounded at such audacity, supposed that they were being attacked by fresh troops, and fled from their first line, after having disarmed the redoubt. Their guns were all this time maintaining a terrific fire, the grape carrying destruction and death even into the ranks of the Royal Grenadiers and Light Infantry who were in reserve, and plunging into the groups formed by the viceroy's staff. It was here that General Gifflenga received a wound in the throat which compelled him to quit the field.

The success of the day was now decided; we were occupying the town and all the neighbouring heights, when the fifth division of the first corps arrived to take position on our left, and the third division of the same corps, which had also arrived after the action, occupied a wood on our right. Our batteries and infantry kept up their fire at close range on the enemy, whose retreat was covered by a cloud of skirmishers. The night and exhaustion at last stopped this bloody combat, but it was not till ten o'clock that the viceroy and his staff could seek the repose so necessary after the terrible exertions of the day. We encamped below Malo-Jaroslavetz, between the town and the river Louja. The troops bivouacked along the whole extent of the positions they had so gloriously taken.

We recognised next day that the obstinacy with which the Russians had defended Malo-Jaroslavetz was due to their determination to cover Kaluga, and to prevent our retreat through the southern provinces. We then regretted our delay at Fominskoe; had we not lost a day, the entrenchments of the enemy would have been turned, and he could not possibly have arrived in time to defend the positions between Malo-Jaroslavetz and Kaluga. Those who were in the Emperor's secrets assert to this day that, in conducting his movement on Smolensk he intended first of all to destroy the arsenal at Tula, and then proceed by the road to Serpeisk and Elnia, through a country which had not been desolated.

Towards four in the morning, the viceroy mounted his horse and we went over the plateau which had been the scene of the battle. We saw the plain covered with Cossacks, whose field artillery opened fire on our troops, and on the left we observed three large redoubts. On the previous evening they had been armed with from fifteen to twenty guns; one of them defended Kutusoff's right flank, with the object, doubtless, of preventing us from turning his position. Towards ten the firing slackened, and at midday it entirely ceased.

The interior of Malo-Jaroslavetz presented a horrible spectacle. The town had been entirely destroyed; the course of the streets could only be traced by the innumerable corpses with which they were covered. Nothing was to be seen on all sides but fragments of limbs and human heads crushed under the overturned guns. The houses were a heap of ruins, and amidst their smouldering ashes could be seen half-consumed bodies. There were also numbers of the sick and wounded who, in quitting the field, had sought refuge in these houses; the few who escaped the flames were a pitiable sight, with bodies blackened and hair burnt off; and their groans of agony were heart-rending. The most callous heart could not but be softened at such a horrid sight, and we turned away our faces to conceal our tears. We shuddered at the misery to which despotism was exposing us, and almost felt as though we were living in those barbarous ages when the wrath of the gods was sought to be averted by the offering of human victims on bloody altars.

During the afternoon, Napoleon having arrived with a numerous suite, coolly rode over the battlefield, and heard without the least emotion the dreadful cries of the unhappy wounded, imploring succour. But even this man, accustomed as he had been for twenty years to the horrors of war, to which he was so insanely addicted, could not, on entering the town, conceal his astonishment at the ferocity of the action, and in spite of his indifference he was compelled to do justice to those who so well deserved it. He warmly praised the behaviour of the fourth corps, and turning to the viceroy exclaimed, "The honour of this brilliant day belongs entirely to you." [3]

While we were engaged with the enemy at Malo-Jaroslavetz, more than six thousand Cossacks pounced upon the emperor's headquarters at Ghorodnia, and captured six guns not far from that village. The Duke of Istria, (Marshal Bessières), promptly pursued them at full gallop, with all the cavalry of the Guard, supported by the fourth division and the corps of General Latour-Maubourg, and the guns were retaken. The Cossacks, sabred and dispersed, effected their retreat and sought refuge on the other side of the Protva; but in the course of their flight, one of their numerous detachments fell upon the train of the fourth corps, and would have captured it had not the cavalry of the Italian Guard rescued it in the same manner as the Imperial Guard had rescued the guns.

---

3. Having lately been at Mantua, I was there told by Sir Robert Wilson, who was present at Malo-Jaroslavetz, that Prince Eugene with twenty thousand men withstood the attacks of nine Russian divisions of ten thousand men each.

CHAPTER 18

Depletion of French Army

The action of Malo-Jaroslavetz convinced us of two sinister facts: first, that the Russians, far from being weakened, had been heavily reinforced, and were fighting us with a determination which made further victories over them hopeless. Two such victories as that, said the soldiers, and Napoleon would have no army left. Secondly, it was obvious that we must abandon the attempt to retire by Kaluga and Tula, and that we had no hope of an unmolested retreat, since the enemy having, as a result of this affair, hemmed us in, not only prevented our columns from proceeding by Serpeisk and Elnia, but also from reaching Viazma by Medouin and Joukhnov, thus reducing us to the disastrous alternative of returning by the high road to Smolensk. Besides these only too well founded fears, we were also confronted with the certainty that the Russians would block our retreat with the army of Moldavia, while the corps of Wittgenstein would also advance to effect a junction with that of Admiral Tschikagow.

After this memorable combat, those who could only form superficial judgments believed that we should advance upon Kaluga and Tula. Great surprise was occasioned, however, by the movements of the enemy's advance-guard, which, instead of proceeding in that direction, outflanked our right by marching on Medouin. It became evident from this that the Russians had seen through Napoleon's designs, and that to forestall the enemy we must make a forced march upon Viazma, so as to get there before him. Thenceforward it was no longer a question of Kaluga and the Ukraine, but solely to regain, with the utmost haste, the road to Mojaisk—in other words, the desert which we ourselves had created. As soon as our retreat was decided upon, the fourth corps effected its retrograde movement, leaving the first corps at Malo-Jaroslavetz with Chastel's cavalry. These troops were to form the rear-guard, marching a day's journey behind us.

26th October.—We found upon our route convincing evidence of the paltry results achieved by the sanguinary action of Malo-Jaroslavetz. On all hands were to be seen ammunition waggons abandoned for want of horses to draw them, and the shattered fragments of carriages and tumbrils left on the ground for the same reason. Such serious losses at the very beginning of our retreat were a gloomy augury of the fate which awaited us. Those who carried with them the loot of Moscow, now began to tremble for their plunder. But there was, above all, a general feeling of dismay at the deplorable condition of our cavalry, especially when we heard the continual explosions caused by the blowing up of our ammunition waggons, the sound of which reverberated from afar like the roar of thunder.

It was nightfall when we reached Ouvaroskoe (26th October). Surprised to see the village in flames, we found on inquiry that orders had been given to burn everything on our route. In this place there was a *château*, which although built of wood, was equal in aspect to the finest palaces of Italy. Its furniture corresponded with the appearance of the exterior: priceless pictures, valuable candelabras and a profusion of lustres of rock-crystal transformed these apartments, when lighted up, into a veritable fairyland. None of these beautiful things were carried off, but next day I was informed that our soldiers, finding that fire was too slow a method of destruction, had blown the château to pieces by means of ammunition waggons full of powder placed in the basement.

The villages which, a few days before, had sheltered us were ablaze when we reached them again. Under their still smoking ashes were numerous corpses of soldiers and peasants, as well as of infants with their throats cut, and young girls murdered after having been ravished. We left on our right the town of Borovsk, which had similarly been burnt, to reascend the Protva, in the hope of finding a ford practicable for our artillery. One had been discovered just above the town, but at this point the river was so choked with abandoned ammunition waggons that we were obliged to seek another. We found, however, that the bridge of Borovsk was still standing, and that it was practicable for our baggage train. The prince immediately ordered the thirteenth division, which formed our advance-guard, to cross this bridge, which gave us access to a much better and shorter road. The great danger we had to fear was the passage of our ammunition waggons through the burning town.

All our waggons, however, got through without accident, and in the evening, after having traversed several very difficult defiles, we arrived at the wretched village of Alfereva (27th October), where the generals could with difficulty find a barn in which to pass the night. Even the quarters of the viceroy were so frightful that commiseration was felt for the peasants who had to live there. As a climax of misfortune, the absence of provisions redoubled our sufferings; the food which had been brought from Moscow was nearly exhausted, and the man who was lucky enough to possess bread, crept off to eat it in secret. Our horses also suffered cruelly; tainted straw, torn from the cottage roofs, being their only fodder. A great many of these poor animals succumbed to fatigue, obliging us to abandon our artillery teams, and each day the explosions of the ammunition waggons went on increasing to a frightful degree.

28th October.—On the following day we recrossed the Protva below Vereia. This town was still burning as we passed through it, and the devouring flames rising amidst dense clouds of smoke, quickly reduced it to ashes. The place was exceptionally unfortunate, as its distance from the main road had hitherto saved it; and with the exception of a fight between the Russians and Poles, it had escaped the horrors of war. Its well-cultivated fields and gardens were stocked with all kinds of vegetables, which in an instant were cleared off by our famished soldiers.

The third corps of the Young Guard, which had been left at Moscow, rejoined us by the direct road. This corps had brought with it the war chest, the commissariat and a large baggage train, and it now resumed its position as advance-guard. At Vereia General Winzingerode and his *aide-de-camp*, who had been made prisoners at Moscow, were taken before the emperor, who received them with great truculence, telling the General that as a Würtemberger he would be sent before a court-martial, as a rebel subject of the Confederation of the Rhine. Fortunately, however, for him he was recaptured in the vicinity of Minsk by Colonel Czernichew who, with a strong body of Cossacks, was on his way to inform Count Wittgenstein of Tschikagow's movement to effect a junction with him for the purpose of cutting off our retreat upon the banks of the Berezina.

We slept at a poor village called, I believe, Mitiaeva, which was even worse than that in which we had passed the previous night. The majority of the officers had to bivouac; a most trying situation, for the nights began to be cold, and the want of firewood rendered them almost insupportable. To procure fuel we went so far as to demolish the huts where the generals were sleeping, so that several of them on waking found themselves under the open sky.

Napoleon, who preceded us by a day's march, had already got beyond Mojaisk, burning and destroying everything on his way. The soldiers of his suite imbibed such a passion for this devastation that they burnt even the places where we were to stop. This exposed us to very great sufferings, but our corps, in its turn, by burning the few houses that were left, deprived that of the Prince of Eckmühl, which formed our rear-guard, of all shelter whatever against the bitter nights. Besides this hardship, the same corps had still to fight continually against an infuriated enemy, who, on learning of our retreat, hastened from all sides to glut his vengeance. The guns which we heard each day at no great distance showed what tremendous efforts were required to keep him at bay.

At length, an hour after passing through Ghorodok-Borisov (29th October) amidst clouds of smoke, we entered a plain, which appeared to have been devastated some considerable time previously. From time to time we encountered the bodies of men and horses. Several half-destroyed trenches, and a town in ruins, enabled me to recognise the environs of Mojaisk, which we had before passed through as victors. The Westphalians and the Poles encamped among these ruins, and as they departed they burnt such of the houses as had escaped the first conflagration; there were so few that the light from the flames was hardly visible. There was one curious circumstance which greatly struck us. The thick black smoke which issued from the *débris* contrasted strikingly with the whiteness of the belfry, which had recently been erected. It was the only building left entire, and the clock still continued to strike the hours though the town had ceased to exist!

The army did not pass through Mojaisk, but diverging to the left, we arrived at the site of Krasnoë, where we had encamped the day after the Battle of the Moskwa. I say advisedly the "site," because the village had disappeared, only the *château* having been saved for the use of Napoleon. We bivouacked around this *château*, and I shall remember to my dying day the delightful sensation of lying down in the hot ashes of the houses which had been burnt the previous evening.

30th October.—The farther we advanced the more depressing grew the landscape; the fields trampled down by thousands of horses seemed as though they had never been tilled. The forests, thinned by the long sojourn of the troops, also bore witness to this frightful devastation; but the most horrible sight of all was the multitude of corpses which, lying unburied for fifty-two days, scarcely preserved the form of humanity. Near Borodino my horror was at its height when I reached the battlefield and found the remains of the twenty thousand men who had been slaughtered, still lying in heaps, the frost having preserved them from entire dissolution. The plain was covered with them; on all sides nothing was to be seen but carcases of horses and human bodies, half interred. There also were to be seen uniforms stained with blood, bones gnawed by famished dogs and birds of prey; here a litter of broken weapons—drums, helmets and *cuirasses*; there the broken staffs of regimental colours, the symbols with which they were covered, revealing how much the Russian eagle had suffered on that bloody day.

Our soldiers in wandering over the theatre of their exploits, showed with pride the places where their regiments had fought; and nearly every one was able to recall some of those deeds of valour which are so flattering to our national pride. On one side were noticed the remains of the hut which Kutusoff had occupied; farther on upon the left was the famous redoubt, which dominated the plain and resembled a pyramid rising in the midst of a desert. Recalling its appearance when last I saw it, it now seemed like Vesuvius in repose. But observing on the summit a soldier, whose immovable figure stood out against the sky, "Ah," said I, "if ever a statue were erected to the Demon of War, here is the pedestal on which it should be set up."

While we were traversing the battlefield we heard at a distance the most lamentable cries for succour. Several of us followed the sounds, and to our infinite surprise found that they proceeded from a French soldier whose legs had been broken. He said:—

I was wounded on the day of the great battle, and being in a lonely spot, remained without assistance. After dragging myself to the side of a brook, I have lived for nearly two months on grass, roots and a little bread which I recovered from the slain. In the night I lay in the insides of dead horses, and the flesh of these animals has served to dress my wounds as well as the best remedies. Seeing you today in the distance, I summoned all my strength, and succeeded in getting near enough to the road to enable you to hear me.

Astonished at such a miracle, we were expressing our surprise, when a general who had heard of the extraordinary occurrence, had the poor fellow removed to his carriage.

Ah! long indeed would be my narrative were I to relate all the calamities engendered by this atrocious war, but if I wished by one instance to give an idea of the rest, I might speak of the three thousand prisoners brought from Moscow. During the march they were herded together like cattle; on no pretext were they allowed to leave the narrow enclosure where they were confined. Without fire, and dying of cold, they had to sleep on the ice, and maddened by hunger they fought like famished wolves for the horse-flesh which was thrown to them, and which they ate raw for want of time and means to cook it. It is asserted, but I dare not believe the story, that when this food failed, they devoured the flesh of their comrades who had died of want.

Let me turn from this awful picture, and resume the thread of my story, of the sufferings, not less cruel, which my companions and myself were soon to endure.

CHAPTER 19

Napoleon Blames the Prince of Eckmühl

We repassed the Kologha with as much precipitation as that with which we had crossed it when spurred on by victory. The descent which led to the river was so steep, and the frozen ground so slippery that men and horses fell pell-mell on one another. Lucky would it have been for us if the many similar passages still to be negotiated had not been more dangerous! We once again saw the Abbey of Kolotskoi; despoiled of its splendour by the war, and having nothing around it now but ruined houses. It more resembled an hospital than a monastery, for it was the only building that we had seen since leaving Moscow that had not been destroyed, and it was filled with sick and wounded.

The fourth corps, still marching in advance, stopped at a wretched hamlet situated half a league to the right of the road between the abbey and Prokofevo. Of all the halting-places we had had up to then, this was the most insupportable. It had nothing but the most miserable sheds, the straw roofs of which had been torn down as food for the horses; in spite of which, it was here that the prince and his suite had to find a resting-place.

31st October.—We left early in the morning, and arrived on the heights of Prokofevo, where we heard the sound of firing so close to us that the Viceroy, fearing that the Prince of Eckmühl might have been overwhelmed, put his troops in order of battle so as to be ready to give him support. For some days the emperor had been complaining of the dilatoriness of the first corps, and censuring the system of retreat by *échelons* which the Prince of Eckmühl had adopted, and which had enabled the advance-guard of Milloradowitch to overtake us. It was also alleged against the prince that he should have passed with more rapidity through the country denuded of supplies. In fairness to him, however, I must remark that a too hasty retreat would have redoubled the audacity of the enemy, who was very strong in light cavalry, and could therefore have attacked us at any moment, and cut the rear-guard to pieces if it had refused to engage. Moreover, this great leader had sufficiently proved in more fortunate circumstances that absolute reliance could be placed in his ability; and he acted on this occasion in accordance with his maxim, "*The more precipitate a retreat, the more is it fatal,*" because the discouragement it creates is even more disastrous than the physical deterioration it involves.

The viceroy had made his dispositions on the heights of Prokofevo in order to be ready to support the Prince of Eckmühl, but having satisfied himself that the marshal was in no immediate danger, he continued towards Ghiat, giving stringent orders to the troops to march in the greatest order, and to halt whenever the first corps might have need of their assistance. It would be impossible too highly to praise the military virtues of Prince Eugene in these circumstances, for he was not only always the last of his column, but bivouacked a league short of Ghiat to be ready promptly to repulse any attacks of the enemy.

The night passed in bivouac was the most trying we had yet had to endure. We were on rising ground, near the spot where the village of Ivachkoua once stood, not one house of which now existed; it having long since been burnt. As the climax of disaster, the wind blew with great violence, and there being absolutely no possibility of procuring firewood, we were deprived of the only means of softening the rigours of the Russian climate.

Although our sufferings were extreme, we could not but be sensible of those experienced by the enemy. On approaching Ghiat we were seized with searchings of heart in finding that this town had been simply wiped out, and had it not been for the *débris* of a few stone-built houses which remained here and there, one would have believed oneself to be upon the site of a burnt forest. Never have cruelty and barbarity been guilty of greater atrocities. Ghiat being built mainly of wood, disappeared in a single day; a deplorable loss in view of its industries and prosperity. It was reckoned to be one of the most flourishing commercial towns in Russia, with manufactures of leather, cloth, tar and rope for the English marine.

The weather, although extremely cold at night, was superb during the day, so that our troops, although very exhausted by the privations they had endured, kept up their spirits, well knowing that to fall into despondency would be the beginning of their ruin. For several days they had had nothing to eat but horseflesh, and by this time provisions had become so scarce that even the generals had to come down to the same diet. In these circumstances the death of a horse was looked upon as a stroke of luck, for without this resource the soldiers would have experienced the horrors of famine.

1st November.—The Cossacks, of whose appearance we were always apprehensive, were not long in justifying our fears. But as so far we had not seen them, we marched with our usual confidence. The baggage train was so enormous that it was divided into several convoys, very carelessly escorted, and straggling along with wide gaps between them. Near the ruined village of Czarevo-Saimiche there was a road about five hundred paces long which previously formed part of the highway. Our artillery had so cut it up, however, that it was no longer practicable; and to continue our march we were forced to pass through marshy fields, intersected by a broad stream. Those who went first crossed it easily on the ice, which, however, soon gave way, and the rest had either to go through the stream or wait until hastily constructed bridges could be got ready.

While the head of the column was thus brought to a stand, fresh vehicles were continually arriving, so that artillery waggons and *vivandiers'* carts were all blocking up the road, while the drivers profited as usual by the delay to light fires, at which they attempted to restore the circulation to their freezing limbs. We were in this state of supposed security when suddenly the Cossacks, uttering frightful yells, rushed out of a wood on our left and fell upon these poor wretches. At this, it was a case of *sauve qui peut*. There was a general panic; some sought refuge in the woods; others scrambled on to their horses, and spurring them with violence, dispersed over the plain, regardless of where they were going. The latter, however, were the worst off, as the stream and the marsh and other difficulties of the ground soon stopped their career and made them an easy prey to the enemy. The luckiest were those who got under the vehicles, and waited for their rescue, which promptly arrived; for as soon as the Cossacks saw infantry appearing they made off, having only succeeded in wounding some stragglers and looting a few waggons.

After this, the escorts began to take advantage of the disorder created by these Cossack raids to appropriate everything entrusted to their care. Robbery and swindling thus spread throughout the army, and grew to such proportions that there was no more safety for one's property amongst our men than there would have been had it fallen into the hands of the enemy. Whoever had charge of anything belonging to another, took advantage of any alarm to steal it; and many, encouraged by so easy a method, often created the desired occasion by themselves shouting "hurrah, hurrah!"

The Royal Guard had just passed through the defile of Czarevo-Saimiche when the train was attacked; it was immediately ordered to halt, and we then saw Cossacks at about two hundred paces to our left, who had evidently come to observe our movements. It was even said that several of them had crossed the road between the gaps left in our straggling column. This swagger, which had produced such an effect upon our camp-followers, had none whatever when directed against the troops. The Royal Guard, although they saw the Tartars hovering on their flanks, did not trouble themselves about them, and halted near a wood close to Velitschevo; the other divisions encamped around the Viceroy, who had always remained in the rear, since the Russians manifested the intention to impede our retreat.

2nd November.—Next day at three hours before dawn, we abandoned this position. Our night march was terrifying; the darkness was impenetrable, and each of us fearing to stumble against his neighbour, went along slowly feeling his way, and plunged in the most harassing despondency. In spite of all our precautions several fell into the ditches which lined the road; others rolled down the ravines with which it was intersected. We awaited daylight with extreme impatience, hoping that its welcome appearance would facilitate our march, and enable us to guard against the ambuscades of an enemy who, by his intimate knowledge of the ground, had such an immense advantage in this campaign.

We knew we should soon be attacked. Those who were acquainted with the country looked with anxiety to the position of Viazma, because that town was situated at the junction of the roads from Medouin and Joukhnow, which a part of the Russian army had followed after the action at Malo-Jaroslavetz, and which was much shorter than the route taken by us. Moreover, the Cossacks seen the previous evening were regarded as the advance-guard of the numerous cavalry commanded by Platow, and of the two divisions of General Milloradowitch, which were debouching near Viazma.

Our pioneers and the escort of the viceroy were only a mile from that town, and still there were no signs of the enemy. The prince found that the distance between the two extremities of his column threatened to compromise the safety of his army, and he therefore ordered the troops in front to halt. During this interval Lieut.-Col. Labedoyère arrived from Viazma, and on his describing the dangers he had run, we had no doubt that next day there would be fighting.

The viceroy halted at Federovskoe, although he was expected at Viazma. His divisions encamped around him; the Poles were on his right, facing the enemy; a little farther forward were the divisions of the first corps, which, although forming the rear, were so hard pressed that they were almost in contact with us, and it was to remedy this that the prince suspended his march.

CHAPTER 20

Difficult Passage of the Osma

3rd November.—The day following we were in motion about six o'clock, and were nearing Viazma; already our leading troops had entered the town, when the Cossacks showed their presence by attacking some vehicles posted around a small church near by. The arrival of our troops soon dispersed them, but when these same troops resumed their march, the first brigade under General Nagle, which formed our rear-guard, was attacked on its left flank about a league and a half from Viazma. Several squadrons of Russian cavalry threw themselves into the short space which separated the fourth corps from the first.

The viceroy seeing the danger of his position, halted his divisions and recalled his artillery, so that well-directed batteries might control the enemy, whose manifest intention was to cut off our retreat by possessing himself of Viazma.

While the manoeuvres were in progress for defeating the Russian plans, we saw with regret that the first corps, no doubt worn out by their unparalleled sufferings and constant fighting, had lost that fine appearance which used to excite our admiration. The soldiers observed but little discipline. Most of them had been wounded in the different actions, or were sick from bad diet and extreme fatigue, and these swelled the ranks of the stragglers.

At first our corps not only sustained single-handed the attack of a large body of cavalry, but also the repeated efforts of a division of Russian infantry more than twelve thousand strong. During this time the first corps took position to the left of the road between Viazma and the point of attack, replacing the troops of the fourth corps, which had been engaged since the action commenced.

The fourteenth division, which was in advance of the thirteenth, remained with the Royal Guard near Viazma, where both were held in reserve. This order of battle having been established, the enemy's infantry advanced, and the action began with much spirit, but with great superiority of artillery on the Russian side, for the wretched state of our horses prevented us from working our guns with the same rapidity.

In spite of their inferiority, our troops held their positions during the whole time required for the passage of our baggage train. While they were traversing the town of Viazma in the most perfect order, part of the enemy's cavalry attempted to envelop our two wings. This manoeuvre of the Russians created consternation amongst those whom exhaustion and starvation had forced out of the ranks to march as best they could; there were many of these, especially among the cavalry, who were nearly all dismounted. These scattered stragglers had become useless and were dangerous in present circumstances, for they not only impeded the manoeuvres, but created alarm and disorder by precipitately bolting whenever the enemy attacked. This increased the difficulty of our situation, as the audacity of the Cossacks was redoubled by seeing this stampede of what they believed to be armed troops.

Fortunately the large redoubt upon the left of our road, and especially the strong position of the Duke of Elchingen, checked the efforts of the Russians, who had got us into a very critical situation. It was close on four in the afternoon when our corps passed through Viazma. In traversing the forest, which extends below the plateau on which that town is situated, we met a convoy of the sick which had left Moscow before us. These unfortunates had for several days been deprived of all assistance, and were bivouacking in the forest which served them both for hospital and grave, for the difficulty of getting the horses to move forward had compelled the drivers to abandon them all. We encamped close by, and at nightfall made a huge fire upon the side of a hill covered with brushwood.

From this hill we saw the distant sky all ablaze; it was the houses in Viazma which had escaped the first conflagration and which had been given to the flames on our retiring. The third corps, which still maintained its position to cover the retreat, although separated from the Russians by a stream and steep ravines, appeared to be frequently attacked. In the silence of the night we were often awakened by gun fire, the din of which, reverberating through the dense forests, was grand and terrible; it rolled along the valley, repeated by a hundred echoes, and died away in low growls among the distant hills.

4th November.—At about one in the morning the Viceroy deemed it prudent to profit by the darkness to effect his retreat, and so obtain some hours start of the Russians, whom we could no longer fight, as hunger prevented us from remaining in the wasted country. We groped our way along the high road, which was entirely covered with baggage and artillery; both men and horses, utterly worn out, could hardly drag themselves along, and when any of the latter fell, the soldiers shared it between them, and grilled the flesh on red-hot cinders. Many, suffering far more from the extreme cold than from hunger, abandoned their accoutrements, and lay down beside a large fire they had lighted, but when the time came for departing, these poor wretches had not the strength to get up, and preferred to fall into the hands of the enemy rather than to continue the march.

It was broad daylight when we arrived before the village of Polianovo, through which runs the little river Osma. The bridge was very narrow and extremely bad, while the crowd that had to cross it was immense, and as there was a desperate struggle to get over, the viceroy directed the officers of the staff to interpose their authority to maintain order during this difficult passage; and he himself ,was not above attending to all the measures needed to facilitate the progress of the convoys of artillery in the midst of the crowd of equipages which were trying to enter the defile. The emperor, who was a day's march ahead of us, having heard that we were attacked, halted between Jalkow Postaja-Dvor and Doroghoboui, but when he learnt that we had forced the passage he resumed his progress towards the latter town.

Below the hamlet of Semlevo there is another branch of the River Osma, much larger than the first, but it did not serve to check the advance of the army, which crossed by a wide and well-constructed bridge, to pass a position which the enemy could have utilised with great advantage if he had been able to take possession of it.

Towards the close of the day, the prince had taken up his quarters in a small chapel situated on this side of a large, marshy stream. Scarcely had this been done when the retinue was attacked by Cossacks and hastily fled, some with the loss of their horses and clothes, while others were badly wounded by sabre cuts and lance thrusts.

It was time to think of escaping, and as the retinue of the viceroy evacuated their quarters the enemy's cavalry advanced. This affair showed very forcibly the necessity for assuring the passage of rivers during a retreat. This one, although comparatively small, was barely fordable, and had no bridge. To get across it, men, horses and vehicles plunged into the water; a most trying situation, as the Russians, profiting by our difficulties, commenced to harass the end of our column, and spread consternation among the immense throng who found themselves confronted by a broad and deep stream, half frozen and bordered by marshes, with the bullets of the enemy whizzing about their ears. In spite of this, however, the passage was unattended by any serious loss, and as night was approaching, and the Cossacks feared to compromise themselves, they desisted from their attacks. We lost a few vehicles, which had to be left in the middle of the water.

This obstacle having been surmounted, we entered a forest. At its extremity, towards the left, was a large *château* built of wood, which had long since been sacked, near the village of Rombki, where we established ourselves. We had no meat but horseflesh, but there still remained a little bread which had been brought from Moscow in one of the waggons belonging to the staff. To economise our resources we made soup, and each officer had his fixed quantity. As to the horses, they had to be satisfied with the straw which, during our advance to Moscow, had served them as litter.

5th November.—We started very early in the morning, and without encountering the enemy arrived at a large village, a few houses in which remained standing. One was built of stone, and was of some size, so that we called the place the *Maison en Pierre*. Seldom knowing the names of the villages through which we passed, it was our custom to call them by such names as their different characteristics suggested, either from their peculiarity of construction or the misery associated with them. We never, however, gave them a name suggesting our hunger, as that calamity was common to all.

CHAPTER 21

Arrival at Doroghoboui

So far, we had supported our privations with calmness and resignation, in the pleasing delusion that they would soon come to an end. In leaving Moscow, we had looked upon Smolensk as the termination of our retreat, where we should unite with the corps left upon the Dnieper and the Dwina, making those rivers our line of defence, and going into winter quarters in Lithuania. It was said, also, that Smolensk was well supplied with provisions, and that there would be found the ninth corps, numbering about twenty-five thousand fresh troops, to relieve us of further duty. That town was therefore the goal of our fondest hopes; we burnt with impatience to reach it, in the full persuasion that once within its walls our sufferings would cease.

6th November.—We were marching with all possible urgency on Smolensk, and had nearly reached Doroghoboui, which was only some twenty leagues distant from the former city. The thought that we should be there in three days filled every heart with joy, when suddenly the sky, which up to then had been so brilliant, became darkened with a cold and gloomy mist. The sun, hidden behind dense clouds, vanished from our sight, and snow, falling in large flakes, in an instant obscured the day and confounded earth and sky. The wind, blowing with fury, filled the forests with its frightful whistling and up-rooted the black fir trees covered with icicles, which fell to the ground with a crash; and almost as if by magic the whole country became one universal white and savage waste.

In the midst of this gloomy horror, the soldiers, overwhelmed by snow and wind, which came down upon them in a freezing mist, could no longer distinguish the road from the ditches with which it was lined, and often fell into the latter, and there found a grave. The rest, making frantic efforts to hasten forward, could hardly drag themselves along; badly shod, insufficiently clothed, without food or drink, groaning with pain and shivering with cold, they showed absolute indifference to those who fell exhausted and expired around them, and who, stretched out along the roads, were only to be distinguished by the heaps of snow which covered their corpses, and which formed along the route little mounds such as are seen in cemeteries. Finally, great clouds of ravens, abandoning the plain to seek refuge in the forests, came wheeling over our heads, uttering dreadful and sinister cries, while packs of savage dogs coming from Moscow, which had been feeding on the dead, came howling around us as if greedy to hasten the moment when we also should furnish them with a meal.

From that moment the army utterly lost its morale and its military organisation. Soldiers no longer obeyed their officers; officers paid no regard to their generals; shattered regiments marched as best they could. Searching for food, they dispersed over the plain, burning and sacking everything in their way. These scattered detachments were soon assailed by the remainder of the population, armed to avenge the horrors of which they had been the victims; and the Cossacks, coming to the aid of the peasants, captured the miserable stragglers who had escaped the carnage.

Such was the condition of the army when we arrived at Doroghoboui. This town, although a small one, would, in our distressed condition, have been a haven of refuge, had not Napoleon's rage blinded him to such an extent that he entirely forgot that his soldiers would be the chief sufferers from the devastation which he himself caused. Doroghoboui had been burnt down, its stores pillaged, and the brandy, of which there was abundance, was running down the gutters, while the rest of the army was perishing for want of it. The few houses that remained were occupied exclusively by a small number of generals and officers. The armed troops which were still left to face the enemy were exposed to all the rigours of the season, while those separated from their corps found themselves everywhere repulsed, being driven away even from the very midst of the bivouacs.

One can imagine the situation of these unhappy creatures; tormented with hunger, they rushed on every horse as soon as it fell, and like famished wolves fought for the fragments. Worn out for want of sleep and with long marches, they saw nothing around them but snow, and not a single place where they could find rest. They wandered about, palsied with the cold, searching for wood to make a fire,

167

but the snow had covered everything, and even when they found any their labour was in vain, for what with the wind and the wet it was impossible to set it alight. The soldiers herded close together like cattle, huddled up under the shelter of birch trees or firs, or under the waggons. Some tore down trees, and others burnt the houses of the officers, and could be seen like spectres lying motionless beside those huge bonfires throughout the night.

Chapter 22

Napoleon's Fatal Blunder

When Napoleon evacuated Moscow, he left it with the intention of combining all his troops behind Witepsk and Smolensk, and so making the Dnieper and the Dwina a line of concentration, from which he would issue in the following spring to attack simultaneously Kiow and St. Petersburg. The days of the 6th and 7th November having, however, destroyed his army, he made this a pretext for abandoning this plan. But the real and only motive which prompted him to do so was the news received at Smolensk that Wittgenstein had stormed Polotsk, and that Witepsk had also been taken with its garrison! These two events involved such sweeping changes in the projects of the Emperor that I think it as well here to describe in some detail the operations which had been in progress upon the Dwina during our retreat.

The very day on which we issued from Moscow, all the Russian armies which Napoleon had left in his rear put themselves in motion. That under the command of Count Wittgenstein, besides its vicinity to the Berezina, was the more to be feared seeing that it had just been reinforced by seventeen thousand recruits and a division of veterans from Finland. Marshal Gouvion Saint-Cyr, entrusted with the duty of holding it, had long been without reinforcements, and saw his army dwindling away, not only owing to continual fighting, but also to their prolonged stay in a wretched country which had been the theatre of the most bloody operations for four months.

Wittgenstein, emboldened by such advantages, at last resolved to take the offensive at a moment when our weakness compelled us to abandon it. On the 15th October, at six in the morning, he debouched before Polotsk with four columns, and profiting by his numerical superiority, advanced to turn the position held by Marshal Gouvion Saint-Cyr upon the left bank of the Polota. His first attack was directed against an advantageously placed battery, which we had to defend at all costs in order not to expose the weak point of our entrenched camp to the enemy—that is to say, the front of the town of Polotsk, the defences of which were too imperfect to cover our extreme left, but which nevertheless were defended by General Maison with great firmness and bravery.

While the Russians were vigorously pressing General Maison, they brought up another of their columns to attack Legrand's division, chiefly directing their efforts against a redoubt upon the left of the Polota, which, owing to the enemy's manoeuvres, had become the centre of this division. The attack failed, and their courage gave way under the fire of our guns.

During the whole of this day Wittgenstein did not dare to advance to the right bank of the Polota, where we were strongly entrenched; but towards four o'clock, having doubtless concentrated all his forces, he debouched *en masse* by the Riga and Sebei roads. His troops, supported by a column from Nevel, the road from which joins the other two near Polotsk, attacked the left flank of the town with so much rashness, that the Swiss and Croats of Merle's division, who opposed them, slaughtered large numbers, and closed the day with the retention of the position they had been charged to defend.

Count Gouvion Saint-Cyr gloriously withstood the assault of greatly superior numbers, confident that so long as it was a mere question of courage he had nothing to fear. But he was not without anxiety as to being able to defeat the enemy's manoeuvres, against which in an open plain the greatest valour could not contend. In order, therefore, to assure the safety of his rear, he had sent General Corbineau to the banks of the Ouchatsch during the night to watch the movements of the corps of General Stengel, whose intention was to turn the Marshal's position by the left bank of the Dwina, while continuing the battle on the opposite side of the river. General Corbineau, as the result of his first reconnaissances, informed Saint-Cyr that on the banks of the Ouchatsch there were only weak bodies of the enemy; but towards ten in the morning he reported in all haste that he saw in front of him five thousand infantry and twelve squadrons of cavalry. He was at once reinforced with a regiment from each division, and the 7th Cuirassiers under General Amey.

The marshal recognised that his position was becoming critical, and that he had no alternative but to repass the Dwina; but wishing to conceal his plan of retreat from the Russians, he announced that it would only begin towards the close of the day, and that it must be made in absolute silence, so as to screen a movement which might have proved fatal had the enemy opposed it. Unfortunately, at nightfall, some reckless soldiers set fire to the barracks of General Legrand, and in a moment the fire extended to the whole line.

Wittgenstein, who had only waited for our retreat to recommence his attacks, at once grasped the fact that we were about to recross the Dwina, and opened fire with his artillery on Polotsk, hoping to set it on fire, and thus prevent our ammunition waggons from getting through the town. The troops which were inside, protected by a double palisade, fought bravely and kept up a sustained fire, entrenching themselves behind baulks of timber and in the houses, which they had loopholed. The bombardment was terrific and the fire of the batteries became general. The flames which rose on all sides lit up this night combat, and illuminated the country for miles round, so that the fight went on as if in broad day. The ferocity of the two sides was extreme, and although greatly outnumbered, our rear-guard defended the town until all the baggage train and troops had cleared the Dwina.

Polotsk having been evacuated at about three in the morning, the Russian general Cazanova took possession of it, and only found some wounded, brought in from the battlefield. But our enforced retreat was glorious, seeing that in so critical a position, which might have been disastrous, the enemy only captured one gun at a loss triple that of ours. That same day, the Russian general staff, having given a grand dinner in the monastery of the Jesuits, Wittgenstein rose towards the end of the banquet, and by a spontaneous impulse, which reflected honour on both victor and vanquished, proposed the health of the brave Gouvion Saint-Cyr.

The marshal, seeing that he had not an instant to lose in opposing the troops advancing by Ouchatsch, which had been held in check by General Amey in the defiles of Sedlitchtche, sent him a reinforcement of seven hundred Bavarians, and gave the command of all these troops to General de Wrede, who promptly marched against Stengel. On coming up with him, he attacked and drove him to the other side of the Bononiia, taking from fifteen to eighteen thousand prisoners; among them two colonels and several officers of various grades.

The marshal having been wounded in the foot was obliged to transfer the chief command to General Legrand, until the Duke of

Reggio could arrive to assume it.

Such were the events which had occurred during the retreat of the Grand Army upon Smolensk; events which were honourable to our arms, but disastrous in their consequences. Wittgenstein having re-crossed the Dwina, detached upon his left the troops which captured Witepsk. Upon his right he employed Stengel's corps to oppose the Bavarians, and with the rest of his army he pursued the corps under the Duke of Reggio. In order to support that marshal, who com-manded the only force able to check Wittgenstein, Napoleon found himself compelled to send the Duke of Belluno to his assistance, in the hope of being able to force the Russians to recross the Dwina, a fatal move, as this corps was annihilated by want of food and the extreme severity of the winter; while, had it remained inactive until our arrival at Mistislavl, where it was securely cantoned, it would have remained intact to oppose Tschikagow, and by its presence would have encouraged Schwartzenberg's corps of thirty thousand men to with-stand the attacks in Volhynia. The Austrians would thus, by defending Minsk and closing the Borisow road against the enemy, have saved the French Army the horrors which it afterwards experienced on the banks of the Berezina.

Through intercepted letters our leader was aware of all these ma-noeuvres, but made no use of the knowledge. The Russians made no secret of their intention to take Napoleon alive, and then put his army to the sword; but we were in such profound ignorance of these hostile movements, and had such complete confidence in the capacity for resistance of the corps by which our flanks were guarded, that we all expected the speedy end of our troubles at the very place where they became more terrible than ever.

It was by no means the severity of the winter that spoilt the em-peror's plan, since, had he remained originally between Smolensk and Witepsk, he could easily have repaired the losses he had sustained up to that period. The chief, indeed the only cause of his ruin, was his proceeding to Moscow in contemptuous disregard of the forces which he left in his rear, and in attempting, at the price of our blood, what the most imprudent of monarchs [1] shrank from attempting. The desire to sack that capital, the boast of there dictating laws, [2] led him

---

1. Charles XII., to whom Napoleon often applied the epithet of "Madman."
2. He gave laws only to the *Comédie Française*. See his regulations for the theatre, dated Moscow, 15th October 1812, appearing in the *Moniteur* of the 15th January 1813.

to risk everything; and forgetting winter and its rigours, he burnt the Kremlin without remembering that he was. supported only by allies whose loyalty was doubtful ;that Wittgenstein had never abandoned the Dwina, and lastly, that Tschikagow, hastening up from Moldavia, would inevitably attack him on his retreat.

CHAPTER 23

Sufferings of the Women and Children

Napoleon, still ignoring the rapid progress of the enemy on the Dwina, resolved that the fourth corps should cross the Dnieper and proceed to Witepsk to relieve the garrison under General Pouget. In order to ascertain whether, in spite of the weather, this route was still practicable, General Sanson was ordered to inspect it, and particularly to examine the banks of the Vop. The engineer officers Delahaye, Laignelot and Guibert accompanied him on this mission; but the whole party had hardly reached the other side of the river when they fell into the hands of a party of the Cossacks who infested the district.

7th November.—Our corps having, however, been ordered to Witepsk, we left Doroghoboui and crossed the Dnieper by a bridge of rafts opposite the town. The artillery teams experienced great difficulty in mounting the opposite bank. The road having become as slippery as glass, these worn-out animals could no longer haul, and from twelve to sixteen of them had often to be harnessed to one gun, and even then had barely strength enough to climb the slightest hill. It had been intended that day to go as far as Zazele, but the road was so bad, that even next day the guns and waggons had not reached the appointed place. A number of horses and ammunition waggons were abandoned, and it was on this dreadful night that looting of the vehicles commenced. The ground was covered with portmanteaux, clothes and papers. A great quantity of articles secretly brought from Moscow now began to appear.

The handsome Château of Zazele presented during the night a

repetition of the scenes of the previous evening; and with the exception of the soldiers into whom the pillage of the vehicles had put new life, nothing was to be seen on all hands but wretches dying of hunger and cold, and horses which, maddened by thirst, endeavoured to break the ice with their hoofs to find water.

8th November.—Our baggage was so enormous that our losses in that direction were still unappreciable. We kept advancing, still full of hope, and congratulated ourselves that by leaving the high road to Smolensk we should follow one less desolated by the calamities of war, where we might find villages undestroyed, which would afford us shelter from the fearful cold, furnish us with food, and above all supply forage for our starving horses. Alas! this hope was soon dissipated. The village of Sloboda, where we halted for the night, only plunged us into fresh dismay. It had been completely sacked, and the Cossacks, hovering upon our flanks, captured, despoiled or slew all those who, forced by necessity, were foraging in the outskirts. In these terrible circumstances General Danthouard, who was continually to be found where danger was greatest, directed our artillery upon all the points where it could be made effective, but while riding along our lines a cannon-ball fractured his right leg after having killed the orderly at his side.

The viceroy, knowing that next day we should have to cross the Vop, had sent General Poitevin with several engineers to construct the necessary bridge. Next day (9th November) at an early hour we arrived at the river, but what was the dismay of the prince and our despair, when we saw the whole army and its baggage train ranged up along the banks of the stream utterly unable to get across it. The bridge had been constructed by the sappers, but during the night a flood having destroyed it, it was neither possible to use nor to repair it.

The Cossacks whom we had seen the previous evening were not long in advancing when they ascertained our critical situation. Already the fire of our skirmishers was heard attempting to check them, but the din of battle rapidly nearing us, showed only too clearly that the Russians had gained fresh courage at the sight of our predicament. The viceroy, whose great soul had always been calm in the midst of the greatest dangers, preserved a *sang-froid* which was invaluable in this desperate dilemma. To tranquillise those who were more terrified by the appearance of the enemy than by the difficulty of crossing the

H. Bellangé 1853

Vop, he brought up fresh troops, who, by protecting our flanks and rear, enabled us to devote all our energies to effecting the passage of the river.

The prince, seeing that it would be desirable for some of his suite to afford an example to the rest by being the first to cross, requested his *aide-de-camp*, Bataille, and his orderly officer, Colonel Delfanti, to place themselves at the head of the Royal Guard and ford the Vop. These brave officers eagerly accepted the duty; and in view of the whole corps plunged into the river. The water was up to their middle, and was full of floating ice, but, accompanied by the grenadiers, they succeeding in reaching the opposite bank.

A few moments afterwards, the viceroy followed with his staff. The vehicles next commenced to cross and the first got over safely, as well as some of the guns. As the Vop ran in a very deep bed, its steep and slippery banks made it impassable except at one place where a slope had been cut. But the guns sank into such deep ruts that it was impossible to extricate them, with the result that the only practicable ford was so blocked that it became impossible for the artillery and the rest of the army to use it.

In this fearful position despair became universal, for in spite of all efforts to keep the Russians at bay, it was only too certain that they were advancing. Terror redoubled our dangers; the river being half frozen, and the vehicles not being able to pass, those who had no horses were compelled to throw themselves into the water, while we were forced to abandon a hundred guns, a large number of ammunition waggons, carts and waggons which contained the small remains of the provisions brought from Moscow. Men threw away their accoutrements to load the horses with the most valuable of their effects. No sooner was a carriage abandoned than the mob of soldiers did not even give the owner time to select from among his property what he wished to preserve. They looted everything, but showed a marked preference for flour and liquor.

On a report that the enemy was upon us, the gunners spiked and abandoned their pieces, hopeless of getting across a river which was everywhere encumbered with mud-embedded vehicles, and by innumerable corpses of the drowned. The cries of those struggling in the water, the terror of others who were in the act of crossing and who at each moment rolled back into the bed of the stream with their horses, owing to the slipperiness of the steep banks; and lastly the despair of the women and the tears of the children, combined to make this passage such a scene of horror that the very recollection of it sends a shudder through my veins.

Although it is distressing to recall such dreadful events I cannot forbear to record an example of maternal love, so affecting in itself and so creditable to human nature, that it was some relief to witness it amidst our unparalleled sufferings.

A *vivandière* of our corps who had been through the whole campaign, returned from Moscow bringing in her carriage five young children, and all the profits of her industry. On arriving at the Vop she regarded with speechless dismay the river, which compelled her to leave on its banks the savings upon which the subsistence of her family depended. For some time she ran hither and thither trying to find a new passage, but all in vain, and addressing her husband she said, "*Mon ami*, we must abandon our all, and try to save the children." With these words, she took the two youngest out of the carriage and placed them in her husband's arms. I saw the poor father tightly clasp those two little creatures, and with tottering steps attempt to ford the stream, while his wife, falling on her knees on the bank, regarded alternately the earth and the heavens, with streaming eyes.

As soon as her husband had safely crossed, she clasped her trembling hands in gratitude to God, and rising, exclaimed in a transport of joy, "They are saved, they are saved!" But the two little ones who were deposited on the opposite bank, believing themselves to be deserted by their parents, called imploringly to them, so that on each side of the river there was a scene of pathetic grief. At last tears ceased to flow and gave place to the joy which the family displayed on finding themselves all reunited.

We left this scene of desolation towards the close of the day, and encamped near a miserable village about half a league from the Vop, where, in the middle of the night, we heard the lamentable cries of those still attempting to cross. Broussier's division had been left on the other bank, so as to hold back the enemy, and endeavour to save some part of the immense baggage which had been abandoned. Early in the morning (10th November) I was sent to recall this division, which in quitting the spot, revealed to me the full extent of our losses. For more than a league nothing was to be seen but ammunition waggons and guns; the smartest *calèches* that had come from Moscow were scattered in heaps along the road and the banks of the river. As to the objects stolen from these carriages, such as were too heavy to be carried away had been thrown promiscuously into the fields.

There were to be seen valuable candelabras, antique bronzes, and priceless paintings and porcelain. I myself saw an exquisitely worked bowl, on which was painted a beautiful design. I took it and drank out of this chalice the water of the Vop, full of mud and ice; and after I had done so, threw the bowl away with the utmost indifference. Hardly had our troops quitted the other bank, when clouds of Cossacks descended upon the unfortunates who, through weakness, had not been able to get across. Although our enemies were already weighed down with booty, they nevertheless stripped their prisoners, leaving them naked in the snow. From our bank we saw the Tartars dividing these bloody spoils. If their courage had been equal to their love of plunder the Vop would have been no barrier to their attacking us. But these prudent foes, always frightened off by the sight of bayonets, contented themselves with firing at us a few cannon-shots, some of which reached our column.

The night which we had passed through had been terrible. To get an idea of it, imagine an army encamped in the snow, in the midst of a Russian winter, pursued by the enemy, and with neither cavalry nor artillery to resist him. The soldiers without boots, and almost without clothing, were worn out with fatigue and hunger; seated on their knapsacks, they slept with their heads on their knees, and only awoke from this stupor to grill steaks of horse-flesh, or shake off pieces of ice; very frequently even firewood was unprocurable; and to obtain it the houses where the generals lodged were destroyed, so that on our waking the village had disappeared.

CHAPTER 24

Splendid Horror of a Night Fire

The Cossacks, who saw along the roads unmistakable proofs of our calamities, observing that we were quitting our position, speedily crossed the river and hung upon our rear, but the fourteenth division covered us with a dozen guns, which they had managed to retain. Meanwhile, the prince and his officers endeavoured to restore order, and to incorporate with their regiments those soldiers who had been compelled by want to stray away in search of food. This attempt, however, had little success; the number of stragglers was so large that it was impossible either to arrest or restrain them, and even when they were discovered and brought back, desertions soon recommenced; as hunger—inexorable hunger—forced them to abandon the flag. The pertinacity of the enemy increased with our misfortunes. They frequently attacked the rear-guard, and compelled us to halt to support it against the superior forces which threatened its destruction.

The rear of our column was being actively followed, when the Royal Guard, which formed its head, was stopped in front of Doukhovchtchina by bands of Cossacks who, issuing from that town, deployed in the plain with the object of enveloping us. Seeing themselves hemmed in on all sides, our corps was thrown into such disorder that it was reduced to the condition of an immense mob, half of whom were sick and without arms. However, on the one side the enemy maintained a firm front, and on the other we pushed on urgently; the prince threw the Italian Guard into squares, with the dragoons and Bavarian light horse, who, marching in squadrons, forced the Cossacks to give us unmolested entrance into Doukhovchtchina.

Our troops were supported by the thirteenth division, whom we succeeded in forming in column in spite of the multitude of stragglers, who, pressing round the platoons, endangered the manoeuvre. To hasten the march of these troops the Viceroy personally superintended the repair of the broken bridge which prevented our passage. In order to hearten us, he did not even hesitate to help in the work himself, and his self-sacrifice greatly stimulated our ardour.

The little town of Doukhovchtchina, which none of our armies had hitherto passed, was absolutely intact. The inhabitants, fleeing on our approach, had left some provisions, which we seized with avidity although they were extremely coarse; but our greatest boon was the possession of decent houses where we could find shelter from the extreme cold and violent wind.

On the previous evening the viceroy had ordered his *aide-de-camp*, Bataille, to take with him the fifteenth division and proceed to Smolensk to inform Napoleon of the disasters which had overtaken us on the Vop. It was doubtless to enable him to receive a reply that the Viceroy remained at Doukhovchtchina (11th November). The capture of Witepsk by the Russians, however, decided him to rejoin the emperor, and with that object to resume the retreat at two in the morning, without waiting for Bataille's return.

We were unmolested all that day, but towards ten at night, while we were enjoying a little sleep, the Cossacks suddenly appeared before the town, and fired some cannon-shots at our bivouac fires. The posts of the 106th Regiment, placed in front of a church, sustained some losses, but the presence of the Viceroy soon put a stop to the confusion created by such an unexpected attack. Our troops were at once called to arms, and disposed in the most advantageous positions to repel this night assault which, however, led to nothing, as the Cossacks took care not to push it further when they saw that we were on the alert.

12th November.—The time for departure having arrived, we set fire to Doukhovchtchina, the houses of which we had found so useful. Although we had long been accustomed to the effects of fire, we could not help being struck with the horrible but superb spectacle presented in the darkness by a snow-clad forest lit up by a vast torrent of flames. The trees enveloped in a coating of ice, dazzled the eyes and produced, as through a prism, the most vivid colours and the most delicate tints; the branches of the birches looked like those of the weeping-willow, bending towards the earth with the effect of chandeliers; and the icicles reflecting the light, seemed to surround us with a shower of diamonds.

In the midst of this splendid horror, the troops, having assembled outside the town, took the road to Smolensk. Although the night was extremely dark, the flames which arose from other villages, which had also been set on fire, formed so many aurora borealis, which shed upon our march an appalling illumination until daybreak. Near Toporovo we passed on our left the road to Pologhi, which we had followed on our march from Smolensk to Doroghoboui. The snow had almost buried the villages, and seen from a distance they were only black specks on a vast expanse of white. Their difficulty of access alone saved them from general destruction. In comparing these peaceful refuges with the torments we were enduring, I could not help exclaiming:—

Fortunate people! exempt from ambition, you live in tranquillity, while we succumb to the most frightful privations. Winter preserves your lives while it destroys ours! When the sweet Spring brings you deliverance, you will, while gazing on our ravages, find in your fields our mouldering remains, and will experience the twofold satisfaction of having escaped the horrors of war, and of being guiltless of our sufferings.

The little River Khmost was frozen when we crossed it; the bridge, which is a very good one, enabled us to make the passage without delay or obstacle. On arriving at Volodimerova the viceroy took up his quarters in the same *château* where he had lodged during our advance. We there found that the Cossacks, who had been continually hovering about our flanks, had halted upon the same heights as ourselves. We soon ascertained this by their swoops upon our foragers, who, forced by the most dire necessity, were ransacking such of the neighbouring villages as had not hitherto been entirely cleared out.

13th November.—We were only one day's march from Smolensk, and it was there that plenty was to succeed to want, and repose to fatigue. Impatient to enjoy these longed-for delights, we left Volodimerova long before daylight, burning, as usual, the cottages where we had sheltered. Arrived at the hill of Stabna where the road from Doukhovchtchina branches off from that of Witepsk, we found the greatest difficulty in climbing it. The side by which we had to ascend was one sheet of ice; men and horses rolled down one on top of the other, and those were fortunate who, after all their fatigues, were able to get over.

Before arriving at Smolensk, where our misery was expected to be at an end, dreadful scenes were encountered which made us all the more anxious to reach that town. In the midst of all the horrors with which we were overwhelmed, none suffered more than the French women who had come from Moscow, and who, in escaping from the vengeance of the Russians, imagined they would find a safe refuge with us. Mostly on foot, with cloth shoes, and scantily clad, they wrapped round them fragments of cloaks, or soldiers' capes, taken from corpses. Their pitiable situation would have drawn tears from the hardest heart, if our dreadful surroundings had not banished all sentiments of humanity.

It was horrible to see and hear those enormous longhaired wolfhounds, which, abandoning the burnt dwellings, followed us all along our route; dying of hunger, they bayed as if they had gone mad, and in their fury often fought with the soldiers for the dead horses strewn along the road. The ravens, also, with which Russia swarms, attracted by the stench of the dead bodies, came wheeling in black clouds above us, with dismal cries of sinister omen, and, striking terror into our hearts, added to the intensity of our misery.

Fortunately, we were now only two leagues from Smolensk, and the tower of its famous cathedral, which we saw in the distance, was the most delightful view we had ever seen.

CHAPTER 25

News of Attempted Rising in France

An hour before arriving at Smolensk we left Broussier's division, with the few Bavarian light horse that remained to watch and hold back the Cossacks, who, in continually increasing numbers, seemed determined to follow us to the very gates of the town. But what was our despair when, on reaching the suburbs, we learnt that the ninth corps had long since departed, and that it was impossible to remain in Smolensk, where all the provisions had been consumed. A thunderbolt falling at our feet could not have overwhelmed us more than this dreadful news. We were so horror-struck that at first we could not believe it. But alas! we soon had ample proof of its truth, by seeing the garrison of Smolensk seeking subsistence from the horses which were falling dead from the fatigue of our march. We no longer doubted that famine reigned in the town which we had hitherto regarded as a land of plenty.

In entering, we were plunged into the depths of depression. To relieve our immediate necessities we were promised a distribution of rice, flour and biscuit. This for a moment raised our spirits, but an instant afterwards we were shocked by a most distressing scene. Hardly had we passed the barrier, when we saw a number of stragglers arriving, dripping with blood, who told us that the Cossacks were only two hundred yards behind. Captain Trezel, *aide-de-camp* to General Guilleminot, then came up.

This officer had been entrusted with the most harassing duties, and had always discharged them with a zeal beyond all praise. That day he had been left behind to get the fourteenth division into position, and on his return he told us that it had been placed in a village behind a small wood which bordered the road; that the enemy had surrounded it, but that as it was strongly entrenched near a *château*, the grounds of which were palisaded, it had given such a good account of itself that the Cossacks, despairing of attacking it with success, had retired to pick up stragglers, of which they secured a large number, slaughtering some and wounding many more. The road was covered with these poor wretches, and presented a most deplorable scene, particularly on the hill of Smolensk, the slope of which was so precipitate, and rendered so slippery by the frost, that these unfortunates were unable to climb it, and lay down on the other side, where death soon put an end to their sufferings.

At last, after leaving the Royal Guard upon the summit to protect Broussier's division, which formed the rear-guard, we descended towards the Dnieper, and sought to enter the town. Near the bridge was the junction of the roads from Doroghoboui and Valontina which all the other corps had followed, and as these corps had not passed the Vop they still possessed a large part of their artillery and vehicles. This huge train, which rolled in from all directions, got mixed up with the infantry and cavalry, who, eager at all costs to enter Smolensk, where they had been promised bread, caused such confusion that it was three hours before we could penetrate into the town.

13th November.—Today the wind was violent and the cold extreme. We were assured that it was twenty-two degrees below freezing-point; in spite of which we all thronged through the streets to buy provisions. Smolensk being built on the side of a hill, the ascent was so steep that in order to climb it we had to cling to rocks which jutted out of the snow. We managed at last to reach the top, and arrived at the great square and the houses which had suffered least from the conflagration. Although the weather was frightfully severe, we sought for food rather than for lodgings. Some soldiers of the garrison, to whom a little bread had been distributed, were compelled to sell us some; and those who had bought it were implored by the others to give them a morsel. Officers and soldiers could thus be seen merged in one common herd, eating together in the middle of the streets. During this time the Cossacks arrived, and could be seen distinctly hovering upon the heights and firing on the troops who were marching below the town.

We found great difficulty in obtaining a lodging. There were but few houses standing, and the crowd seeking shelter was immense. At last, packed together in great chambers, the vaulted roofs of which had withstood the fire, we awaited with the greatest impatience the distribution of rations. But the preliminary formalities were so long that night arrived without our having received a morsel. We were thus compelled again to perambulate the streets and, gold in hand, try to find something to eat among the soldiers of the Imperial Guard, who, being more favoured than the rest of the army, had often plenty when we were starving.

This town, therefore, where we had expected to find the end of our misery, most cruelly shattered our fondest hopes, and became, on the contrary, the scene of our deepest humiliation and the acme of our woes. The soldiers, deprived of shelter, camped in the middle of the streets, and some hours afterwards were found dead around the fires they had lighted. The hospitals, the churches and other buildings could no longer hold the sick, who could be counted by thousands. These unfortunates, exposed to all the rigours of a freezing night, rested in the carts and ammunition waggons, or died vainly seeking for refuge. To sum up, we had been led to expect everything in Smolensk, and yet no provision had been made for our sustenance; nothing had been prepared to relieve an army which had to depend entirely on this town for its salvation.

From that moment, despair filled every heart, and each man thinking of nothing but his own existence, forgot honour and duty, or rather, did not consider honour and duty to consist in obeying the orders of a callous leader who did not think it necessary to trouble himself about those who had sacrificed their lives for his sake. Men were to be seen, formerly the gayest of the gay and the bravest of the brave, who had totally lost their nerve, and now dreamt of nothing but disasters and catastrophes. [1] We had now only one thought—our country, and only one prospect—death. By a gloomy foreboding, each man, full of terror at his impending fate, spoke tremblingly and with an air of deep mystery of the armies from whom we might expect deliverance. "Where is Marshal Gouvion Saint-Cyr?" they asked in whispers.

"He attempted to defend the Dwina, but has been forced to abandon Polotsk and to fall back on Lepel," was the gloomy reply.

"And the Duke of Belluno? He has not been able to reach the Oula. And the Russian Army of Volhynia? It has driven Prince Schwartzenberg behind the Bug, is marching on Minsk, and advancing against

---

1. Much has been said about twenty thousand waggons intended for the transport of biscuits and flour, drawn by forty thousand bullocks, but I can affirm that very few of these arrived at Smolensk. The bullocks which got that far, owing to fatigue and bad food, contracted diseases which rendered their flesh so poisonous that the army doctors forbade its consumption.

us."

Ah! if this news is true, repeated each to himself, our position becomes frightful, and we can only expect that on the banks of the Dnieper or the Berezina a great battle will complete our destruction.

What fresh thoughts of gloom came to torment our harassed souls, when a vague and terrifying rumour began to circulate that a great agitation had sprung up in France; that the towns of Nantes and Caen had risen, and that Paris, which for nearly twenty years had decided the fate of Europe, was also in a state of effervescence, which boded ill for our beloved fatherland. We learnt that the men who were known as the partisans of popular government had conceived the project of disseminating false news of Napoleon's death, and the complete destruction of his army, so as to profit by the grief and consternation with which this falsehood would overwhelm the existing authorities, and persuade them that all was lost. If this plot had been concocted by responsible men anxious to distinguish themselves as saviours of their country, and to deliver it from an intolerable yoke to save it from the shame of being emancipated by the foreigner, the scheme would unquestionably have been heroic.

But instead of so noble an enterprise, we learnt that the conspirators had no other object in view than to rescue us from despotism in order to plunge us once more into the horrors of anarchy. Far from approving of this attempt, we desired that our country should be saved from the fury of parties; for the perfidious policy of our oppressor had been so contrived that the welfare of a whole people was dependent upon him alone. By his monstrous Machiavellism he plunged France into war with the whole human race, so that the salvation of the nation might depend on the preservation of his person.

CHAPTER 26

The Fourth Corps Leaves Smolensk

We were littered about on beds of dirty straw, and plunged in the gloomiest reflections, when suddenly we were startled by shouts of "Get up, get up, they are looting the food stores!" We promptly sprang from our miserable beds, and hastily throwing on our clothes, seized whatever receptacles came first to hand—a sack, a basket or a bottle, and there were cries of "I am going for flour; you go for brandy; let the servants run for meat, biscuits and vegetables." In an instant the room was almost empty, every one rushing off helter-skelter for anything he could get hold of. Some time after, our friends began to return, and told us that the soldiers, dying of hunger, and not being able longer to endure the dilatoriness of the distributions, had overpowered the guards, and broken in the doors of the magazines to loot them.

Those who first came back were as white as millers, and some had their clothes pierced with bayonet thrusts, having had a tussle with the sentries over a sack of flour. The rest returned half dead with fatigue, and deposited on the table a large basket full of biscuits, an enormous round of beef, and other comestibles. An hour later the servants arrived, bringing rice, peas and brandy. At the sight of such plenty, our hearts expanded; some indulged in laughter while kneading the bread, another sang joyously while cooking the meat, but many, resorting to the bottle, passed from the deepest melancholy to extravagant mirth.

Although the weather was superb, the air was so sharp that one got frozen while passing through the streets. At almost every step many dead bodies were encountered, stretched upon the snow, having succumbed to the cold while hunting for shelter. These terrible disasters, and particularly our sojourn in Smolensk, prompt me to refer more especially to the sad fate of the Italian Guard of Honour, which by this time had been annihilated.

It was composed of young men, selected from among the first families of the kingdom of Italy. Their parents had to guarantee them an allowance of twelve hundred *francs* a year as a condition of their joining the corps, the admittance to which was considered a very high distinction. Among these young fellows were often found men of great talents and ample fortunes; several being the only sons of illustrious houses. To these advantages were added great culture and all the qualities essential to the making of first-class soldiers. It was, in fact, the school from which issued the best officers of the Italian army. They acquired a consummate knowledge of military affairs by submitting to the rules and regulations of their corps, for although on joining each had the honorary rank of sub-lieutenant, they had nevertheless to serve as private soldiers.

This Guard, after having greatly distinguished itself on all occasions, was conspicuous by its smart appearance and its rigid discipline, but it had suffered more than any other corps from the terrible privations we had undergone; not at all a surprising matter, seeing that the Guards of Honour, being unskilled in the shoeing of horses and the repairing of their clothes and boots, were the first to feel the hardships which befell us, when the artificers and servants attached to their regiment had been lost. No longer possessing horses, and having to wear the heaviest and clumsiest boots, they were unable to endure the fatigue of our perpetual marches.

Mixed up with the stragglers, they remained in the rear without food or shelter; so that these sons of good family, born in a happier lot, perished even more miserably than the ordinary run of our soldiers, as their sense of honour prevented them from descending to acts of baseness to supply their wants. Some were to be seen enveloped in fragments of half-burnt cloaks; others mounted upon wretched little native ponies, when they dropped from sheer fatigue and want, never rose again. Out of a total of three hundred and fifty, all except eight perished miserably.

The night had been perfectly quiet, but next day (14th November) we heard cannon firing at intervals of about five minutes. The viceroy, convinced that it was a signal of distress from General Broussier, at once mounted and, accompanied by his aides-de-camp and orderlies, rode towards the position, and on arriving at the hill of Smolensk, placed himself at the head of the Italian Guard. The cold was so intense that thirty-two grenadiers fell frost-bitten in attempting to get into line. General Broussier, who since daybreak had been engaged with the Russians, was forced to evacuate the village where he was entrenched. In his retreat the division slaughtered the enemy's posts which they encountered on their march, and by sheer pluck succeeded in reaching the viceroy, who was advancing to their support.

The prince, however, being extremely anxious to get the remnants of our forces into Smolensk, ordered the second brigade to drive away a Russian battery that was firing on the bridge over which the vehicles had to pass. General Heyligers at once brought two guns and a mortar into position, while about fifty men clambered up the hill to turn the enemy's field artillery; but on seeing this movement it made off at a gallop. Our convoys issued from the defile, cleared the bridge, and continued their route under the very eyes of the Cossacks, who appeared rather to be escorting our baggage train than trying to capture it.

14th November.—The emperor, who was at Smolensk when we arrived there, daily received news of fresh disasters to his armies. That which affected him most was the forced retreat of Count Baraguay d'Hilliers, who had been sent with General Augereau towards Elnia to check Count Orloff Denisoff, who was advancing with fresh troops. Although General Augereau was entrenched, he could not, with only three thousand men, hold out for more than an hour against five thousand cavalry. Baraguay d'Hilliers, who was three leagues in his rear, fearing also to be enveloped, was compelled to fall back upon Smolensk, bringing with him the guns and the convoys. [1]

Out of his wits to know what to do in these terrible circumstances, Napoleon convened a Council of War, in which all the chiefs of corps and marshals of the Empire took part. Immediately afterwards he gave orders to burn a portion of our equipment, and then left in a carriage, accompanied by some *chasseurs* and Polish lancers of the Guard. At the close of the council a report became current that we were to leave next day with the first corps, and that the third would leave last, in order to blow up the fortifications of the town and to form our rear-guard. The same day the viceroy was closeted with General Guil-

---

1 The results of this unfortunate campaign, and all the evils which it produced, have been ascribed to General Baraguay d'Hilliers; but it is easy to understand that a few weak battalions could not possibly hold back an entire army. Besides which, every fair-minded man can see clearly enough that Napoleon, embittered by defeat, only sought by this accusation to ascribe his own follies and blunders to a general of known capacity, whose soul was so pure and noble that this base calumny killed him.

leminot for a long time, and we awaited the result of their conferences with great anxiety.

15th November.—Today the order was at last given to continue our march, but we started late owing to the delay caused by the distribution of all the stores which the depots contained. The greater part of our women were left in Smolensk, a most dreadful position for them, as these poor creatures knew well enough that the remains of the city were to be destroyed, the houses given to the flames, and the churches and fortifications blown up. This would have been done had it not been prevented by the sudden arrival of the Hetman Platow, who entered the town a few hours after we left.

When we marched out of Smolensk we beheld a sight which filled us with humiliation. Under the ramparts, once the witnesses of our triumph, was collected an immense number of guns which had to be left to the enemy. From this point up to the poverty-stricken village of Loubna, a distance of about three leagues, the road was completely covered with guns and ammunition waggons, which there had been no time to spike or blow up. Dying horses covered the road, more than thirty thousand being dead in a few days. All the defiles through which the vehicles could not pass were choked with weapons, helmets, shakos and *cuirasses*. Trunks broken open, valises torn asunder, and clothes of all kinds were scattered along the valley. From time to time we saw trees, at the foot of which soldiers had tried to light fires, but these poor fellows had fallen dead while attempting to procure the means to warm their freezing bodies. They could be seen by the dozen, lying near green boughs which they had vainly endeavoured to ignite, and the multitude of corpses would have blocked our road had they not frequently been used to enable us to get across ditches and ruts.

Such horrors, far from arousing our emotions, only hardened our hearts. Our cruelty no longer being able to vent itself on the enemy, we directed it against each other. The closest friendships were broken; whoever showed the least sign of illness, if he were not lucky enough to be well mounted and to have about him faithful servants, was absolutely certain never to see his native country more. The greater number much preferred to save the loot of Moscow than their own comrades. On all hands were heard the groans of the dying and the dreadful lamentations of those who were being left behind; but every ear was deaf to their cries, and if anyone approached those who were on the point of death it was only for the sake of plunder, or to discover if they still possessed a morsel of food.

At Loubna, we could only save from destruction two miserable hovels, one for the viceroy, and the other for his staff. Hardly had we established ourselves, when we heard a heavy cannonade in our front. As the sound seemed to be to the right of our position we concluded that it proceeded from the ninth corps, which, unable to hold its own against Wittgenstein, had been compelled to retreat. Those, however, who were better informed had no doubt that the emperor and his Guard had been attacked before arriving at Krasnoë by Milloradow-itch and Orloff Denisoff, who, having come up from Elnia, had closed the road to our army while we remained in Smolensk.

The scene presented by our bivouac was deplorable and gloomy in the extreme. Under the remnants of a shed, about twenty officers and as many servants were huddled round a small fire. Behind were all the horses littered in a semi–circle, to shelter us against the violence of the wind. The smoke was so dense that one could hardly see the figures crouching round the fire and blowing the embers upon which pieces of meat were being grilled. The rest, enveloped in pelisses or mantles, lay on their stomachs, huddled close together for the sake of warmth, and never moving except to curse any one walking over them, damn the horses for kicking, or extinguish the sparks which the fire shot out on to their *pelisses*.

CHAPTER 27

Napoleon's Danger and Ill-Temper

Before daybreak (16th November) we resumed our march, littering the road with our enormous *débris*. The horses could no longer haul, obliging us to abandon our guns at the foot of the smallest hill; and the only duty remaining to the artillerymen—and a sad one too—was to shake the powder out of the cartridges and spike the guns to prevent them being turned against us. We were thus reduced to the most cruel extremity, when two hours before reaching Krasnoë, Generals Poitevin and Guyon, who were in advance, saw a Russian officer coming towards them, followed by a trumpeter who sounded a parley. Surprised at such an unexpected apparition, General Guyon stopped, and allowing the officer to approach, asked him whence he came and what was the object of his mission. "I come," he replied, "from General Milloradivitch to inform you that yesterday we beat Napoleon with the Imperial Guard, and that today the viceroy is surrounded by an army of twenty thousand men; he cannot possibly escape, and if he will surrender, we will offer him honourable terms."

At those words General Guyon sternly rejoined: "Return immediately to those who sent you and inform them that if you have twenty thousand men, we have here eighty thousand."

These words, uttered with an air of the most entire assurance, so completely silenced the envoy that he promptly returned to the camp whence he had come. Just after this interview the viceroy arrived, and heard of it with mingled astonishment and indignation. Although his corps was practically destroyed, and he knew about the affair of the previous evening between Kutusoff and the Imperial Guard, the glorious way in which the latter had extricated itself inspired him with the hope of cutting his way through the enemy to rejoin it; and he was resolved, in any case, to die with honour rather than accept terms which would have left a blot upon his reputation. He at once ordered the remains of the fourteenth division to face the enemy, taking with them the only two guns which we still had left.

The viceroy then took General Guilleminot apart, and conversed with him for some time, and the conclusion they arrived at was that we must press on at all costs. Meanwhile our troops continued to advance, the Russians withdrawing before us as far as the foot of the plateau on which they were encamped. There they unmasked their guns (mounted on sledges to enable them to be moved with rapidity) and pounded our squares, while their cavalry, having descended from the heights, prepared to charge. The veterans of the 35th, although worn out with fatigue, hardly able to stand, and nearly all wounded, received the enemy with French valour, and their heroism can only be fully appreciated by those who grasp the desperate situation we were in.

Through the fire of the enemy General Ornano advanced with the rest of the thirteenth division to support the troops of the fourteenth, who were very hard pressed, when a cannon-ball passed so close to him that it threw him from his horse; he was thought to be dead, and the soldiers went up to plunder him, when it was found that he had only been stunned by the violence of his fall. The prince then sent an orderly, Colonel Delfanti, to reanimate the troops. This brave officer, throwing himself into their midst through a hail of grapeshot, encouraged them both by voice and example; but two dangerous wounds compelled him to quit the field. A surgeon having given him first aid, he left the battle with much difficulty, and on his way was met by Monsieur de Villeblanche, who, as auditor to the Council of State, should have left Smolensk with General Charpentier, the governor. Unfortunately for him, however, he asked and obtained from the viceroy permission to accompany him.

This young gentleman perceived the wounded Colonel Delfanti, supported by an officer, and moved solely by sympathy, offered him his arm. All three were slowly leaving the field when a cannon-ball struck the colonel between the shoulders and took off de Villeblanche's head. The two hundred men, who had been brought by Colonel Delfanti, advanced to support the square of the 35th, which was commanded by General Heyligers, but deprived of their leader, they placed themselves partly in front and partly behind the square. The enemy's cavalry, profiting by this confusion, renewed their charge, slaughtered the soldiers, and captured the last two guns, which had only fired a few shots for want of ammunition. General Heyligers was attempting to rally his feeble remnant, when he received three sabre cuts on the head, and when two Russian *chasseurs* were on the point of running him through with their bayonets, a cavalry man, who recognised him as a general, seized him by the collar and took him prisoner.

A large number of distinguished officers fell during this bloody day. The guns continued their heavy fire and carried death and destruction everywhere; the battlefield was covered with the dead and dying, and many of the wounded, throwing away their arms, swelled the numbers of the stragglers. The same discharges which had torn the front ranks, carried death into the rear of the army, where many dismounted officers were collected. It was there that Captains Bordoni and Mastini fell, two of the small number of the Italian Guard of Honour who yet survived.

The viceroy seeing the determination with which the enemy blocked our passage, feigned, by an adroit movement, to be desirous of prolonging the action on our left by rallying and reanimating the fourteenth division; and while the Russians concentrated the majority of their forces on that point, so as to surround the division, the prince ordered all who still survived to move off to the right and join the Royal Guard, which had not been engaged. During this movement Colonel Kliski gave a remarkable example of presence of mind. He was familiar with Russian, and was riding in advance of our column, when he was seized by one of the enemy's vedettes, who called out in Russian, "*Qui vive?*" The intrepid officer, not at all disturbed by so annoying a *rencontre*, advanced towards his challenger, and said to him in his own language, "Shut up, you fool; don't you see that we belong to the corps of Ouwarow, and that we are on a secret expedition?" To this the soldier made no reply, and allowed us to pass in the darkness without another word.

We had all managed to elude the vigilance of the Russians except the fifteenth division which, under the command of General Triaire, was left as rear-guard, with orders to march as soon as the prince had completed his manoeuvre. We were just about to pass before the enemy when the night, instead of affording us a welcome obscurity, was suddenly illuminated by the most brilliant moonlight. The snow rendered our march all the more visible, and it was not without great anxiety that we saw ourselves flanked by clouds of Cossacks who, approaching unpleasantly close to us as if to reconnoitre, returned immediately to the squadrons from which they had been detached. Several times we believed we were about to be charged, but General

Triaire, by halting his column, imposed sufficiently on the enemy to deter him from attacking us. At last, in spite of the ravines and the snowdrifts that obstructed its march, this division succeeded in regaining the high road. An hour afterwards we effected our junction with the Young Guard, which was encamped on this side of the river, at a short distance from Krasnoë. The emperor was there, and that fact went far to dissipate our fears.

In describing to the soldiers of the Guard the action we had fought, they told us that they, too, had had to cut their way through the enemy, and that the fusiliers, under General Rouget, had carried at the point of the bayonet a village where the enemy had concentrated to bar the passage. In this fight Napoleon had been exposed to great danger, and had only escaped through the valour of his troops. In this connection it is stated that the band of the Guard, having rejoined him after a prolonged separation, struck up the air of "Home, Sweet Home!"[1] But as in the midst of icebound deserts this ditty was capable of a double meaning, Napoleon took it in very bad part, and growled out to the musicians, "You would do better to play 'Let us watch over the safety of the Empire.'"

The emperor's staff, his Guard, his cavalry and the fourth corps being all assembled together in this small town, choked it up to such a pitch that there was hardly room to move about the streets. They were filled with soldiers lying around their fires, which they could only make by demolishing the wooden houses, and burning the doors and window-sashes of such as were built of stone. The viceroy was well received by the emperor, in spite of his bad temper over his unaccustomed humiliations, and he approved particularly of the stratagem by which the enemy had been circumvented. Their conference lasted all through the night, and meanwhile the prince's suite camped in the streets until Napoleon and he appeared, and placing themselves at the head of the Guard, marched upon the position occupied by the Russians, in order to extricate the first, third and fifth corps, which formed the rear-guard, and were in the same fix that we had been in on the previous evening.

A fresh action now took place, and it was obstinate and bloody. Only by bravery combined with ability could the Prince of Eckmühl succeed in saving the troops under his command. The Duke of Elchingen who remained to the last, found himself opposed by such superior

---

1 At all events that appears to be the best rendering of the French title, "*Où peut-on être mieux qu'au sein de sa famille?*"

forces that he was unable to rejoin us. Hoping against hope, the emperor was reluctant to quit Krasnoë, but the enemy getting round to our rear compelled us to evacuate the position. We frequently paused to listen for the sound of firing which might herald the arrival of our rear-guard. We listened, however, in vain, and at last had to depart, sad at being unable to relieve a Marshal of France who, far from accepting the offers of the enemy, threw himself across the Dnieper with the remnant of his troops, fighting incessantly. The Russians, on their side, found it impossible to believe in the success of such audacity, and redoubled their efforts to compel him to surrender.

Such overwhelming disasters, however, far from detracting from our fame, increased it. Kutusoff and Milloradowitch, less astonished at the immense wreckage we left behind us than at our indomitable pluck and perseverance, admitted to our captured officers that they only owed their success to the elements, and loudly eulogised our generals, who, reduced to the most cruel extremity, returned a dignified refusal to every summons to surrender.

Twenty-five guns and several thousand prisoners were the fruits obtained by the Russians from four successive actions, in which all we had to oppose to an entire army was a miserable remnant of exhausted troops, harassed by unparalleled marches, and for two months almost without food, ammunition and artillery.

The Russians have divided our retreat into three principal epochs, which have each a separate character, besides recording the progress of our disasters. The first ends with the action of Krasnoë; the second with the passage of the Berezina, and the third with that of the Niemen. From this record it will be found that up to the close of the first epoch, the period at which we have now arrived, we had lost thirty thousand prisoners, twenty-seven generals, five hundred guns, and in addition to our immense train of baggage, all the plunder of Moscow which we had not burnt. If to these be added the forty thousand men dead of cold or hunger or killed in battle, it will be found that our army was reduced to thirty thousand men, out of whom, including the Imperial Guard, there were not more than eight thousand effective. The twenty-five guns which the Guard had saved were not worth counting, as it was a matter of certainty that they would have to be abandoned. As to the cavalry, it had almost ceased to exist. Such is the exact tale of the losses which we had sustained during one month's march! It filled us with gloomy forebodings, for we were scarcely half-way to the Niemen, with three rivers to cross.

CHAPTER 28

Napoleon Harangues His Guard

The terrible disasters which had befallen us between Moscow and Krasnoë seemed to justify the hope that we had seen the worst, and that the future had better things in store for us. This appeared all the more probable as Jomini held the strong position of Orcha, which should enable us to cross the Dnieper without opposition, and thus effect our junction with the corps of Dembrowski and the Dukes of Reggio and Belluno. Moreover, we were now approaching the line within which were our magazines, and were about to enter an inhabited country, which we looked upon as belonging to our ally; added to which, Prince Kutusoff, with a view to concerting his plan of attack with the army of Moldavia, which was about to join him, abandoned the pursuit and restricting himself to harassing us with Cossacks, reserved his final *coup* for the banks of the Berezina.

All these flattering hopes were, however, speedily dissipated when we learnt that Admiral Tschikagow, coming from the Danube, had repulsed the troops opposed to him and had driven them nearly as far as Warsaw; that the Austrians, retiring behind the Bug, had abandoned the important position of Minsk, where all our *dépôts* were situated, with an immense quantity of provisions; and finally, that the admiral was marching on Borisow to intercept our passage of the Berezina, and there to effect his junction with the corps of Wittgenstein and Stengel. As a matter of fact, these two generals, ever since the fatal battle of Polotsk (18th October), being no longer held in check by our second and sixth corps, had marched, the first towards Tschachniki to get into communication with the army of Moldavia, and the other upon Veleika to cut off the Bavarians. The union of all these corps meant the complete ruin of the French Army, and it was to avert this frightful danger that Napoleon was advancing by forced marches to the Berezina.

17th November.—As soon as the Prince of Eckmühl had effected his junction with us, and the Duke of Elchingen had thrown himself to the other side of the Dnieper, we put ourselves in motion at about eleven in the morning to proceed to Liadoui. While we were at Krasnoë, the Cossacks surrounded the town, and formed in column, followed us all along the road. We made a feint to attack them so as to give the baggage and the convoy of wounded time to get away. The Russians, however, refused the engagement, having observed that the rest of our force had halted, and was in great disorder, owing to the difficulty experienced by the horses in getting through the valley, which separated the town from the plateau. They fell, accordingly, upon a section of the vehicles, and captured them without resistance; amongst others taken being the waggon of the general staff, containing the records of correspondence and all the plans, maps and memoranda relative to the campaign.

As the enemy continually advanced, subjecting us to a galling cannonade, the emperor placed himself in the centre of a square of the Guard, and posted the cavalry on his wings, while the remnants of the first corps, with the *voltigeurs* and the fusiliers, under the Duke of Treviso, formed our rear-guard. Napoleon could not bring himself to abandon the Duke of Elchingen, and therefore ordered frequent halts, each of which resulted in a sanguinary struggle with the enemy.

We entered Liadoui towards nightfall. Above the little river which had to be crossed before reaching the town, there is a very elevated plateau, the slopes of which were so slippery that we had to slide down them. Liadoui presented an unaccustomed sight—there were inhabitants to be seen. Although they were all Jews, we forgot the dirtiness of that sordid nation, and succeeded in buying from them a few necessaries in a town which at first sight appeared absolutely ruined; so that the very cupidity for which we hold them in contempt was exceedingly lucky for us, as it prompted them to run any risk to drive a good bargain.

Liadoui being in Lithuania, we imagined that it would be spared, as belonging to the ancient kingdom of Poland. Next day (18th November) we left while it was still dark, and to our great surprise found ourselves lighted on our way as usual by the burning houses. This particular destruction resulted in one of the most horrible scenes of our whole retreat, and I would recoil from describing it if the recital did not serve to render more hateful the devilish ambition to which this barbarous expedition was due.

Among the houses that were in flames, there were three large barns full of soldiers, mostly wounded. It was impossible to issue from the last two of these without passing through the first, which was in a blaze. The nimblest saved themselves by leaping out of the window, but those who were ill or crippled, saw the flames advancing to consume them, without being able to move. At the shrieks uttered by these poor wretches some of the less callous among the soldiers tried to save them. But their efforts were in vain, and soon nothing could be seen but bodies half buried under burning joists. Through the clouds of smoke, they implored their comrades to put them out of their agony, and it was considered true humanity to do so. Those who still lived screamed, "For God's sake, shoot us—through the head, through the head. Shoot straight!" and these heart-rending cries continued until an appalling death put an end to them.

By this time the cavalry was entirely dismounted, and Napoleon requiring an escort, united at Liadoui all the officers who still possessed horses in order to form four companies of a hundred and fifty men each. Generals Defrance, Saint-Germain, Sebastiani and others acted as captains, colonels and subalterns. This squadron, to which was given the name of "sacred," was commanded by General Grouchy, under the direction of the King of Naples. It was a fundamental law of its organisation that it was never to lose sight of the emperor; but its horses, which had hitherto survived only because they had been better looked after than those of the rank and file, soon perished when exposed to the rough work of the campaign, so that at the end of a few days the "Sacred Squadron" had ceased to exist.

The enemy continued to follow us at a distance of some two to three musket-shots, while the remnants of our army, having no longer the means of defence, marched in extreme disorder, continually harassed by the Cossacks, who in every defile fell upon the rear of our column, and captured the baggage, obliging us to abandon the guns which the horses could no longer haul. Up to this time Napoleon had travelled in a comfortable weather-proof *calèche*, filled with furs, and he wore a pelisse and cap of sables, which prevented him from feeling even the most extreme cold. After passing Krasnoë, however, he often marched on foot, followed by his staff, and beheld without the least emotion the miserable wreckage of a once powerful army. And yet in spite of all that had happened, his presence never excited the slightest murmur. On the contrary, it seemed to infuse courage, even into the hearts of cowards, who always appeared reassured when the emperor was by.

Nevertheless, we were rapidly nearing the lowest depths of misery, and "Bread! Bread" was the only cry of the feeble remnant of the most formidable army that ever existed. The employees of the various administrative departments were much to be pitied, especially the commissaries and store-keepers, a class little accustomed to endure privations. But even those were less worthy of commiseration than the doctors, and particularly the surgeons, who, without the slightest hope of promotion, were exposed to the same dangers of battle as the soldiers whom they tended on the field. While I was in Doubrowna I happened to be near a house which a great crowd of soldiers were trying to enter, under the belief that provisions were being sold there. My attention was caught by a young surgeon, who appeared to be in an extreme state of depression and who with a disordered look was trying to enter this dwelling. Seeing that he was continually being kept back by the crowd and that he showed unmistakable signs of acute despair, I ventured to ask him the cause.

"Ah, Captain," said he, "I am a ruined man. Having had nothing to eat for two days, I heard on arriving here that bread was being sold at this house. On giving six *francs* to the sentry he permitted me to enter, but as the bread was still in the oven, the Jew who was in charge of it refused to promise me any unless I paid him a *louis* in advance. I gave it him, and now when I have returned, I find the sentry changed and am brutally kept from entering. Ah, sir! I am the most unlucky wretch on earth. I have spent the whole of the money I had left for nothing, and have not tasted bread for more than two months."

The day on which we arrived at Doubrowna, Napoleon, as was now his custom, marched a great part of the way on foot. As the enemy did not attack us, he had ample opportunity of observing the deplorable condition of his army, and how little he could rely upon the reports of the leaders who, knowing what danger they ran if they told him the truth, concealed it from him, to avoid being ignominiously dismissed. He seemed to think that his discourses partook of the nature of magic, and that by bullying the officers and cracking the lowest jokes with the men, he could inspire the former with fear and the latter with courage. But the day had passed when his slightest word worked miracles; his iron despotism had destroyed the illusion, and having by his own example stifled in our hearts every generous sentiment, his appeals had entirely lost their force.

But what must have disquieted Napoleon most of all was the fact that his Guard was infected with the general discouragement. With an impassive countenance concealing the agitation of his heart, he assembled a part of these veterans before leaving Doubrowna, and placing himself in their midst, impressed on them the absolute necessity of maintaining discipline, adding that they were the pride of his armies and had been the means of obtaining his greatest victories. These fine sentiments were, however, somewhat out of place at this juncture; and it was brought home to this man, who aspired to heroism in contempt of morality, that no true glory can be achieved by schemes, however vast, which are not directed to laudable ends, and carried out in accordance with the laws of humanity and justice.

CHAPTER 29

Ney's Heroism

Half an hour after quitting Doubrowna (19th November), we traversed a very wide and deep ravine, through the middle of which ran a river, the opposite bank of which completely dominated the one by which we had arrived. On seeing this important position, we thanked Heaven that the Russians had not occupied it to stop our passage, especially as this showed that they were not in possession of the town of Orcha. As a matter of fact, a picked body of *gendarmerie*, recently arrived from France, had maintained themselves there, and we struck the Dnieper towards two in the afternoon without having been molested even by Cossacks; a rare stroke of luck, for in our present state of disorder it would have been quite impossible to have forced these two terrible positions.

Two bridges had been constructed over this great river, and the *gendarmerie* were guarding them. As everyone wanted to be the first to cross, the crowd was enormous, but happily no fatalities occurred. Napoleon arrived at Orcha shortly after us, and the wooden houses of which the town consisted were at once occupied by the general staff, and a swarm of soldiers. As usual, the Jews at first supplied us with a few necessaries, but the number of buyers was so great that the stock was soon exhausted.

The further I examined the position of Orcha the less could I understand why the enemy had not attempted to occupy it. This town, situated on the right bank of the Dnieper, which is considerably higher than the left, is protected by projecting bluffs, which form what are to all intents and purposes natural bastions. Below them flows the river, which is here about twelve hundred feet broad, and forms an immense moat, which the most formidable army could not cross without exposing itself to total destruction. While we were upon these bluffs we heard the fire of our rearmost skirmishers; and a moment afterwards all who had remained on the other bank rushed across to us, shouting, "The Cossacks! the Cossacks!" The Tartars shortly afterwards appeared, but in such small numbers that a panic of this kind would have excited indignation and contempt had not the fugitives consisted of unfortunate stragglers, entirely without weapons and most of them wounded.

20th November.—Next day we were pretty tranquil, and only heard a few musket-shots, which were fired occasionally at the Cossacks; but as by this time we were quite used to their game of advancing and then bolting at the sight of armed troops, their performances had ceased to interest us. We were thus enabled to enjoy the unaccustomed delight of a day of complete rest; and some provisions which General Jomini, the Governor of Orcha, had reserved for the passage of the army, were all the more welcome, as since leaving Smolensk, we had received no distribution of food, the stores at Krasnoë having been looted by the Cossacks before our arrival.[1]

The Poles were in such utter ignorance of the deplorable condition into which Napoleon's army had fallen, that a deputation from the province of Mohilow reached Orcha the very day of our arrival to congratulate him on his return. But his actual situation contrasted so painfully with the vainglorious boasting with which he had heralded his march to Moscow, that he could not bring himself to face these deputies. Wishing to save himself the humiliation of such a painful interview, he politely begged to be excused, while assuring them that they might always count upon his protection.

The day had been very quiet; but what was our joy when in the middle of the night we learnt that a great commotion in the town was caused by the arrival of the Duke of Elchingen who, as already stated, had been compelled to abandon the line of retreat that we had followed, and seek another on the other side of the Dnieper. For three days he never ceased fighting the enemy, and displayed on this occasion the most extraordinary courage and capacity. Having to traverse an entirely unknown country, he marched in square, successfully repelling the attacks of six thousand Cossacks, who day after day fell upon him with the object of forcing him to capitulate. This

---

1. I should state that only soldiers present at roll-call were included in the distributions, and they numbered less than a fifth part of the army. Apart from that, in the space of two months only three distributions were made, namely, at Smolensk, Orcha and Kowno.

heroic resistance put the copestone to his already brilliant reputation, and proved that there is more merit in rising superior to the blows of Fortune, than in profiting by her favours.

21st November.—We left Orcha just as it was being set on fire. In climbing the mountain to regain the high road we heard several musket-shots, which came from the soldiers of the first corps, left in the town as a rear-guard, and who were already attacked by the Cossacks. During our sojourn at Orcha, Napoleon foreseeing that he must soon find himself in a still more critical position, exerted himself to the utmost to rally his troops. To the sound of the drum he had it proclaimed by three colonels that stragglers who did not at once rejoin their regiments would be punished with death, and that officers and generals who abandoned their posts would be cashiered. When we reached the high road we saw what little effect had been produced by this measure. Everything was in the most frightful confusion; and the soldiers, without weapons and insufficiently clad, showed their contempt for it by continuing to march in the same disorder as before.

An hour before arriving at Kokhanovo we camped in a poor village where there were two or three hovels left. Kokhanovo itself, where we passed the next day, was absolutely destroyed, with the exception of the posting-house, which the *gendarmes* had occupied. Proceeding, we were traversing a road which the thaw had made into a sea of mud, when we received an order not to proceed as far as Toloczin where the emperor was established, but to stop at a large château about half a league short of it. In order to hoodwink the enemy Napoleon often adopted the expedient of sleeping at an entirely different place from that which had been announced in the morning; and this frequently involved his camping on the road in the middle of squares formed by the Guard. In these bivouacs, cold and want of food so enfeebled the soldiers, that his escort diminished daily to a fearful extent.

The road from Orcha to Toloczin is unquestionably one of the finest in Europe. Running in a straight line, it is flanked by double rows of birch trees, the branches of which were then covered with snow and icicles, and descended gracefully to the earth in a manner suggestive of weeping-willows. But alas! this majestic avenue was for us a *via dolorosa*; nothing was to be heard on all sides but groans and lamentations; some, protesting that they could go no farther, lay down on the road and implored us to convey their papers and money to their families; a little farther on could be seen others clasping their children in a last embrace, or attempting to restore life to the inanimate forms of women who died of hunger and fatigue.

The emperor learnt that the combined armies of Volhynia and Moldavia had taken Minsk (16th November) and were marching towards the bridge of Borisow to bar our passage of the Berezina. It is said that on hearing this fatal news he calmly observed, "It has then been ordained that we are to do nothing but make fools of ourselves in this campaign," an extraordinary observation to make in such critical circumstances. He knew also that the armies of Wittgenstein and Stengel, which had been victorious on the Dwina, were vigorously pressing the second and sixth corps, with the object of gaining Borisow, and effecting a junction with Admiral Tschikagow and Prince Kutusoff. In order to prevent the execution of a plan which would have completed our ruin, Napoleon had ordered General Dembrowski to raise the siege of Bobruisk in order to march on Minsk, which it was of vital importance to us to retain.

But the gross incompetence of the governor of that place resulted in its surrender before succour arrived. Dembrouski then marched on Borisow, where he found the remains of the garrison of Minsk. He established himself in the *tête de pont*, but on the 21st November, after a sanguinary engagement with the divisions of Langeron and Lambert, he found himself compelled to evacuate his position, and retire upon Nemonitsa. The enemy having then passed the Berezina, marched upon Bobr and appeared on our front. The Duke of Reggio, who was at Tschereia, having learnt of the loss of Borisow and the bridge, marched to the assistance of Dembrowski, so as to secure the passage of the river for the army. On the next day (24th November) the Duke of Reggio encountered Lambert's division near Nemonitsa. At four o'clock he attacked and beat it. At the same time General Berkheim, by a charge of the 4th Cuirassiers drove the enemy back across the Berezina, capturing seven hundred prisoners and a large quantity of baggage.

CHAPTER 30

Brutalising Effect of Disasters

The Army of Moldavia, having in its march cut off the great bridge of Borisow, commanded the whole of the right bank of the Berezina, and occupied with four divisions the principal points by which we might attempt to debouch. During the day of the 25th, Napoleon manoeuvred to elude the enemy's vigilance, and succeeded by stratagem in establishing himself in the village of Weselowo, situated on a hill commanding the river which we had to cross. In spite of the opposition of the Russians he there superintended the construction of two bridges, by which the Duke of Reggio passed the sixth division over the river. Attacking the troops which opposed his passage, he defeated and pursued them without a moment's respite up to the *tête de pont* of Borisow. Napoleon by this manoeuvre was able to satisfy himself that the admiral was alone on the right bank, and that Wittgenstein's army had not yet effected its junction with him.

The Duke of Belluno who, since the actions of Smoliani (where he took three thousand prisoners) had held the corps of Wittgenstein in check, having received orders to support the movement of the Duke of Reggio, was followed in his retreat by the Russian army of the Dwina. By this retrograde march he effected a junction with the rest of the army returning from Moscow, but Wittgenstein, instead of continuing the pursuit, manoeuvred to co-operate with Kutusoff, whose advance-guard under Milloradowitch was still five days' march from us. During these operations, which occupied from the 23rd to the 27th November, we marched without molestation. The days were so short that although we made little progress we had to march partly by night, which resulted in many of the soldiers going astray and losing themselves.

The second and the ninth corps, and the Poles under Dembrowski not having been to Moscow, had such an enormous quantity of baggage that from Borisow to Weselowo the road was covered with carriages and ammunition waggons. The reinforcements which they brought us were a very powerful help, but it was alarming to reflect that this mass of men, in the midst of a vast desert would, in the long-run, only redouble our difficulties. However, marching always amidst extreme confusion with the corps of the Duke of Belluno, we found ourselves, two hours later, stopped by such an enormous crowd that there was no longer any possibility of moving. In the midst of this rabble there were a few wretched barns built on the summit of some rising ground, and as the chasseurs of the Guard were encamped around them, we concluded that Napoleon had taken up his quarters there, and that we were close to the banks of the Berezina. It was at this precise spot that Charles XII. passed that river in his march to Moscow.

What an appalling spectacle was this multitude of men, overwhelmed with every kind of misery, crowded together in an icy swamp! That army which only two months since had triumphantly overrun half the surface of the greatest Empire in the world! Our soldiers, pale, dejected, dying of hunger and cold, having nothing to defend them from the rigours of the season but tattered fragments of pelisses, or half-burnt sheepskins, despairingly wandered along the bank of this horrible river. Germans, Poles, Italians, Spaniards, Croats, Portuguese and French, all jumbled together, each lamenting his hard fate in his own language; the officers and even the generals wrapped in filthy and ragged cloaks, mixed up with the soldiers and cursing those who jostled them or defied their authority—all these together produced a confusion and tumult which it is beyond the power of language to describe.

Those who from weariness and ignorance of their danger were indifferent as to passing the river, tried to light fires and seek repose from their fatigues. These bivouacs showed to what a degree brutality could be engendered by excess of suffering. Men could be seen fighting each other for a morsel of bread; if, perishing with cold, a shivering wretch approached one of these fires the soldiers to whom it belonged inhumanly drove him away; and if another, dying of thirst, implored a drop of water from some one carrying a pailful, the refusal was accompanied by a torrent of oaths. It was the commonest thing to hear educated men who had hitherto been bosom friends, quarrelling over a wisp of straw or a piece of horse-flesh which they were cutting up. This campaign was also horrifying in that it entirely changed our natural characters, breeding in us vices to which previously we had been utter strangers. Even those who had formerly been honest, compassionate and generous, became selfish, avaricious; bloodsuckers and depraved.

The pretence which had been made at Borisow of repairing the great bridge, had considerably reduced the number of the enemy's troops opposite Weselowo, especially as Kutusoff, being badly informed of the point at which we would cross the Berezina, had told Tschikagow that we would debouch below Borisow. Napoleon, availing himself of this circumstance, and also of the arrival at Weselowo of the Duke of Belluno, put himself at the head of his Guard at about two in the afternoon, in order to make his way through the immense crowd that was pressing towards the river. The army also passed, although slowly, owing to the frequent necessity of repairing the bridges.

The viceroy, who had been throughout the day with the emperor, told his staff that the troops of the fourth corps would cross the river at eight in the evening. Many, however, could not tear themselves away from the fires they had lighted, arguing that it was just as well to wait until next day, when the bridges would be clearer of people. This vicious argument prevailed with so great a number that only the prince's household and some of the staff officers actually crossed the river at the appointed hour.

In point of fact, only a true sense of the danger of remaining on the left bank could have induced any one to cross to the right. The viceroy and his suite were obliged to encamp on marshy ground, and sought out the most frozen places in order to avoid being engulfed in the bog. The darkness was horrible; the wind, bitter and blowing with violence, drove against our faces great flakes of icy snow. Most of the officers, to avoid being frost-bitten, raced or walked rapidly to and fro, stamping their feet. As the climax of misfortune, firewood was so scarce that a fire could hardly be made for the viceroy, and to obtain some faggots it was necessary to remind the Bavarian soldiers that Prince Eugene had married the daughter of their king!

26th November.—Napoleon having gone towards Zembin, left behind him this immense crowd, which, placed upon the other bank of the Berezina, bore an appalling resemblance to the unhappy shades who, according to the myth, wander on the shores of the Styx, waiting to cross the fatal ferry. The snow fell in huge flakes; the hills and forests only appeared as great white masses looming through the misty atmosphere; nothing could be seen distinctly except the dreadful half-frozen river, rolling its turbulent waters like a great black serpent through the midst of the snow-clad plain.

Although there were two bridges, one for the vehicles and the other for the infantry, the crowd was so great and the approaches were so dangerous, that on reaching the river the multitude got wedged into a mass, unable to move. In spite of these difficulties, however, those on foot managed, by great exertions, to save themselves; but towards eight in the morning the bridge reserved for the vehicles having broken down, the baggage train and artillery advanced towards the other and attempted to force their way across. A frightful struggle immediately took place between the infantry and horsemen. Many perished by mutual slaughter; a greater number still were suffocated towards the entrance to the bridge, and the bodies of men and horses blocked the approaches to such an extent that in order to reach the river it was necessary to climb over the corpses of those who had been crushed. Some there were who still breathed, and who, struggling against the horrors of death, endeavoured to raise themselves by seizing those who were trampling on them. While this appalling struggle was in progress, the multitude which followed, like an angry sea, continually engulfed fresh victims.

CHAPTER 31

Horrible Scenes of Carnage

The Duke of Belluno, who was still on the left bank, took up a position on the heights of Weselowo, with the two divisions of Girard and Daendels to cover the passage, and protect it amidst this frightful confusion, against Wittgenstein's corps, the advance-guard of which had appeared the previous evening. General Partouneaux, after having repulsed the attacks of Platow and Tschikagow, left Borisow at three in the afternoon with the third brigade to oppose the Russians, who were advancing in columns. Informed that he would have to deal with considerable forces, he recalled the first and second brigades which had remained at Borisow, commanded by Generals Blamont and Lecamus. On arriving at Staroi-Borisow, instead of taking the road to Weselowo, he took that of Studentzy. This mistake took the division right into the middle of Wittgenstein's corps. Although it only numbered three thousand men, it attempted to cut its way out, and during the whole evening sustained a combat which lasted more than four hours, and in which Generals Blamont and Delaitre were wounded.

In the midst of the snow and in terrible weather, our troops formed squares, remained on foot throughout the whole night without anything to eat, and refrained even from lighting fires so as not to reveal their position. This dreadful situation lasted until the morrow, when the division found itself completely surrounded by the whole of Wittgenstein's corps, numbering some forty-five thousand men. Despairing then of escape, it surrendered, having no longer more than twelve hundred men, and two weak squadrons of cavalry, to such an extent had the horrors of famine, the severity of the cold, and the fire of the enemy diminished the number of these veterans who, in their misfortunes, proved that French soldiers, even in defeat, know how to cover themselves with glory.

Borisow having been evacuated, the three Russian armies effected their junction, and the same day (28th November) towards eight in the morning, the Duke of Belluno was attacked on the left bank by Wittgenstein, at the same time that the Duke of Reggio was attacked on the right by Tschikagow, who united all his forces and fell upon us at a short distance from the bridges of Weselowo. All that remained to us of effectives thereupon rushed to arms; the fight was beginning with great fury, when the Duke of Reggio, who seemed destined never to win a victory except at the cost of his own blood, was wounded and had to quit the field, leaving the command to the Duke of Elchingen.

That marshal having reanimated his troops, the action against the army of Moldavia was renewed with redoubled ardour. Doumerc's *cuirassiers* delivered a brilliant charge at the moment when Claparède, at the head of the legion of the Vistula, was endeavouring to pierce the enemy's centre. These brave *cuirassiers*, although worn out by fatigue and privations of all sorts, performed prodigies of valour, broke the squares, and took several guns, and three or four thousand prisoners whom we were unable to keep; for in our cruel situation we no longer fought for victory, but solely for our own existence and the honour of our arms.

In spite of the courage of our soldiers and the efforts of our leaders, the union of the Russian armies pressed heavily on the ninth corps, which formed our rear-guard. Already we heard the thunder of cannon, and it dismayed every heart. It gradually drew nearer, and soon we saw on the neighbouring hills the fire of the enemy's batteries. There could no longer be any doubt that the ground occupied by so many thousands of men, either unarmed or sick and wounded, besides women and children, could not possibly become a battlefield.

The position occupied by the Duke of Belluno to oppose the progress of Wittgenstein was not at all favourable; for although its right rested on the river, its left could not be extended far enough to secure the protection of a wood in that direction. In order to link it with that wood a brigade of cavalry was posted in the gap under the command of Count Fournier, who delivered two brilliant charges, which checked Wittgenstein's corps, while a battery of the Guard protected the right of the Duke of Belluno. Even the heroic valour of these troops was obliged to yield, however, to superior numbers, and the ninth corps, overwhelmed by such a concentration of forces, found itself compelled to abandon its position.

During the heat of the combat several of the enemy's cannon-balls passed over the heads of the unfortunate crowd which for three days had been huddled around the bridges across the Berezina; and some shells even burst in their midst. Terror and despair then seized every heart; the instinct of self-preservation became uncontrollable; those women and children who had survived such incredible sufferings seemed only to have been reserved for a more horrible death. Many rushed from their carriages and screamed to be taken to the other side of the river The sick and wounded, propped up against the trunks of trees or supported by crutches, sought in vain for help! In this dire emergency pity was dead in every heart; each thought only of himself.

At last the Russians, continually reinforced by fresh troops, advanced *en masse*, and drove before them the Polish division of General Girard, who up to then had kept them in check. At the sight of the enemy, those who had not yet passed, mixing themselves with the Poles, rushed towards the bridge. The artillery, the baggage train, the cavalry, the infantry—each struggled to get over first. The stronger threw into the water the weaker who impeded their progress, and trampled over the bodies of the sick and wounded. Several hundred men were mangled out of recognition under the wheels of the guns; others, hoping to find safety by swimming, were frozen to death in the river, or perished by trying to cross on pieces of floating ice, which sank from under them. Thousands and thousands of victims, having lost all hope, threw themselves pell-mell into the Berezina, where almost all perished miserably.

Girard's division, by sheer physical force, succeeded in overcoming the obstacles in their way, and by clambering over the mountain of corpses, reached the other side, where the Russians would probably have followed them had not the bridge at that moment been set on fire.

The miserable wretches left upon the Berezina had now an even more horrible fate in front of them. To avoid it, some endeavoured to cross the flaming bridge; but when half-way over drowned themselves to escape being burnt to death. At length the Russians, having possessed themselves of the battlefield, our troops retired, the passage of the river ceased, and to the frightful din succeeded a silence as of death.

On our march to Zembin we reascended the right bank of the Berezina, from which could be distinctly seen all that was passing upon the other side. The cold was excessive, and the whistling of the wind in the distant forests was frightful. At the close of day the darkness was only lit up by the innumerable fires of the enemy along the neighbouring hills. At the foot of these heights we heard the dying groans of our comrades, and no imagination is vivid enough to realise the miseries they endured on this terrible night. The elements appeared to have conspired to add to its horror. Victors and vanquished both suffered, but at all events the Russians had fire and shelter, while we lay without light and without covering.

More than twenty thousand sick and wounded soldiers or servants fell into the enemy's hands. Two hundred guns were abandoned; and all the baggage of the two corps shared the same fate.

CHAPTER 32

Napoleon's Narrow Escape

In the fatal passage of the Berezina we appeared to have reached the nadir of our misfortunes. The reserve corps, which had alone escaped the horrors of the retreat from Moscow, had now been reduced to the same appalling condition as the rest of the army. The cup of bitterness therefore seemed to have been drunk to the dregs, and destiny accomplished. Our leader alone appeared to have been reserved by the Almighty for that most dreadful of punishments, the remorse and despair felt by the wicked at the remembrance of their misdeeds.

But what torture for this conqueror, to lose his conquests even more rapidly than he had achieved them! To find himself crowned not with laurels but with cypress; to have for incense the smoke of burning villages; and to grace his triumph only twenty thousand disarmed soldiers, ragged and unshod; their feet encased in boots made out of old hats, and their shoulders covered with odds and ends of sacks, capes, and even the raw skins of horses. Such were the miserable remnants of four hundred thousand warriors who, had it not been for the unbridled ambition of one man, would have lived to be an honour to France and the dread of her enemies.

29th November.—The continually increasing severity of the winter greatly intensified our disorder and made our losses simply incalculable. The second and ninth corps followed the general example; and at last the rear-guard was reduced to less than three thousand men, of which the Duke of Elchingen took command. We arrived pretty early at the town of Kamen, and were continuing thence towards Plescenkovice, in accordance with our instructions, when Captain Colaud, who had been ahead, returned and told us that Cossacks to the number of two thousand had entered the town with their usual "*Hourra!*" massacring everyone they found in the streets. He added:

> The Duke of Reggio, who had been wounded the previous evening, had just arrived. Fortunately, several officers having offered him their services and expressed their readiness to die at his side, they managed to deceive the Cossacks into the belief that a trap had been laid for them. The Tartars therefore retired to the top of a neighbouring hill, and bombarded the town where the marshal was staying, with a view to forcing him to capitulate. By the strange fatality which seems to dog the footsteps of the Duke of Reggio, one of their shots smashed a beam, and a splinter wounded him while he lay in his bed.

This news determined us to remain in Kamen. Next day (30th November) we left before daybreak, and in passing through Plescenkovice we received confirmation of what we had already heard. On seeing the house in which the Duke of Reggio had lodged, we were astonished that two thousand Cossacks had not had the pluck to take by force a marshal who had had only some twenty wounded officers to guard him. Napoleon stopped in this town, but the viceroy, continuing his march, camped in a deserted village which we believed to be Niestanovitschi, near Zavichino.

1st December.—On the following day, towards seven in the morning, Prince Eugene, followed by a few officers, placed himself at the head of some grenadiers of the Royal Guard, who still remained faithful to their flag. After a march which for worn-out men was very long, we arrived at the town of Iliia. The Jews, who formed the majority of the population, had not fled from their homes, and their greed for gain induced them to unearth the provisions which their first instinct had led them to conceal. We paid them handsomely, for in our situation the vilest stuff was preferable to gold. But for these supplies we should have lost the brave and estimable Colonel Durieu, our chief of the staff, whose health had undergone a terrible alteration, less owing to his sufferings than to the indefatigable zeal with which he devoted himself to his duties.

2nd December.—On the morrow we proceeded to Molodetschino and the march was still longer and more demoralising. For twelve hours, without a single halt, owing to the frightful cold, we had to march through an immense forest. The only comfort we had was the knowledge that the Cossacks would not worry us upon our right.

Captain Jonaud, who had been sent to General de Wrede at Vileika, assured us that the Bavarians, although hard pressed by Stengel's corps, still held that important position.

We were indeed in the most pitiable plight when we arrived at Molodetschino. Fortunately the houses were good, and some of the owners still being there, we were able to procure the means of subsistence. Next morning, Napoleon's carriages started, but had hardly got clear of the village, when a swarm of Cossacks appeared to attack them, and they would have been captured had they not been rushed back into the village and placed under the protection of some still-armed troops. The Viceroy was preparing to leave, when he was informed that we were to stay at Molodetschina, but that he would have to turn out of the *château* where he was lodging to make room for Napoleon.

This rest was all the more welcome as it enabled us to improve the occasion by hunting up some food. In spite of that, however, a considerable number of soldiers expired in the streets, while in the houses where the officers were lodged, things were almost as bad. One poor fellow was so worn out with marching that he protested he could go no farther; another was suffering from frost-bitten feet, and having no horse, was compelled to remain in the hands of the Russians. The generals were exposed to the same dreadful fate, for many of them having lost their servants and carriages could find nothing to replace them, and if in such circumstances they were overtaken by the slightest illness, all hope of saving their lives was at an end.

4th December.—On leaving this village we did not follow the high road which goes direct to Smorghoni *via* Zachkevitschi. We marched to the left of that road (which was anything but safe), and took one which makes a *détour* through Lebioda to Markovo. We halted in this village with a few soldiers of the first corps, while the emperor and his Guard were at Bienitsa, about half a league away. On leaving for Smorghoni (5th December) we marched continually through marshy swamps, which would have been utterly impassable except for the frost; proving how well Nature has protected this country, for had we not experienced the terrible rigours of winter, the bogs of Lithuania would have engulfed us in a common tomb. When we reached Smorghoni, we found none of the supplies we had been led to expect; every house was full of the sick, and most of the Jews had fled. Our only comfort was to find in the stores some barrels of biscuits, the contents of which we promptly devoured.

By this time Napoleon was thoroughly terrified at the extent of our disasters, but what alarmed him far more was the prospect of the loss of his power and prestige in France. He therefore began to turn over in his mind the desirability of deserting the miserable wreckage of his army, so that he might hasten to his obsequious Senate in order to obtain from it another.

Full of this resolution, on arriving at Smorghoni he satisfied himself, in the first place, that the route was open to the Niemen, and then summoned a meeting of the leaders of the various corps. He next had a private consultation with the Viceroy, at the close of which Napoleon issued from his cabinet followed by the Grand Equerry, the Marshal of the Palace, Count Lobau and General Lefèbvre-Désnouettes. In passing through one of the ante-chambers, he met the King of Naples and said to him with much gaiety, "À vous, roi de Naples!" With these words he departed, accompanied by four of his suite, who were to be his fellow-travellers.

Having got into his carriage, he selected the Count de Lobau and General Lefèbvre to remain with him. The Grand Equerry and the Marshal of the Palace entered a second carriage, and both took the road to Wilna. No address to the army, no words of comfort to the Lithuanians, were issued to calm the anxiety of the former at having no longer a leader, and of the latter at seeing themselves deserted by the man who had promised them so much.

The King of Naples took command of the army, but it marched in such disorder and precipitation that it was only at Wilna that the soldiers were informed of a flight as discouraging as it was unexpected. They said one to another:—

What! Is it thus that he forsakes those of whom he used to say he was the father? What has become of the genius who at the height of his prosperity exhorted us to bear our sufferings with patience? Is he, who so freely poured out our blood, afraid to die with us? Is he going to treat us as he treated the army of Egypt, which, after having served him with such devotion, became a matter of indifference to him the moment he was out of the country?

Such were the opinions which passed current among the soldiers, who accompanied them with all the most vigorous epithets our copious language can supply; and verily never was indignation more justifiable, for never had men been more basely betrayed.

CHAPTER 33

General Demoralisation Caused by Napoleon's Flight

The presence of the emperor had kept the leaders of the army up to the mark. Immediately his flight was known, the majority, debauched by his example, threw to the winds all honour and sense of shame, and callously deserted the remains of the regiments confided to them. Up to that time there were to be seen occasional parties of armed soldiers, who, with their officers at their head, marched beneath the flag which they had sworn to defend. But as soon as they found themselves without leaders, and when unheard-of calamities had reduced their numbers to vanishing point, these veterans were reluctantly compelled to hide their eagles in their knapsacks. Several of these brave men when they felt death approaching, knowing that the honour of the French soldier depends on preserving his flag, dug with feeble hands a last resting-place for this hallowed emblem, to preserve it from the desecrating touch of the Russians.

Loison's division, and the Neapolitans who had come from Wilna to secure a passage for Napoleon, had been obliged to encamp in a temperature of twenty-two degrees of frost, and were totally destroyed. Out of six thousand men, there were now only to be seen through the thick fog a few feeble battalions, who ran about like madmen, stamping the iron earth with their feet to ward off the attacks of a cold so frightful that the unfortunate sick, in satisfying the calls of Nature, lost the use of their hands and fell stone dead by the roadside, before they had time to readjust their clothes. Even those who were in good health, although they could by continual marching prolong their sufferings, could always end them at any moment simply by standing still.

On the road we were following could be seen almost at each step gallant officers clothed in rags, leaning heavily on staffs of pine, their hair and beards bristling with icicles. These same warriors, once the terror of our enemies, and the conquerors of two-thirds of Europe, having entirely lost their dignity of demeanour, dragged themselves along with faltering steps, and without obtaining so much as one glance of pity from the soldiers who once obeyed them. The horror of the situation was intensified by the fact that whoever lacked strength to march was abandoned, and to be abandoned meant certain death within an hour. Every bivouac bore the appearance next day of a battlefield. Whenever a soldier succumbed, his nearest comrade pounced on him even before the breath was out of his body, and stripped him of his clothes to wear them himself.

At each moment could be heard one or another of these poor famished wretches appealing for help. "Comrades," would cry one of them in heart-rending tone, "help me to get up; for God's sake lend me a hand to enable me to continue the march." But each passed on without so much as glancing at him. "Ah! I beseech you by all that you hold most dear not to abandon me to the enemy. In the name of humanity give me the trifling aid I require; help me to get up." But those who were passing, far from being touched, looked upon the man as already dead, and anticipating his end, threw themselves upon him to strip him. "Help, help! they are killing me. Why are you trampling on me? Why are you stealing the money and bread I have left? You are even stripping me of my clothes!" And if some officer, less callous than the rest, did not happen to come up in time to rescue him, he was certain to be murdered by his own comrades.

7th December.—We reached Joupranoui a little before nightfall. Utterly worn out, we were compelled to rest there, but the houses open to the sky afforded us no shelter against the fearful cold, and we left very early (8th December), reaching Ochmiana at about eleven. The winter was so terrific that to prevent themselves being frozen to death, the soldiers set complete houses on fire, around which could be seen the half-consumed bodies of those who, having gone too near for the purpose of warming themselves, and being too weak to get away, had become the prey of the flames. There were also to be seen poor wretches blackened with smoke, and stained with the blood of the horses they had been devouring, flitting like spectres around these burning houses. They stared vacantly at the bodies of their companions, and then falling heavily to the ground, perished in the same manner.

We counted on stopping in this town to receive rations, but learnt that the stores had been looted by the Cossacks, and that on the previous evening Napoleon had arrived only half an hour after they had disappeared. We therefore continued our course, still in the most fearful weather; and marching amidst the dead and dying, we at last arrived at the stone-built Château of Rovno-Polé, where the prince and his staff passed a most distressing night. Misfortune having brought everyone down to one common level, attempts to assert authority were treated with contempt. The colonel found himself compelled to beg for a morsel of bread from any of his men who happened to have some. The lowest menial, if he was possessed of food, was immediately surrounded by a crowd of courtiers, who were driven by hunger to resort to the most abject devices to gain his favour.

To realise the frightful disorder to which famine and cold had brought us, imagine the forty thousand men[1] who still remained, marching promiscuously irrespective of rank, without the slightest order or discipline, ignorant as to where they were going, and halting when fatigue or caprice prompted. The leaders, accustomed to command, and unable to forage for themselves, were the worst off. Soldiers avoided them so as to escape having to render them services, for to give any one a glass of water or offer a hand to raise one who had fallen was at that time an event that excited wonder.

The road was covered with soldiers who had lost the form of humanity, and whom the enemy disdained to make prisoners. Each day these poor creatures were actors in scenes which it is harrowing to relate. Some had lost all sense of hearing, others the power of speech, and many, owing to the frightful cold or to hunger, were reduced to such a condition of brutish ferocity as to roast the dead bodies and devour them, or to gnaw off the arms and hands. Some there were so weak that they were unable to carry a log or roll a stone, but sat down upon the corpses of their comrades, and with vacant faces stared into the camp fires; ere long the fire would begin to die out, when those livid corpses, not having strength to rise, would fall dead beside the bodies upon which they had been resting.

Others were to be seen, driven mad by suffering, who to warm

---

1. This number may appear large in view of the enormous losses we were daily suffering. But it must be remembered that Loison's division, the garrison of Wilna, and those of all the towns of Lithuania had joined the *débris* of the army in its retreat.

themselves came and placed their naked feet in the middle of the fire. Some, with a bloodcurdling laugh, threw themselves into the midst of the flames and perished, uttering the most frightful screams, and amidst the most horrible contortions; while others in the same condition of raving madness followed them, and met with the like appalling death.

We were in this state morally and physically, when we arrived at the village of Roukoni, of which there only remained a few miserable hovels filled with corpses. Being now only three leagues from Wilna, many of us continued their march to get first to that town, where they hoped not only to find food, but to remain there for some days and enjoy the sweets of repose, of which we were in such urgent need. The fourth corps, however, of which only a hundred and fifty men now answered to the roll-call, stopped in this miserable village. At daybreak (9th December) all haste was made to get out of Roukoni, where cold and smoke prevented us from getting a wink of sleep. On leaving, the Bavarians under General de Wrede, composing the rear-guard, rejoined us from Wileika, crying that the enemy were at their heels. The previous evening a report had been current that they had had a success, but the confusion in which they arrived emphatically gave the lie to the rumour. Apart from that, however, it is only just to say that they still possessed a few guns, but the horses were so weak that they could no longer draw them.

Each successive day brought a renewal of the dreadful scenes of which I have only been able to give a faint idea. Our hearts grew so callous that these terrible tragedies ceased to affect us, and a brutal selfishness reigned supreme in the state of abasement to which we had been reduced. Our whole thoughts were now centred on Wilna, and the idea that we should there find relief from our awful privations filled all who were able to continue the march with such transports of joy, that they were utterly indifferent to the sad fate of those who felt themselves unable to proceed another step forward. And yet Wilna, the object of our fondest hopes, towards which we hurried with such eagerness, was destined to be for us another Smolensk!

At last we arrived at the outskirts of this longed-for town. But imagine our bitter disappointment when we found the large suburb obstructed by a vast crowd of vehicles, men and horses. The confusion was so terrible that it reminded me of the passage of the Berezina. Our faculties were so dulled by suffering that, accustomed as we were to follow mechanically the column to which we belonged, we dared not separate ourselves from it, for fear of being lost. The consequence of this was that while the multitude were jostling each other in their frantic efforts to get through the same gate, there were other gates to left and right which were available, both for ingress and egress, but which were entirely overlooked. Having at last, after a long and arduous struggle, managed to get into the town, we found it a perfect pandemonium. Soldiers were rushing about in all directions trying to find their appointed quarters.

Those assigned to the fourth corps were at the Convent of St. Raphael, on the opposite side of the Wilia, but before taking up their quarters the starving soldiers ranged through the town in search of food, going from house to house demanding bread. The shops, the inns, and the *cafés* being unable to satisfy the enormous mob of customers, promptly put up their shutters. But goaded by hunger and resolved not to starve to death, we smashed in the doors, while others, money in hand, chased after the Jews, who, in spite of our generosity, found it impossible to meet the full extent of our needs.

At Wilna, we learnt that Napoleon had passed through the town incognito, having for escort only a small detachment of three entire regiments of Neapolitan cavalry, which had been sent on in front of him to assure his escape. These unhappy southerners were half dead when they arrived at Wilna, and hardly had they left the town when about a third of them had to return with their feet, hands and noses frost-bitten. The flight of Napoleon in such circumstances spread consternation among the Lithuanians, who were devoted to us, and greatly discouraged the French.

The former bewailed their cruel fate in finding themselves abandoned to the vengeance of their savage masters, while the latter were alarmed for their own safety, as in our critical situation we looked upon the desertion of our leader as sealing our doom. There were some, however, who, anxious to make the best of things, argued that this occurrence would redound to our advantage. "Napoleon, once in Paris," said they, "will promptly organise another great army, reassure the anxious country, and by fear secure the fidelity of our allies, whose defection would be disastrous."

Towards three in the afternoon, the rear of our long column had only just gained the suburbs, when a report was spread that the Cossacks had taken possession of the heights commanding the town. Immediately afterwards we heard gun-fire, and at this sound the fresh troops in Wilna beat the *générale*, and sounded trumpets. In a moment the place was bristling with arms; but it was a strange irony of fate that the colossal power of Napoleon was now reduced in this iron-bound climate to the remains of one Neapolitan division, composed of the garrisons of Taranto and Capua. These troops having been quickly dispersed, a general panic ensued at the one word "Cossacks," and the majority of the soldiers, demoralised by suffering, rushed from their quarters and took to flight. The King of Naples, throwing his dignity to the winds, bolted from his palace and, followed by his officers, fled on foot through the mob to establish himself outside the town on the road to Kowno.

While some of the men flew to arms, others, when night approached, availed themselves of the evacuation of the stores to carry off every movable they contained; but the majority, only desiring to allay the pangs of hunger, went hammering at every door and carried the terror of universal pillage into the hearts of the wretched inhabitants.

CHAPTER 34

Conclusion

We were now reluctantly driven to the conclusion that it was hopeless to remain in Wilna; and as our feeble remnant could no longer contend with the enemy, it was necessary to take advantage of the darkness of night to get away from so dangerous a position. It was therefore decided to evacuate the town at about eleven o'clock; at which hour we started in absolute silence, leaving the streets covered with drunken, sleeping or dead soldiers. The courts, landings and stairs of the houses were full of them, and not one even condescended to notice the commands of the officers. At last, having got clear of the town with as much difficulty as we had experienced in getting into it, the prince and his staff visited the King of Naples, with whom all the officers remained closeted until one in the morning.

In the midst of a pitch-black night we plodded along the Kowno road, but the snow which covered the country caused us frequently to lose our way, and we were for some time unable to determine our whereabouts; for the Poles in going to New-Troki had trampled out a new road which was very misleading. Two hours afterwards we reached the foot of a small mountain, which was inaccessible, owing to the steepness of the ascent and the sheet of ice with which it was covered. All around were the remains of Napoleon's escort, the baggage, the army chest, and the waggons containing the sinister trophies brought from Moscow. We knew then only too well that we were on the road to Kowno.

We were groping round the base of this mountain without being able to get over it, and all the time heard the fusillade between the Cossacks and the skirmishers of the 29th Chasseurs, who had only just joined the army and who in this critical moment well sustained their reputation. In the spirit of querulous discontent which misfortune

225

always engenders, there were universal grumblings among the men that we had not taken the road by New-Troki, so as to avoid this fatal hill. Those who found themselves stopped by it were for the most part sick or wounded, and were practically delivered into the hands of the enemy. To meet this fate after having come through the terrors of Krasnoë and the Berezina added to the bitterness of their anguish, which deepened to despair when they reflected that the Cossacks had passed Wilna, were pursuing our rear-guard and advancing towards us. Nevertheless, there was no alternative but to remain where we were until daylight, when we could ascertain if there were any way of getting round the mountain instead of over it. We lit a fire and all anxiously awaited the return of day.

It was all in vain, however. We had examined every point, but the ascent was so slippery and the horses so tired that we despaired of proceeding. We then conceived the idea of employing the soldiers of the escort to carry off the money belonging to the Imperial Treasury. As it amounted to about five millions, mostly in crowns, this involved the employment of such an enormous number of men that it was impossible to look after them properly, with the natural result that each man helped himself liberally to the spoil. The standards taken from the enemy, which in our debased condition had ceased to interest us, were perforce left at the foot of the mountain, as was also the famous cross of St. Ivan.

Many who came up later joined in this looting, and it was a most grotesque spectacle to see men dying of hunger weighed down with riches they could hardly carry. There was, however, a general preference for the food found in the carriages over the money they contained. Scattered around in every direction were trunks broken open, portmanteaux half torn asunder, magnificent court dresses and rich furs adorning the persons of the most hideous and repulsive soldiers, who, loaded down with booty, were offering to exchange sixty *francs* for one *louis*. There were some who gave ten crowns for a glass of brandy; and I myself saw one man offer a cask full of money for a few gold pieces.

It is quite impossible to convey an adequate idea of the demoralisation of our army. Far from being braced by the presence of some battalions which had recently arrived from Prussia, the terror with which it was saturated was communicated to the newcomers, who, yielding to the effects of the frightful cold, threw away their arms and joined the crowd of stragglers. Finally, our soldiers, transformed into Cheap-

Jacks, thought only of selling the property stolen along the road, and from morning to night there was one perpetual round of bargaining and bartering. The talk on all sides was of ingots and jewellery; every soldier staggered under a weight of money, but not one had a musket. After that the terror inspired by the Cossacks is not a matter for surprise.

It was in this state of demoralisation that after fifteen hours of a most trying march we arrived at Eve, about ten leagues from Wilna. Great hardships were also suffered by the superior officers. The Prince of Eckmühl prostrated by fever, was obliged to travel in a sledge. Generals Lariboissière, Eblé, Laboussaye and others suffered the most cruel torments. Great anxiety was felt for the fate of several sick officers who had remained in the sledges of the viceroy, but that evening we learnt that they had avoided the Wilna mountain by going via New-Troki, and that only the length of the road had obliged them to halt before arriving at Evé.

11th December.—On leaving that village we heard from those who had last come from Wilna, that the Russians had arrived there at dawn. A crowd of generals, colonels and other officers, and more than twelve thousand of the rank and file, fell into their hands. The officers had been well treated, but all the soldiers and servants were ordered off to Moscow, where it was said they were to be employed in rebuilding the city. These poor wretches, stretched about the streets and public places, without fire and food, and most of them sick or wounded, presented so afflicting a spectacle that the enemy did their utmost to soften their miserable fate. It is sad to think that many who managed to drag themselves from Moscow to Wilna gave up the struggle when only a few leagues more would have brought them to safety. We also learnt that the Jews had basely murdered a large number of our soldiers, particularly those of the Imperial Guard, desiring thus to avenge the ill-treatment they had received. The Emperor Alexander, moved by that sense of justice which distinguished him, had many of these Jews hanged, to teach their people not to interfere in the quarrels of sovereigns.

Our long column plodded wearily on, continually leaving behind it a line of the dead or dying. Its rear continued to be followed by a cloud of Cossacks, who stripped the stragglers and then turned them over to the peasants, who took them to the rear after subjecting them to a thousand ignominies. At last, the Tartars, getting tired of taking prisoners, set free all the soldiers of the Confederation of the Rhine, only keeping officers of distinction. But when they captured a Frenchman, however miserable his condition was, they stripped him, accompanying the operation with the most inhuman jests. If he was still able to march with them up to the evening, they ordered him to fetch wood or water, and then brutally drove him away from the fire which he himself had lighted—an example of the awful fate of the common soldier who, forced into war, is always the victim of the calamities engendered by the quarrels of kings, without deriving one single advantage from them.

Before arriving at Zismori, we heard in our rear the sound of a cannonade, and at no great distance either, which made us suppose that our feeble rear-guard was being relentlessly pursued. In spite of this, however, some of us were so utterly played out that they preferred rest to safety and stopped at Zismori; but the viceroy pressed on to the village of Rounchichki.

12th December.—Worn out with one of the longest and most tiring marches we had yet gone through, we at last arrived at Kowno, where all the fragments of each corps were united. As usual, they camped in the streets, and as it was common knowledge that our deplorable condition would not permit us to remain long in any one place, the stores, which were amply supplied, were given over to pillage. In an instant clothes, flour and rum were looted on all sides. The principal quarters were filled with broken barrels, and the liquor formed a small lake in the centre of the chief square. The soldiers who had for so long been deprived of this luxury, now gave themselves over to excess, and abused the opportunity to such an extent that more than twelve hundred of them got dead drunk, and falling senseless on the snow, rapidly passed from sleep into death.

In the evening we were instructed to take the road to Tilsit, and as many of us, in order to avoid confusion, were in the habit of halting for the night one or two leagues ahead of the general quarters, it followed on this occasion that a large number proceeded towards that town. In the middle of the night the chief of the staff arrived to find the whole of the fourth corps *assembled in one room*. He informed us that the order had been revoked, and that it was to Gumbinnen and not to Tilsit that we must direct our steps. These conflicting instructions completed our ruin; and thenceforth our corps only existed in the household of the prince, and in the persons of eight to ten officers of the staff.

13th December.—On the following day we found the same tumult in the outskirts of Kowno that had prevailed at the gate of Wilna. The crowd was struggling to cross the bridge, while the Niemen was frozen so hard that it would have borne the weight of artillery had we had any. In Kowno and its neighbourhood we saw large numbers of unfortunates stretched out on the snow who had broken down just as they had reached the end of our fatal expedition. Poor Colonel Vidman's death particularly affected us. He was one of the small number of the Italian Guard of Honour who had survived up to then. Feeling unable to go a step farther, he fell while leaving Kowno to reach the bridge, and expired without having had the satisfaction of dying beyond the Russian frontier.

The calamities which had overwhelmed the army had by no means spared the Imperial Guard, and every day several of these soldiers perished, like the others, of hunger, cold or fatigue. I saw one who was indeed worthy of admiration. He was an old grenadier; stretched out on the bridge of Kowno, the passing throng showed marked respect for his uniform, his decoration and particularly for his three stripes. This veteran, with dry eyes calmly awaited death, and disdained to resort like so many others to useless entreaties. By chance, there happened to come up one or two men of his own regiment. He then made a final effort to rise; but the attempt was vain, and feeling death approaching he summoned all his remaining strength, and in faltering accents said to one of these friends:—

> Thine efforts are useless, my friend; the only favour I ask of thee
> is to prevent the enemy from profaning the marks of honour
> which I gained in fighting them. Take to my captain this deco-
> ration which was presented to me on the field of Austerlitz;
> take him also my sabre, which I used at Friedland.

His comrade obeyed him, and taking the sabre and the cross, rejoined the old Guard, of which there were only about three hundred left. They still marched, however, in serried platoons, and preserved even unto death their proud and martial bearing. This soldier, on reentering the ranks, showed with respect the sword and the decoration of the grenadier who had just died.

At last, on the morning of the 13th December, out of the four hundred thousand warriors who at the opening of the campaign had crossed the Niemen near Kowno, scarcely twenty thousand repassed the river, and of these at least two-thirds had never seen the Kremlin. On arriving at the other side of the stream, like shades returned from Hades, we cast terrified glances behind us, and saw with horror the savage countries where we had suffered such woes. We found it difficult to realise that, not many months before, we had looked upon them as a promised land, which we deemed it dishonour to be among the last to enter.

On leaving the bridge we turned to the left for Gumbinnen. Many persisted in conforming to the order of the previous evening, to march to Tilsit, and most of these fell into the hands of the Cossacks. Those who took the proper route had hardly gone more than a few yards when they found themselves confronted with a high and extremely steep mountain, which would have been fatal for our equipages, had we not long since got rid of everything of that sort. But several waggons and carriages which had been in store at Kowno, and particularly a superb park of artillery, recently arrived from Koenigsberg, were abandoned at the foot of the hill.

Hardly had we entered the duchy of Warsaw when all our wreckage dispersed by different roads, and marched like ordinary travellers through the same countries which a few months previously had been covered with innumerable armies. The Duke of Elchingen, who commanded the rear-guard up to the Niemen, lost the few troops that still remained to him. This great captain, who had crossed that river at the head of forty-three thousand men, repassed it alone except for the company of his *aides-de-camp*, and the little party had to defend itself with muskets against the Cossacks. In the evening the King of Naples and Prince Eugene stopped at Skrauda; the same morning (14th December) on which we left that village the Russians entered Kowno, passed the Niemen, which was completely frozen over, and spread themselves over the immense plains of Poland, where their cavalry killed or captured large numbers of stragglers who thought themselves safe, in the belief that the enemy would not come beyond the Niemen.

From Skrauda many went towards Thorn, but the Viceroy continued to follow the road to Gumbinnen, where he arrived on the 17th December. From there he sent his *aide-de-camp*, General Gifflenga, to Koenigsberg, to direct all of the fourth corps who had followed the road to Tilsit, to *rendezvous* at Marienwerder.

Koenigsberg being the first great town on the road we were following, was soon crowded with fugitives from Russia, who hoped to restore within its walls their exhausted energies. The *cafés*, the restaurants and the hotels were utterly inadequate to meet the demands upon their resources. As to the shops, one had to elbow one's way through the crowds to enter them. The cold was terrible, but the delicious sensation of being able to protect oneself against it, and the pleasure of getting whatever one desired were all the more appreciated after six months of dreadful privations and unutterable misery.

The King of Naples went to Koenigsberg, where he was coldly received by the chief authorities of the town. The leaders of each corps went into cantonments along the Vistula, and appointed the towns of Plock, Thorn, Marienburg, Marienwerder and Elbing for their headquarters.

At last, on the 27th December, Prince Eugene arrived at Marienwerder, where he busied himself in collecting all who belonged to the fourth corps. After the most careful inquiries he succeeded in getting together about twelve hundred cripples, the miserable remains of fifty-two thousand men, who had come all the way from Italy to perish in Russia, not from the arms of the enemy, but as victims of the fatal madness of a leader, who, not satisfied with the conquest of the fairest part of Europe, next aspired to vanquish the elements as a preliminary to the invasion of deserts.

Such were the frightful calamities which destroyed a powerful army in attempting the most vainglorious and futile enterprise that history records. In searching the annals of antiquity it will be found that from the age of Cambyses to our own day no army equally great has experienced such frightful reverses. Thus were fulfilled the pompous prophecies uttered by Napoleon at the opening of the campaign, with this difference, that it was not Russia but himself who, drawn on by Fate, was struck down by the inexorable decree of Providence, the results of which are seen in the restoration of the liberties of Europe and the happiness of France.

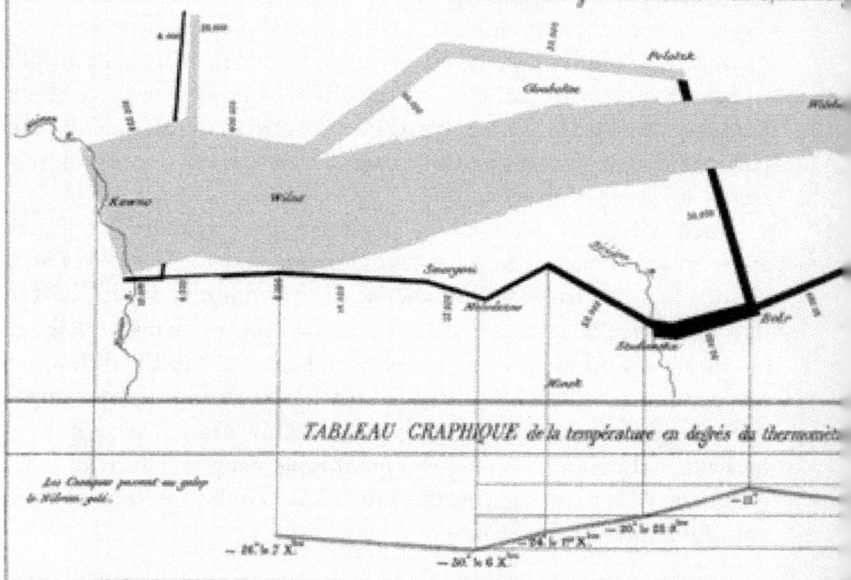

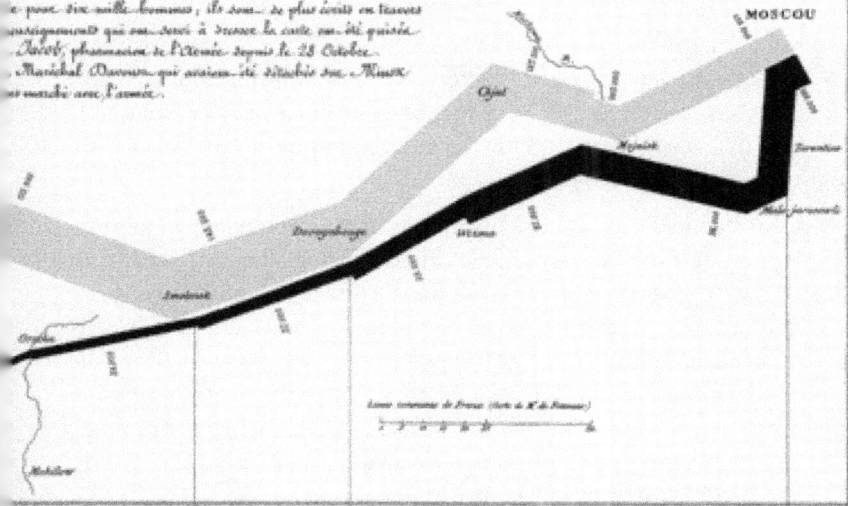

la Campagne de Russie 1812–1813.
transisse en retraite

Paris, le 20 Novembre 1869.

MOSCOU

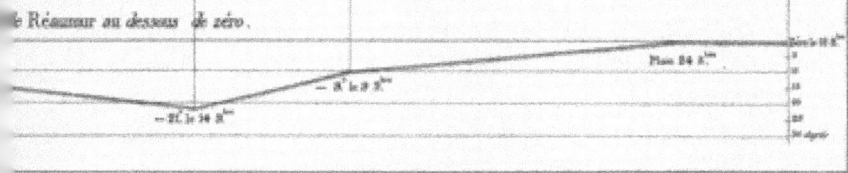

le Réaumur au dessus de zéro.

The Principal Leaders of the Army During the Moscow Campaign

King of Westphalia.—b. Ajaccio, 15th Dec. 1784. Youngest brother of Napoleon, m. 1st, Elizabeth Patterson of Baltimore, U.S.A.; 2nd, Frederica Caroline, daughter of King of Würtemberg. Commenced his career in French Navy. Made King of Westphalia by Napoleon. Fought at Waterloo, d. 24th June 1860.

King of Naples.—Joachim Murat. Son of an innkeeper at Cahors. b. 1771. Intended for Church, but escaped from College of Toulouse and enlisted in *Chasseurs*; dismissed for insubordination. At revolution obtained a commission. With Napoleon in Italy and Egypt. In 1800 married Caroline, sister of Napoleon. In 1804 made Marshal and Prince. In 1808 made King of Naples. Deserted Napoleon after Leipzig. Took up arms for him in Italy; tried by court-martial and shot, 13th Oct. 1815. One of the greatest cavalry generals that ever lived; but otherwise a rash, feather-brained, unreliable man.

Viceroy of Italy.—Eugène de Beauharnais. Son of Josephine by her first husband, Alexandre de Beauharnais. b. 1781. *Aide-de-camp* to Napoleon 1796. With him in Egypt and Italy. Made Prince in 1804 and Viceroy of Italy. In 1806 adopted by Napoleon. After his fall retired to Munich, d. 1824.

Prince of Eckmühl.—Louis Nicolas Davoust. b. 1770. Fellow-student of Napoleon at Brienne. Fought in nearly all his campaigns. War Minister during Hundred Days. d. 1823.

Prince of Neuchâtel.—Alexandre Berthier. b. 1753, and served in American War of Independence. With Napoleon in Egypt, Italy and Germany. Made peer by Louis xviii. Retired to Bamberg during the

Hundred Days, and committed suicide through remorse in 1815, by throwing himself out of window.

Duke of Reggio.—Charles Nicolas Oudinot. b. 1767. Distinguished himself at Austerlitz. Adhered to Bourbons, and retired to his country-seat during the Hundred Days. d. 1847.

Duke of Elchingen.—Michael Ney. b. 1769. Entered army as private hussar 1787. Exhibited great bravery with army of Rhine. m. Mlle Anguié, friend of Hortense Beauharnais. In 1804 made Marshal. Called in army "the Bravest of the Brave." Made Duke of Elchingen and Prince of the Moskwa. In 1814 adhered to Bourbons. Deserted them for Napoleon during the Hundred Days. Fought at Waterloo. Tried by Court of Peers and shot 7th Dec. 1815, to the eternal disgrace of the Bourbons.

Prince Poniatowski.—Joseph. Born at Warsaw 1763; nephew of Stanislaus Augustus, last King of Poland. Served against Russians under Kosciusko. In 1809 served against Austria. After Leipzig, when Napoleon created him Marshal, was drowned when attempting to swim his horse across the Elster, 19th Oct. 1813.

Marquis de Gouvion St. Cyr.—Laurent. Distinguished in many campaigns. Adhered to Bourbons and appointed Minister of Naval Affairs. One of the greatest of Napoleon's generals, d. 1830.

Duke of Abrantes.—Andoche Junot. b. 1771. Entered army 1791. Attracted Napoleon's attention by coolness under fire at Toulon. In 1806 commanded French army in Portugal, and capitulated to Wellesley. Committed suicide by throwing himself out of window, 1813. Noted for his extravagance and licentiousness.

Duke of Belluno.—Claude Perrin Victor, b. 1766. Entered army in 1781. Fought at Montebello and Marengo; and at Friedland was created Marshal. Defeated at Talavera by Wellesley. Adhered to Bourbons. Followed Louis XVIII. to Ghent, and after Waterloo was created Peer of France and Minister for War. d. 1841.

Duke of Taranto.—Etienne Jacques Joseph Alexandre Macdonald. b. 1765. Descended from Scottish family who took refuge in France after the rising of 1745. Entered French army 1784. Commanded army of Rhine 1796. With Napoleon in Italy. Governor of Rome. In 1800 commanded army in Switzerland, where he won great fame Fell under Napoleon's displeasure as a friend of Moreau. Taken again into favour in 1809. In 1810 created Duke of Taranto. Adhered to Bourbons and held aloof during the Hundred Days. He was a great captain, and probably the finest character among all the marshals, d. 1840.

Duke of Treviso.—Edouard Adolphe Casimir Joseph Mortier, b. 1768. Entered army 1791. Held many commands under Napoleon, in which he greatly shone. In 1808 made Duke of Treviso. Commanded in Spain. Adhered to Bourbons and remained faithful to them during the Hundred Days. In 1819 made Peer of France. In 1834 succeeded Soult as War Minister. Killed by Fieschi's "infernal machine," 28th July 1835.

Duke of Istria.—Jean Baptiste Bessières. b. 1768. Distinguished himself in Italian campaign 1796, and became intimate friend of Napoleon. Went with him to Egypt. Fought at Marengo. In 1804 was created Marshal and Duke of Istria. Killed while reconnoitring at Lützen, May 1813, the day before the battle.

Duke of Friuli.—Michel Duroc. b. 1772. Accompanied Napoleon to Egypt, and fought in nearly all his campaigns, besides being closely associated with him personally. Killed at Wurschen, 1813.

Prince Schwartzenberg.—Carl Philipp, Austrian field-marshal, b. 1771. Entered Austrian army at an early age. Served against the Turks, and afterwards against the French, and fought at Austerlitz and Wagram. Commanded against Napoleon in 1814, and afterwards was made President of the Aulic Council, d. 1820.

ITINERARY

Of the March of the Fourth Corps in the Russian Territory, during the Campaign of 1812.

		Leagues.
1 July, 1812, from Pilony to Kroni		1
2 —— Melangani		7
3 —— Rouicontoui		6
4 —— New-Troki		3
5 —— Halted.		
6 —— Halted.		
7 —— Rudniki		7
8 —— Paradomin		3
9 —— Halted.		
10 —— Paulovo		4
(At the castle of the Count of Choiseuil).		
11 —— Ochmiana		6½
12 —— Smorghoni		8
13 —— Halted.		
14 —— From Smorghoni to Zachkevitschi		3½
15 —— Vileika		8
16 —— Kostenevitschi		6
17 —— Dolghinow		4½
18 —— Dokzice		7
19 —— Halted.		
20 —— Berezino		6½
21 —— Pouichna		6½
22 —— Kamen		6
23 —— Botschaikovo		3¾
	Carried forward	96¾

The Emperor Napoleon passed the Niemen at Kowno, the 24th June; the 22d, being at Wilkowiski, he declared war against Russia. The fourth corps, commanded by the Viceroy of Italy, passed the Niemen at Pilony, the advanced-guard effected its passage on the 29th; but the Prince and the fifteenth division passed on the 1st of July. On the 28th Napoleon was at Wilna.

24 July, From Smorghoni to Bezenkovjtschi 4
25 —— Soritza (three leagues on this side Ostrowno) 4½
26 —— Combat (Bivouack at small castle Dobrijk) 5½
27 —— Bivouack before Witepak 2⅚
28 —— Bivouack at Aghaponovchtchina 5¼
29 —— Sourai 5
30 —— Halted.
1 August Ditto.
2 —— Ditto.
3 —— Ditto.
4 —— Ditto.
5 —— Ditto.
6 —— Ditto.
7 —— Ditto.
8 —— Ditto.
9 —— From Sourai to Janowitschi 4
10 —— Halted.
11 —— Velechkovitschi 3½
12 —— Liozna 2⅔
13 —— Liouvavitschi 5¼
14 —— Rasasna 4
15 —— Siniaki 7½
16 —— Katova 3
17 —— Bivouack (at a league from Korouitnia) 5
18 —— Bivouack (near the *chateau* of Novoidvor) 5
19 —— Suburb of Smolensk 1½
20 —— Passed the Dnieper (Bivouack above Smolensk) ½
21 —— Bivouack same place.
22 —— Ditto.
23 —— Volodimerowa 6
24 —— Pologhi 7½
25 —— Zazelé 5⅔
26 —— Mikaelovskoe 7½
27 —— Agopochina (passed the Niemen at Blaghove) 4½
28 —— Bivouack (round a *chateau*) a league beyond
Bereski 4
29 —— From Agopochina to Novoe 9
30 —— Halted.
31 —— Pokrow 6⅔
1 September Paulova 6⅓
2 —— Woremiewo 2

Carried forward 224½

238

		Leagues.
	Brought forward	224½
3 September	Halted.	
4 ———	Louzos	5½
5 ———	Encamped on the heights of Borodino	4
6 ———	Ditto.	
7 ———	Battle.	
8 ———	Ouspenskoe, or Krasnoë	3¼
9 ———	Rouza	6¼
10 ———	Halted.	
11 ———	Alpalchtchouina	4½
12 ———	Zwenighorod	3¾
13 ———	Buzaievo	6¼
14 ———	Khorechevo	4¾
15 ———	Moscow	2
Total from Pilony to Moscow		264¾
	Stopped in this city from 15th September, until	
18 October.	Village on the road from Kaluga, a league from Moscow	1
19 ———	Little village, near Batoutinka bivouack	5
20 ———	Inatowo	7½
21 ———	Fominskoe	3
22 ———	Halted.	
23 ———	From Fominskoe to a village half a league beyond Borovsk bivouack	7¼
24 ———	Battle of Malo-Jaroslavitz. Bivouack	4¼
25 ———	Halted.	
26 ———	Ouvarovskoe bivouack	4
27 ———	Alfereva	4½
28 ———	Village a league beyond Borisov, supposed to be Mitïaéva	2½
29 ———	Ouspenskoe, called Krasnoë bivouack	5½
30 ———	Village ½ league on the right of the road between Kolotskoi and Prokofevo, bivouack	6
31 ———	Ghiat, bivouack	8¼
1 November.	Near Velitschevo, bivouack	5
2 ———	Fœderovskoe, bivouack	6¼
3 ———	Battle of Viazma bivouack, ½ league further	3½
4 ———	Rouibki, a league beyond Semlevo	7
5 ———	Jolkov Postola Door	3½
6 ———	Doroghobouï bivouack	6
	Carried forward	90

7	November.	From Fominskoe to Zazelé bivouack	7
8	————	Sloboda bivouack	4
9	————	From Sloboda passed the Wop, bivouacked at a little village half a league from this river	1
10	————	Donkhovchtchina	4
11	————	Halted.	
12	————	Wolodimerowa, bivouack	6¾
13	————	Smolensko	5¼
14	————	Halted.	
15	————	Hamlet three leagues from Smolensko, supposed to be Loubna	3½
16	————	Krasnoë	7
17	————	Liadoui	4½
18	————	Doubrowna	8
19	————	Orcha	4
20	————	Halted.	
21	————	Half a league before Kokanovo, bivouack ..	5
22	————	Bivouack round a castle half a league this side Tolschin	5
23	————	Bivouack three leagues from Toloschin, near Jablonka	4
24	————	Bobr	4
25	————	Natscha five leagues from Bobr, where there is an insulated church, bivouack	5½
26	————	From a village at Memonitsa, to two and a half leagues on this side Borisov, bivouack	5½
27	————	Studzianca, passage of the Beresina, bivouack	4⅝
28	————	Zembin, bivouack	4⅝
29	————	Kamen	3¼
30	————	Niestanovitschi, near Zavichino	6
1	December.	Iliia	4¼
2	————	Molodetschino	6
3	————	Halted.	
4	————	Village supposed to be Markovo, bivouack ..	7
5	————	Smorghoni	4½
6	————	Joupranoui	5
7	————	Rovno-Pole, bivouack	5
8	————	Roukoni, bivouack	5¼
9	————	Wilna	5

Carried forward 234½

240

A LIST

Of all the Persons mentioned in this Work, with their Rank during the Campaign of Russia.

NAPOLEON.

Jerome Buonaparte, King of Westphalia, Commander of the 8th Corps.

Joachim Murat, King of Naples, Commander of all the Cavalry.

Eugene de Beauharnois, Viceroy of Italy, Commander of the 4th Corps.

Berthier, Prince of Neufchatel and of Wagram, Major-General.

Davoust, Prince of Eckmuhl, Commander of 1st Corps.

Oudinot, Duke of Reggio,   do.   2d.

Ney, Duke of Elchingen,   do.   3d. Prince of Moskwa.

Prince Poniatowski,   do.   5th.

Marshal Count St. Cyr,   do.   6th.

General Count Regnier,   do.   7th.

Junot, Duke of Abrantes,   do.   8th.

Victor, Duke of Belluno,   do.   9th.

Duke of Tarentum,   do.   10th.

Duke of Treviso, Commander of the Young Guard.

Prince Schwartzenberg, Commander of the Austrian Auxiliary Corps.

Bessieres, Duke of Istria, Commander of the Cavalry of the Guard.

Caulincourt, Duke of Vicenza, General of Division, Master of the Horse.

Durock, Duke of Frioul,   do.   Grand Marshal of the Palace.

Count Rapp,   do.

Count Lauriston,   do.

Count de Lobau,   do.

} Aides-de-Camp to the Emperor.

Count Lefebre Desnouettes, General of Division, Colonel of the Horse-Chasseurs of the Guard.

Count Nansouty,

Count Grouchy,

Count Montbrun,

Count Latour Maubourg,

} Commanders of Cavalry Corps, and Generals of Divisions.

General Dessoles, Chief of the Viceroy's Staff.

Baron Guilleminot,   do.

Count Danthouard, Commander of the Artillery of the Fourth Corps.

Count Lariboissier, General of Division, Inspector-General of Artillery.

Count Sortin,   do.   Commander of the Artillery of the Guards.

Baron Pernetti,   do.   Commander of the Artillery of the 1st Corps.

Baron Fouche,   do.   do.   4th Corps.

Count Eblé, General of Division of Artillery, Commander of the Bridge Equipages.

Count Gudin,

Baron Gerard,

Count Dessaix,

Count Friant,

Count Compans,

Count Morand,

} Generals of Division—1st Corps.

Count Verdier,

Count Legrand,

Count Maison,

Baron Merle,

} Generals of Division—2d Corps.

Baron Ledru, Commander of a Division—3d Corps.

Count of Clasparede, General of Division, Commander of the Legion of the Vistula.

Baron Delzons,

Count Broussier,

Count Pino,

} Generals of Divisions—4th Corps.

Baron Wrede,

General De Roy,

General Sierbein,

} Bavarian Generals—6th Corps.

Dombrowski,

Zoionsheck,

} Do. 7th Corps.

Count Parthonneaux,
Baron Girard,
General Daendals,
General Damas,
} Generals of Divisions—9th Corps.

Baron Grandjean, Commander of a Division—10th Corps.
General Grawert,
General Kleist,
} Prussian Generals—10th Corps.

Baron Roquet, General of Division, Commander of the Fusileers of the Imperial Guard.

Count Charpentier, General of Division, Governor of Smolensko.

Count Baraguay d'Hilliers, General of Division.

Count Loison, Commander of a Division, from Koningsberg.

General Frederic, Commander of the 4th Division (1st Corps).

Count Sanson, General of Division, Chief of the Topographical Bureau.

Baron Haxo, General of Division of Engineers.

Count Sebastiani,
Baron Lahoussaye.
Count Bruyères,
Baron de St. Germain,
Count Defrane,
Baron Chastel,
Count Ornano,
Baron Wathier,
Count Fournier,
Baron Pajol,
Baron Castex,
Baron Doumerc,
} Generals of Divisions of Cavalry.

Count Preyssing, Commander of a Division of Light Bavarian Cavalry.

Prince Czartoryski, Grand Marshal of the Diet of Warsaw.

Count Mejean, Counsellor of State of the Kingdom of Italy, and Secretary of the Viceroy.

General Poitevin (Baron Maureillan), Commander of the Engineers of the 4th Corps.

Baron Aubrey, Commander of Artillery of 2d Corps.

Baron Dode, Commander of Engineers.

GENERALS OF BRIGADE.

Barons Ricard, Roussel, Huard, Plausanne, Bonami, Nagle, Augereau, Marion, Compere, Villata, Fontane, Levie, Chastel, Berkheim, Colbert, Castex, Saint Geniez, Aug. Caulincourt, Pajol, Guyon, Bourdesoult, Bachelu, Thiry, Lanabarc,

Graudeau, Dalton, Dommarget, Laurency, Grabowski, Fischey, Delantre, Le Camus, Blandont, Pampelone, Poltré, Chouard, Ameya, Corbineau, Heyligers.

Pouget, General of Brigade, Governor of Witepak.

Lecchi, ditto ditto, Commander of the Italian Guard.

Lepel, Aide-de-Camp to the King of Westphalia.

Dery, Aide-de-Camp to the King of Naples.

Klengel, General in the Saxon service.

General Jomini, Governor of Orcha.

Marthod,
Letort, } Major of the Dragoon Guards.

Baron Triaire, General of Brigade, Aide-de-Camp to the Viceroy.

Baron Gifflenga ditto ditto.

Baron Lacroix, Colonel, ditto.

Count Louis Tascher Lapagerie,
—— Charles Labedoyerè,
—— Maurice Mejan,
—— Jules Deseve, } Chiefs of Squadrons.

Bellisomi, Master of the Horse to the Viceroy.

Colonel Delfanti, Officer of the Ordnance to the Viceroy.

André Corner, Lieutenant ditto.

Sanoi, ditto.

Liedot, Colonel of Engineers.

Marbœuf, Colonel of Lancers.

Kliski, Polish Colonel, with the Viceroy.

Radzivil, Colonel of the 8th Polish Hulans.

Dalbignac, Adjutant-Commander of the 2d Corps.

Durieu, Adjutant-Commander, Sub-Chief of the Staff of the 4th Corps.

De Bourmont,
Asselin, } Adjutant-Commanders attached to this Staff.
Forestier,

Colonel Grosbon, of the 53d Regiment.

—— Battaglia, Commander of the Italian Guards of Honour.

—— Gueheneue, 26th Light Troops.

—— Vidman, Commander of the Company of the Venetian Guards of Honour.

—— Demay, Commander of the Artillery of the 13th Division.

—— Banco, of the 2d Italian Horse Chasseurs.

—— Rambourg, of the 3d ditto.

—— Peraldi of the Chasseurs of the Italian Guard.

D'Oreille, Major of the Spanish Regiment of Joseph Napoleon.

Vives, Major of Artillery.

Turenne,
Grammont, } Aides-de-camp to Count Grouchy.

Colaud, Chief of Battalion, Waggon-Master-General of the 4th Corps.

Sevelinge, ditto, attached to the Staff.

Tempie, Lieutenant-Commander of the Marines of the Italian Guard.

Delahage,
Laiynelot, } Captains of Engineers.
Guibert,

Boutarel, Captain of Horse Chasseurs, Adjutant of the Palais Royal of Monza.

Trezel, Captain, Aide-de-Camp of General Guilleminot.

Maisonneuve,
Jouard, } Assistant Captains of the Staff of the 4th Corps.
Evrard,

Morlaincourt, Captain of Engineers to the 4th Division.

Bonardelle, Captain of Artillery.

Octave de Segur,
Ferrari, } Officers of Hussars.

Guyard,
Savary, } Captains of the 9th of the lines.

Lelande Maupertius, Lieutenant of the Reg. of the Voltigeurs of the Guard.

Bordoni,
Mastini, } Lieutenants in the Italian Guards of Honour.

Saint Marcellin de Fontanes, attached to the Staff of the 4th Corps.

Lesseps, French Consul at Moscow.

Villeblanche, Auditor of the Council of State, Intendant of Smolensko.

———

ALEXANDER I. Emperor of Russia.

Grand Duke Constantine.

Prince Kutusoff, Commander-in-Chief of the Russian Army.

Barclay de Tolly, Commander-in-Chief before the arrival of Prince Kutusoff.

Count Wittgenstein, Commander of the 1st Russian Corps.

Generals {
Bagawout, ... ditto .... 2d do.
Schomoaloff, .. ditto .... 3d do.
Tutschkoff, ... ditto .... 4th do.
Prince Bagration, ditto .... 5th do. } Forming the
Doctorow, ... ditto .... 6th do. } Second Army
Tormasow, ... ditto .... 7th do. } of the West.
}

Admiral Tschikakoff, Commander of the Russian Army of the Danube.

General Langeron,
——— Lambert,
——— Woinow,
——— Tschaplitr,
——— Paklin,
} Commanding the Divisions of the Army of the Danube.

Platoff, Hetman of the Cossacks.

Platoff, son.

Orlow Dennisow, General of the Advanced-guard.

Kamenski,
Ertel,
Sacken,
Marcoff,
Repnin,
Casanowa,
} Generals Commanders in Volhynia;

Koulniew,
Stengel,
} Generals, Commanders in the Corps of Prince Wittgenstein.

Sicverse, General, employed in the 2d Army of the West.

Ostermann,
Bennigsen,
Skallon,
Woronsow,
Otschakoff,
Kanovitzen,
Gregoff,
Rajewski,
Kropswitski,
Strogonoff,
Boekmetieff,
Ouvarow,
Balla,
} Generals employed in the Centre of the Russian Army.

Koulniew, General of Light Cavalry.

Koff, General of Cavalry.

Milloradowitch,
Winzingerode,
Czernichew,
} Generals commanding the advanced-guard of Prince Kutusoff.

Archbishop Platon.

Bishop Augustin, Vicar of Moscow.

Rastopshin,
Momonoff,
Orlow,
Saltikoff,
Sherimitow,
} Nobles of Moscow.

A STATEMENT

Of the different Corps composing the Grand French Army, which marched against Russia, from March 1st, to September 1st, 1812.

		Men.	Horses.
The Staff. — The Prince of NEUCHATEL Major-General (Berthier).	Badeners, Hessians, Saxons, Neuchatalese, 28th Chasseurs, &c.	4000	1150
First Corps. — The Prince of ECKMUHL (Davoust).	1st Division, General Morand, 13th Light Infantry, 17th, 30th of the line, Badeners, &c.	14,400	1050
	2d Division, General Friant, 15th Light Infantry, 33d, 48th of the line, Spaniards, &c.	15,900	1100
	3d Division, General Gudin, 7th Light Infantry, 12th, 21st, 127th of the line, Strelitzers, &c.	15,500	1050
	4th Division, General Dessaix, 33d Light Infantry, 85th, 108th of the line, Hessians, &c.	13,700	1100
	5th Division, General Compans, 25th, 27th, 61st, 111th of the line, &c.	17,500	1200
	Cavalry, General Girardin, 1st, 2d, 3d, Chasseurs, 9th, Poles, &c.	3800	3800
	Artillery, Engineers, &c.	2300	2200

		Men.	Horses.
Second Corps. — The Duke of REGGIO (Oudinot.)	6th Division, General Legrand, 26th Light Infantry, 55th, 19th, 128th of the line, Portuguese, &c.	14,000	800
	8th Division, Gen. Verdier, 11th Light Infantry, 2d, 37th, 124th of the line, &c.	13,200	900
	9th Division, General Merle, 123d of the line, Swiss, Croats, &c.	12,200	800
	Cavalry, General Castex, 7th, 20th, 24th, 28th, Chasseurs, 8th Light Horse, &c.	3200	3200
	Artillery, Engineers, &c.	1800	1300
Third Corps. — The Duke of ELCHINGEN (Ney).	10th Division, General Ledru, 24th Light Infantry, 46th, 72d, 129th of the line, Portuguese, &c.	13,000	800
	11th Division, General Razout, 4th, 18th, 93d of the line, Illyrians, Portuguese, &c.	14,000	880
	25th Division, General Marchand, Wirtemburghers, &c.	10,000	500
	Cavalry, General Woelwarth, 4th, 28th, Chasseurs, 6th Light Horse, 11th Hussars, Wirtemburghers, &c.	4000	4000
	Artillery Engineers, &c.	2800	2600
Fourth Corps. — The Prince VICEROY (Eugene de Beauharnois).	13th Division, General Delzons, 8th Light Infantry, 84th, 92d, 106th of the line, Croats	13,700	800
	14th Division, General Broussier, 18th Light Infantry, 9th, 35th, 53d of the line, Spaniards	13,000	800
	15th Division, General Pino, Italians, Dalmatians.	14,000	900
	Cavalry, General Guyon, 9th, 19th, Chasseurs, Italians.	2900	2700
	Royal Italian Guard, General Lecchi	6200	2800
	Artillery, Engineers, &c.	2600	2500

248

		Men.	Horses.
Fifth Corps. — Prince PONIATOWSKI.	16th Division, General Zaionsheck, Poles, &c..........	12,000	800
	17th Division, General Dombrowski, id.	12,000	800
	18th Division, General Kamieniecki, id.	9300	700
	Cavalry, General Kaminski, id.	4000	4200
	Artillery, Engineers, &c........	22,000	2600
Sixth Corps. — Marshal GOUVION SAINT-CYR.	19th Division, General Deroy, Bavarians, &c............	2200	400
	20th Division General Wrede, id.	12,700	500
	Cavalry, General de Seydewitz, id.	2000	2100
	Artillery, Engineers, &c......	500	800
Seventh Corps. — General REGNIER.	21st Division, General Lecoq, Saxons, &c..............	7,800	800
	22d Division, General de Funck, id.....................	7600	700
	Cavalry, General de Gablentz, id.................	2300	2600
	Artillery, Engineers, &c.	1200	1400
Eighth Corps. — The Duke of ABRANTES (Junot).	23d Division, General Tharreau, Westphalians, &c.	10,600	400
	24th Division, General d'Ochs	5200	400
	Cavalry, General Chabert	19,000	2000
	Artillery, Engineers, &c.	1000	1400
Ninth Corps. — The Duke of BELLUNO (Victor).	12th Division, General Parthonneaux, 10th, 29th, Light Infantry, 36th, 44th, 51st, 55th, 125th, and 126th of the line.	15,000	600
	26th Division, General Daendels, troops from Berg and Baden, Hessians, &c.......	8000	700
	28th Division, General Girard, Poles....................	7,500	2100
	Cavalry, Generals Delaitre and Fournier, troops from Berg, and Baden, Hessians, &c...	2,000	200

		Men.	Horses.
Tenth Corps. — The Duke of TARENTUM.	7th Division, General Grandjean, Poles, Westphalians, &c.	13,000	900
	27th Division, General d'Yorck, Prussians	14,000	
	Cavalry, Gen. Massemback, id.	2700	2700
	Artillery, &c.	1700	1700
Eleventh Corps. — Duke of CASTIGLIONE.	30th Division, General Leudilet, 2d, 4th, 6th, 8th, 16th, 17th, 18th, 21st, 28th, Light Infantry, 14th, 28th of the line, Westphalians, &c.	18,000	400
	31st Division, General Lagrange 27th, 63d of the line, &c. ..	9900	
	32d Division, General Durutte, the regiments of Walcheren, Belleisle, and the Mediterranean	12,700	
	34th Division, General Morant, 3d, 29th of the line, Hessians, Saxons, &c.	12,900	600
	Cavalry, General Cavaignac, Dragoons, Chasseurs	1600	1500
Prince Schwartzenberg.	Austrians.................	30,000	6000
1st Corps of Cavalry, General Nansouty.	1st Division of Light Horse, General Bruyères, 16th Chasseurs, 7th and 8th Hussars, Poles, Prussians, &c.	6500	6700
	1st Division of Heavy Horse, General St. Germain, 2d, 3d, 9th Cuirassiers, 1st Light Horse	3700	3800
	5th Division do. General Valence, 5th, 6th, 11th, 12th ..	3200	3300
2d Corps of Cavalry, General Montbrun.	2d Division of Light Horse, General Pajols, 11th, 12th Chasseurs, 5th, 9th Hussars, Prussians, Poles, &c.	4800	4900
	2d Division of Heavy Horse,		

		Men.	Horses.
2d Corps continued.	General Wathier, 5th, 8th, 10th Cuirassiers, 2d Light Horse	2700	2800
	4th Division do. General Defranc, 1st 2d carbiniers, 1st Cuirassiers 4th do.	2900	2900
3d Corps of Cavalry, General Grouchy	3d Division of Light Horse, General Chastel, 6th, 8th, 25th Chasseurs, 6th Hussars, Bavarians, Saxons	4500	4700
	3d Divisions of Heavy Horse, General Doumerc, 4th, 7th, 14th Cuirassiers, 3d Light Horse	3300	3300
	6th Division do. General Lahousaye, 7th, 23d, 28th, 30th, 50th Dragoons	2800	3000
4th Corps of Cavalry, General Latour Maubourg.	4th Division of Light Horse, General Rozniecki, Poles ..	4600	5000
	7th Division do. General Lorge, Saxons, Westphalians, &c...	3200	3500
Imperial Guard.	Imperial Guard, Infantry, Cavalry, Artillery, &c.........	43,000	16000
	Division of the Vistula, General Claparede, Poles, &c.......	8300	500
Grand Park.	Grand Park of Artillery, General Lariboissiere	9500	4800
	Grand Park of Engineers, General Chasseloup Laubat....	5100	900
	Waggon Train, General Picard	7800	9300
Garrisons.	Magdebourg, General Michaud	900	
	Dantzig, General Lagrange....	3000	1000
	Stettin, General Liobert......		
	Custrin, General Fomier d'Albe	These Garrisons formed part of the different Corps.	
	Glogau, Laplane		
	Berlin, General Durutte......		
	Stralsund, General Morand ..		
	Kœnigsberg, General Loison ..	5000	200

		Men.	Horses.
General Carra St. Cyr.	Troops of the Princes of the Confederation	7300	300
General D'Estrees	Neapolitan Troops............	8000	1000
Garrison of Hamburgh, General Carra St. Cyn.	Cohorts of the National Guard of the first van, &c........	5700	
General Eswald.	Danish Troops	9800	2000
Troops on the March.	Infantry	25,000	
	Cavalry....................	14,000	14000
	Artillery, Engineers, &c........	4000	2500
Depôts of Cavalry, General Boucier.	Detachments of all the regiments of Cavalry	1500	600

RECAPITULATION.

	Men.	Horses.
Staff	4000	1150
First Corps	83,000	11,500
Second do.	44,100	7000
Third do.	43,800	8700
Fourth do.	52,000	10,500
Fifth do.	39,500	9100
Sixth do.	27,400	9800
Seventh do.	18,900	5500
Eighth do.	18,700	4300
Ninth do.	32,500	4500
Tenth do.	31,400	5300
Eleventh do.	55,100	2500
Austrian auxiliary Corps	30,000	6000
Imperial Guard	51,390	16,500
Grand Park	22,400	15,000
Garrisons { Dantzig Magdebourg Kœnigsberg Hamburgh }	14,600	1200
Troops of the Princes of the Confederarion	7300	300
Neapolitans	8000	1000
Danish Troops	9800	2000
Troops on the March	43,000	16,500
Depôt of Cavalry	1500	600
First Corps of Cavalry	13,400	13,800
Second	10,400	10,600
Third	10,600	11,000
Fourth	7800	8500
	680500	176850

The following Statement of the effective Force of the French Army is taken from an excellent Critique on Labaume in the Quarterly Review ;—it is given on the authority of a Westphalian Officer.

Westphalians	30,000
Bavarians	40,000
Wirtemburghers	16,000
Grand Duchy of Berg	3,000
Prussians	20,000
Austrians	30,000
From Baden	5,000
Poles	60,000
Swiss, French, Spaniards, and Portuguese	300,000
Various	20,000
Total	**524,000**